הפך בה והפך בה דכלא בה

"Turn it and turn it again,
for everything is in it."

Mishnah 'Avot 5:25

TREASURES OLD AND NEW

Essays in the Theology of the Pentateuch

Joseph Blenkinsopp

WILLIAM B. EERDMANS PUBLISHING COMPANY
GRAND RAPIDS, MICHIGAN / CAMBRIDGE, U.K.

Wm. B. Eerdmans Publishing Co.
255 Jefferson Ave. S.E., Grand Rapids, Michigan 49503 /
P.O. Box 163, Cambridge CB3 9PU U.K.

Printed in the United States of America

09 08 07 06 05 04   7 6 5 4 3 2 1

Library of Congress Cataloging-in-Publication Data

Treasures old and new: essays in the theology of the Pentateuch / Joseph Blenkinsopp.
p.   cm.
Includes bibliographical references and index.
Contents: Memory, tradition, and the construction of the past in ancient Israel —
Old Testament theology and the Jewish-Christian connection — Creation, the body,
and care for a damaged world — Sacrifice and social maintenance in ancient Israel —
YHVH and other deities — Gilgamesh and Adam — Structure, theme, and motif
in the succession history (2 Samuel 11–20; 1 Kings 1–2) and the history of human
origins (Genesis 1–11) — The Judge of all the earth (Genesis 18:22-33) — Biographical
patterns in biblical narrative — What happened at Sinai? — Deuteronomy and the
politics of postmortem existence — "We pay no heed to heavenly voices".
ISBN 0-8028-2679-2 (pbk.: alk. paper)
1. Bible. O.T. Pentateuch — Criticism, interpretation, etc.   I. Title.

BS1225.52.B54   2004
230'.0411 — dc22
2004043402

www.eerdmans.com

Contents

Preface

This little sketchbook of biblical theology represents a selection of essays of more general biblical-theological interest published over the last four decades or so. Electronic digitization and publication have made it easier for us to shed the illusion that what we write carries the stamp of finality. I have therefore had no qualms about revising these sketches, in some cases fairly drastically. They have no unifying theme; they have in common only the aim to engage topics I presume to be of interest to thoughtful people today, and to do so in dialogue with texts from the Pentateuch. In that sense, they could be considered as a companion to my contribution to the Anchor Bible Reference Library, *The Pentateuch: An Introduction to the First Five Books of the Bible* (New York: Doubleday, 1992).

It will be obvious that this is not a theology of the Pentateuch, much less of the Old Testament. After reading a great number of theologies of the Old Testament, several of which are the subject of a brief comment in the second of the sketches, I arrived long ago at the by no-means-sensational conclusion that, notwithstanding claims made by the authors, all such attempts are necessarily perspectival, and therefore selective and incomplete. I even arrived at the point of wondering whether the Hebrew Bible/Old Testament is capable of generating a theology. The creation of any theological system, biblical or otherwise, begins at a specific starting point dictated by the agenda of the writer and the interest groups to which the writer belongs. What it says or leaves unsaid will also generally be determined by a ruling concept chosen in advance of writing, the choice dictated by the presuppositions and prejudices, conscious and unconscious, of the writer. If, as with Eichrodt, "covenant" is the point of departure, you have the problem what to do with texts like Proverbs that evince little or no interest in the idea. If, like von Rad, you are convinced that "salvation mediated through history" has to be the organizing principle, you are left asking what to do with texts like Qoheleth, which are not only uninterested in salvation history *(Heilsgeschichte)* but also deny its possibility. Yet both can provide interesting and important *perspectives* guiding the reading of biblical texts, and thus complement each other.

There is also the question whether circumscribing the Hebrew Bible/ Old Testament — or even just the Pentateuch — within a coherent theological system can do justice to the conflicting and sometimes mutually exclusive views that it contains. Scholars still widely assume that the idea of canonicity implies the reconciliation of divergent views in a grand harmony. But the fact is that we do not know that this is how those responsible for the final form of the Scriptures worked. For their own reasons, which could be quite different from ours, they may quite deliberately have left mutually incompatible views in simple juxtaposition. Canonicity implies normativity, but normativity is not a straightforward idea either. There are tensions, antinomies, and aporias in what counts as normative that cannot be disregarded, that honesty and good sense require us to take seriously, and that can actually result in a more flexible, interesting, and even exciting approach to our reading of the Bible. With a bit of good fortune, something of this may come through in these twelve sketches.

Now a brief word about method. Some readers will be reassured and others dismayed to hear that my treatment of the texts is critical and basically conservative. It is well known that the historical-critical reading of biblical texts is under attack from several quarters. On one flank are arrayed fundamentalist Christian and Jewish Bible readers, and no one will need to be told that Christian biblical fundamentalism is as strong and influential now as it has ever been, especially in the United States. On the other side, the historical-critical reading of biblical texts is, in large segments of the Biblical Studies guild, fighting a losing battle against different varieties of postmodernist theory that favor indeterminacy and fluidity of meaning. I must confess to skepticism about certain self-indulgent, "readerly" approaches to biblical texts. If reading texts is like a dialogue or conversation, the well-tried critical methods in use in Biblical Studies, when used deftly and imaginatively, can help the text to hold up its end of the conversation. There are, nevertheless, many different ways of carrying on a good conversation. Martin Buber speaks somewhere of the "infinite interpretability" of biblical texts. It is salutary to bear in mind that the text will still be there after the interpreter of any persuasion has worked it over.

Anyway, my hope is that this little sketchbook of biblical theology can be read with ease and perhaps even with pleasure. With that aspiration in view, I have reduced the notes and learned asides to a minimum. Then, too, I have presented the few Hebrew words transliterated and translated, and I have confined bibliographical references as far as possible to English-language items or English translations of foreign works where available. In addition, I have followed the guidelines of the Society of Biblical Literature for biblical and other abbreviations. Finally, I have written the Tetragrammaton as YHVH rather than spelling it out, and I have used my own translations of biblical texts unless I have stated otherwise.

JOSEPH BLENKINSOPP

Acknowledgments

It is a pleasure to express my appreciation to the following for permission to reprint in revised form essays previously published:

- to the editor of *Biblical Theology Bulletin* for "Memory, Tradition, and the Construction of the Past in Ancient Israel" (chapter I)
- to Continuum Books for chapters II and IX earlier versions of which appeared in *Journal for the Study of the Old Testament*
- to the University of Notre Dame Press for "Creation, the Body, and Care for a Damaged World" (chapter III)
- to the editors of *Interpretation* for "YHVH and Other Deities: Conflict and Accommodation in the Religion of Israel" (chapter V)
- to the editor of *Journal of Jewish Studies* for "The Judge of All the Earth (Genesis 18:22-33)"
- to Scholars Press for "We Pay No Heed to Heavenly Voices" (chapter XII).

Memory, Tradition, and the Construction
of the Past in Ancient Israel

1

According to the biblical record, the Babylonian army of Nebuchadrezzar II invested Jerusalem in January 587 B.C., breached its walls in July of the following year, and torched the city with its palaces and temple in the second week of the month of Av, namely, sometime in early August of the same year, about eighteen months after the siege had begun (2 Kings 25; Jeremiah 52). If we leave aside a long-standing dispute as to whether the year in question was 587 or 586, this summary of what happened would, I believe, be widely accepted. Since the Babylonian Chronicle breaks off in 593, about six or seven years prior to the disaster, we have no direct attestation to the event apart from the biblical record. But the same chronicle matches the biblical account of the capture of the city by the Babylonians a decade earlier, and administrative texts excavated in Babylon contain lists of rations for various high-ranking deportees, including the Judean king Jehoiachin, exiled at that time and detained in Babylon (Pritchard 1995: 308, 563-64). Ostraca discovered at Lachish, the most important Judean city after Jerusalem, document the approach of the Babylonian army from the southwest and are therefore consistent with the biblical record (Gibson 1971: 32-49). Physical testimony to the struggle for the city is also provided by charred remains, including Scythian arrowheads used by the Babylonians, at the base of a tower in the Jewish quarter of Jerusalem (Avigad 1980: 49-53). Circumstantial evidence, therefore, favors the essential historicity of the biblical narrative of the fall of the city, and no information currently available contradicts it.

The process by which the historian establishes that this event of major importance took place more or less as described does not seem to leave any place for memory. We cannot appeal to oral history, there are no ethnotexts as there are for the Great War of 1914-18, or the Shoa, or the Armenian genocide now (at this writing) almost a century in the past. It seems, in fact, that the science of historiography as conceived by the great nineteenth-century historians (von Ranke, Mommsen, Langlois, et al.), the detailed chronicling of events, is essentially disconnected from, or even hostile to, memory, since it tends to objectify the event *wie es eigentlich geworden ist* — as it really came about — and to move along a different groove from that of the tradition within which a particular society transmits its collective memories. Historical recording is flat and detached; it lacks the vitality and emotional charge of memory (Wieseltier 1993: 16-18). Here we recall Yerushalmi's comment about Judaism's deep concern to remember, coupled with a relative indifference to recording past and contemporary events (Yerushalmi 1982: 5, 9-10).

There was a time, of course, when the catastrophe of 586 B.C. *was* remembered. As I was writing the first draft of this paper, in November 1993, people were recalling the assassination of President John F. Kennedy almost exactly thirty years earlier, and it was clear that among those who lived at that time memories were still vivid. Unless we assume that the biblical historian was involved in wholesale invention, we may suppose that the memory of that other event long ago — the burning of the city and the temple, the dragging of the blinded king into exile, the refugees, and the deportations — was still vivid to many in the homeland and abroad thirty years afterward, say, around 556 B.C. The chronicler of the "return to Zion" informs us that half a century after the event, at the laying of the foundation stone of the rebuilt temple, some of the people remembered having seen Solomon's temple and maybe even had worshiped in it, and they could not hold back their tears (Ezra 3:12). By the time the work of rebuilding and dedication was finished, more than two decades later, most if not all of these people would have been dead. The primary memory of the event would have died with them, just as the primary memory of the sinking of the *Titanic* (again, at this writing) is about to disappear forever.

Memories are, however, communicable and, once communicated, can become part of the collective consciousness of a society, an ingredient, no doubt the principal ingredient, of the tradition by which a society constructs, maintains, and perpetuates its identity. In this respect collective, social memory functions like biological memory, the genetic code in the individual. In most societies, even today, the primary vehicle for memory transmission at the local level is the kinship network and, along with this, its many analogues — affinity associations of different kinds, such as churches, synagogues, religious congregations, parties, and sects. Within the extended family, what has been called "the grandfather law" enables the memory of the individual to reach back two or three generations (Connerton 1989: 38-39). My own grandfather gave me, as a small child, an emotional and vivid impression of his own memories — transmitted no doubt with advantages — as a combatant in the Great War of 1914-18, with the result that First Ypres, Polygon Wood, the Somme, and Passchendaele were, and still are, more real to me than World War II, which I experienced firsthand at an English boarding school. After reading, much more recently, Paul Fusell's *The Great War in Modern Memory,* I realized that my vicarious recall of those events was part of a larger pool of social memory that was still shaping the consciousness of entire societies in the modern world. Something like that may be assumed to have taken place among Judeans in the homeland and abroad in the aftermath of the disasters of 586 B.C. The memory of the disaster would have remained as an active ingredient of consciousness in the three- or four-generational household and the larger society after the passage of almost a century, thus presumably well into the fifth century B.C. It is not surprising, therefore, if it has insinuated itself in one way or another into practically all the biblical texts that can be dated to the first century following the disaster.

Scholars have often observed that the collective consciousness of societies that have experienced disaster, the Irish and Poles, for example, is more profoundly shaped by memory than those whose experience of disaster is more episodic or, a fortiori, those who have acquired a reputation for inflicting disaster on others. Consider, for example, how pervasive in the ethnic consciousness of the Serbs is the defeat at Kosovo in 1389, or, among the people of the Cévennes region, are the Revocation of the Edict of Nantes in 1685 and the suppression of the Camisards. Few communities known to history have had a closer acquaintance with disaster than the Jewish people, and few are less subject to collective amnesia. But how does such a society preserve its memories when the links of person-to-person transmission are stretched and thinned out with the passage of time?

At one time biblical scholars appealed confidently to oral tradition as a principal constituent of historical reconstruction. They claimed, for example, that stories about Abraham, Isaac, and Jacob had been transmitted faithfully by word of mouth, together with the appropriate social setting, from the Middle Bronze Age, therefore the early second millennium B.C., to the time when the memories were first committed to writing. Until fairly recently there was wide agreement that these earliest sources were written down no later than the tenth or maybe the ninth century B.C., thus about a millennium after the events they purport to narrate, and no doubt some people are still prepared to accept that. But more recent studies in oral tradition have demonstrated, what should have been obvious from the start, that the survival of memories transmitted orally over such an enormously long period of time has a very low percentage of probability even in situations of cultural and political continuity, decidedly not the case in Late Bronze Age and Iron Age Palestine (Culley 1972: 102-16; Van Seters 1975: 158-660; Vansina 1985). The painstaking attempt to authenticate the social and cultural background of the stories with reference to Nuzi customary law (e.g., dealing with adoption and surrogate spouses) and Mari nomadic-pastoral economy has held up no better. The book of Job may serve to demonstrate that creating a plausible social setting does not settle the issue of historicity.

Another problematic aspect of the debate about the place of oral tradition is the common assumption that oral transmission and writing are mutually exclusive. Numerous studies have shown that this is not the case. Oral composition, transmission, and instruction are frequently attested in societies familiar with writing, Western Europe in the Middle Ages, for example (Carruthers 1990; Le Goff 1992: 68-80). A related problem, apparent in recent attempts to determine the degree of literacy or illiteracy at different times in Israel of the biblical period (Harris 1989; Baines 1992: 4:333-37; Young 1998: 239-53, 408-22) arises out of failure to clarify what being literate meant for a society like Israel at different points in its development. We are talking about what was basically, at all times, an agrarian, peasant society, and therefore about people the vast majority of whom had neither the competence nor the motivation to read or write. There were, of course, scribes whose own degree of literacy may in many cases have been confined to the ability to read and reproduce the Hebrew alphabetic script, not a particularly difficult skill to acquire. When the need arose, one would have had recourse to such a "specialist" and paid the going rate, as happened to a day laborer in seventh-century-B.C. Judah who by this means petitioned the local governor at Yavneh-Yam for the return of his confiscated outer garment (Gibson 1971: 26-30). At any rate, nothing much can be deduced from the relatively few inscriptions that have survived from the period of the kingdoms. Outside of small social, economic, and intellectual elites, a significant degree of literacy requires not only a developed urban culture and an appropriate institutional setting (e.g., a palace or a temple) but also the means to produce and disseminate writing, conditions that were absent during most if not all of the biblical period.

2

Let us return to the disaster of 586 and its aftermath. Inevitably, in the course of time, the event was recorded in writing. It was recorded toward the end of the work to which modern scholarship has given the inelegant title the Deuteronomistic History (hereafter the History *tout court,* and its author the Historian), which dates in its finished form to no earlier than the middle of the sixth century B.C., and perhaps considerably later. This kind of historiography seems to have developed from the writing up of court chronicles, a task entrusted to an official known in Judah as the *mazkîr* (recorder, chronicler, or, more literally, "remembrancer"; see 2 Sam 8:16; 20:24; 1 Kgs 4:3; 18:18, 37 [= Isa 36:2, 22]; 1 Chr 18:15; 34:8. Esth 6:1 mentions a *sēper hazzikrōnôt,* literally "a book of things to be remembered," i.e., a record or chronicle). Into this annalistic base different kinds of narrative, including legends about holy men and (less frequently) holy women, were in due course inserted. The Historian's account is quite detailed, but clearly its purpose was not so much to perpetuate the memory of the disaster as to explain why it happened. The fall of Jerusalem and the destruction of its temple raised an intractable and, for some, insuperable problem regarding the reality, power, and ethical character of the national deity. In fact, much of the writing that has survived from that time was written to address this issue. The historian's explanation, which in the post-Holocaust age can hardly fail to appear problematic, is that the people must take the blame since they had been warned continually through YHVH's "servants the prophets" of the consequences of nonobservance of the laws and yet did nothing about it.

Historians are not, in any case, the principal custodians of a society's memories, least of all in a culture in which only a very small percentage of the population has the competence, leisure, and motivation to read history.

At the same time the History, and the book of Deuteronomy, closely related in theme and ideology with it, reflect an educational program that appeals to collective historical memory as a means of reinforcing the frequent injunctions to observe the laws (e.g., Deut 8:11, 14, 18-19; 9:7). Hence the formulation of motivation clauses in the form of historical reminiscence appended to several of the laws, a feature, as far as we know, unique in ancient jurisprudence. An example: "You shall not oppress the resident alien; you know what it is like to be an alien, for you were aliens in the land of Egypt" (Exod 23:9). Those who heard these words were expected to know what it was like to be an alien even though they had never been in Egypt.

Without getting into the long-standing and still inconclusive debate on the identity of these "Deuteronomists," I suggest that this program, implemented in the period of the Second Temple in open-air assemblies (e.g., Neh 7:73–8:12), was the brainchild of Levites one of whose functions was, according to late-biblical sources, religious education. An important point is at issue here. Societies in which collective memory and its perpetuation, either in writing or otherwise, are tightly controlled by a dominant social class will tend to leave nothing behind once that social class, which has identified itself with the nation, disappears from the scene. This seems to have happened to the Etruscans. Once the aristocracy disappeared, the people in effect lost their contact with the past, and therefore their identity as a people, with the result that we can view them today only through the blurred filters of Roman historiography and archaeological discovery (Le Goff 1992: 98). In the province of Judah successively under Iranian, Ptolemaic, Seleucid, and Roman rule, the educational program pursued by Deuteronomists, Levites, and their heirs the Pharisees led to a democratization of social memory and thus created a situation favorable to ethnic survival in spite of almost incessant social and political upheaval.

Orality and writing therefore interact subtly in the ways in which they mediate the past into the present. Even in societies more culturally advanced than sixth-century-B.C. Judah, social memory is shaped, sustained, and transmitted largely by noninscribed means such as rituals of reenactment, commemorative ceremonies, bodily gestures, and, on a smaller scale, public monuments, coins, medals, and postage stamps (Douglas 1986: 69-80; Connerton 1989: 41-104). So it was with the memory of the destruction of Jerusalem and its temple. A prophetic text from the early Persian period, one long lifetime after the event, speaks of public fasts in the fourth, fifth, seventh, and tenth months, corresponding to successive stages of the unfolding disaster, from the beginning of the siege to the assassination of the Babylonian-appointed ruler Gedaliah after the conquest (Zech 7:5; 8:18-19). The ritual itself, therefore, encoded a kind of rudimentary history of the event. In due course the fast of the fifth month, mentioned in Zechariah, became the festival of Tisha b'Av, a commemoration on the ninth of the month of Av (August) of the destruction of the city by both Babylonians and Romans, both Nebuchadrezzar and Titus. In this commemorative liturgy the range is extended even further since it is meant to include the defeat of the second revolt against Rome in A.D. 135 (*m. Ta'an.* 4:6). Some rituals of Tisha b'Av also commemorate, on the preceding sabbath, the sufferings of Jewish martyrs during the terrible period of the Crusades (Idelsohn 1960: 254-55). It would presumably be possible to extend it further by incorporating *anamnēsis* of the victims of the most recent Holocaust; indeed, this may already have been done.

Grieving belongs with remembering, as does rejoicing with pleasure in the present moment or in anticipation of pleasure in the near future. To grieve *is* to remember, to be unable to forget; witness the language of the biblical book of Lamentations, which some scholars suggest was composed for recital on the site of the ruined temple. Psalm 137 follows up the impossibility of singing the old songs or hymns with a vow to remember — "If I forget you, Jerusalem, may my right hand wither" (v. 5). Then there is the practice of praying with one's face turned toward the city, as Muslims at a later time would pray toward Mecca. Writing in the postdestruction period, the Historian attributes a long prayer to Solomon at the dedication of the First Temple in which Solomon speaks, prophetically or anachronistically, of Israelites in exile praying toward the land of Israel and the city of Jerusalem (1 Kgs 8:48). Later still, Daniel, accused by his detractors in distant Susa, kneels in prayer in an upstairs room with its window opened toward Jerusalem (Dan 6:10). The orientation of synagogues toward Jerusalem, beginning in the Roman period, conferred a permanent institutional stamp on this bodily gesture and served to focus the collective consciousness on the past.

Remembering can be related to action in many different ways. Prospective or short-term memory, the kind that enables us to keep a doctor's appointment or a dinner engagement at least some of the time, is an obvious example. And we know that damaged short-term memory resulting from trauma or alcohol intake can result in serious behavioral disorders. But much more important is the complex of long-term autobiographical memories without which we would have no sense of identity or context for meaningful action. We live by necessity out of the past. The past recalled is a necessary precondition for acting in the present. In biblical usage, likewise, remembering is rarely a simple psychological act. Joseph in prison asks the Pharaoh's butler to remember him when he gets out, which is tantamount to requesting that he mention his name and intervene on his behalf with the Pharaoh, which the butler promptly forgets or neglects to do (Gen 40:14, 23). The same is true, it seems, for the deity. God remembers Hannah, with the result that she beats the odds and conceives (1 Sam 1:19-20). The common prayer formula of the "remember me" (*zokrâ-lî*) type, addressed to a deity, is, equally clearly, a request for divine intervention on the petitioner's behalf, whether addressed to Yahveh by Nehemiah or by a pious individual who puts up the money for a mosaic in the local synagogue (Childs 1962: 45-65; Schottroff 1967; Blenkinsopp 1994: 208-10).

We do not need to appeal to the allegedly unique features of Hebrew mentality, or Hebrew psychology, to make the point that the vocabulary of remembering (Hebrew verbal stem *zkr*) very often implies a specific, concrete social embodiment. In the causative conjugation in Hebrew (Hiphil) the verb can connote participation in an act of worship in which the invocation of the deity, or the memorializing of the dead, is of central importance. To pronounce the name in a liturgical context is a significant act of retrieval, a conjuring up from the collective memory of a presence from that other world — a deity, a spirit, or a person long dead. Hence the term *zēker*, related to the same verbal stem, stands for the name pronounced in worship, the name that is to be invoked. So YHVH says to Moses at the burning thornbush: "This is my name forever; this is my *zēker* for all generations" (Exod 3:15).

The Old Testament offers many examples of these social embodiments of memory. The tassels (*ṣîṣîôt*) and phylacteries (*tĕfillin*) worn by the pious are both called *zikkārôn* (from the same verbal stem *zkr*), meaning a kind of mnemonic device or *aide mémoire* recalling the commandments (Exod 13:9; Num 15:37-41). The same term is applied to several significant cult objects, including the precious stones on the high priest's epaulettes (Exod 28:12; 39:7) and the twelve stones set up in the middle of the Jordan at the first entry into the land (Josh 4:7).

But the most significant use of the term *zikkārôn* must surely be in connection with the Passover festival (Exod 12:14). In the Passover the past is both remembered and reenacted. The Passover *sēder* speaks in the plural

— "we were Pharaoh's slaves in Egypt" — but the individual participant is invited to internalize the collectively retrieved past: "In every generation one must look upon oneself as if one had in one's own person come out of Egypt." In the course of a long development every item of food eaten and every gesture performed during the ritual was given its own specific historical referent. The matzoh lifted up by the one presiding for all to see is the bread of affliction eaten by the ancestors in Egypt. It would be difficult to find a better example of the pressure of the past on the present.

Passover is a prime example of a commemorative ritual, and it is no accident that it is carried out in the family circle. It also illustrates how calendars function as fundamental templates or frameworks within which societies organize and structure their collective memories into patterns of recurrence. We shall follow up on this in a moment, but we must first mention a related aspect. In the Old Testament God also remembers, and occasionally forgets, and one of the goals of cultic performance, including common prayer, whether in the family circle or the state shrine, is to activate God's memory. Hence the frequent appeals in the complaint psalms and prophetic intercessory prayers for God to remember and intervene and the frequent complaints that he has forgotten the suppliant. The texts assigned by modern scholarship to the Priestly strand in the Pentateuch, described God as setting up a perpetual covenant *(bĕrît 'ôlām)*, first with all creation, then with Israel's ancestors (Gen 9:8-17; 17:7-8, 13). What is implied in this term is a covenant that does not require periodic review, renewal, and revalidation, as was the case with political treaties. All that is needed is that God *remember* his covenant, which, in the Priestly history, he is called upon to do at times of hardship and crisis (Exod 2:24; 6:5; Lev 26:42, 45). To speak of God remembering is therefore a way of spanning the gap between the past and the present. As a memorial service *(zikkārôn)*, Passover functions to activate God's autobiographical memory. The same may be said of the Christian *anamnēsis* (the Greek translation of *zikkārôn*), as may be seen in the words of institution: "Do this as my memorial service," "Do this so that God will remember me."

3

The account of the Passover ritual in Exodus 12 begins by emphasizing a new calendar and therefore a new beginning: "This month shall be for you the beginning of months; it shall be the first month of the year for you" (Exod 12:2). Signaling a break with the past and a new beginning by instituting a new calendar is a familiar phenomenon; witness the *hejira* of Islam in A.D. 622 and the founding of the French Republic on September 22, 1792, the first day of the first month of a new epoch — later called Vendémiaire. The account of the celebration of the Passover festival in Egypt is meant to mark the birth of the Jewish commonwealth and the beginning of its history. Therefore, from this point on, and only from this point, the Israelites of the first generation are described as an organized congregation or assembly (Heb. *'ēdâ, qāhāl*) under civil and religious leadership. This is the birth of the nation. The care with which the Passover ritual, drafted by temple scribes, specifies who may or may not take part in the festival points in the same direction (Exod 12:43-49). Though its sacrificial aspects have receded with the passage of time, the Passover was considered to be a sacrifice, and is so described in the ritual (Exod 12:27). An important social function of sacrifice in ancient and traditional societies is to serve as a visible confirmation of membership and status in the kinship group by defining who are and who are not sacrificial adepts, and therefore who are and who are not members of the group. It also functions to sustain *communio,* a sense of identity and belonging, among the sacrificial adepts. By defining carefully who may or may not participate in the Passover sacrifice, the ritual in effect stipulates who does or does not qualify for membership in the new commonwealth.

Passover, then, combines the recollection of the past with a new beginning. It re-collects, gathers up, the past, and reconnects it with the present. With this we return to the hiatus in the history of Israel brought about by the disaster of 586 B.C. We can speak of a hiatus rather than a terminus on account of the founding of a new commonwealth within about two generations after the disaster. The author of the third-person narrative in Ezra 1–6, closely related to if not identical with the author of 1-2 Chronicles, tells a story about the return of Judeo-Babylonians to Palestine in the early years of Persian rule, their overcoming of obstacles and opposition from different sources, the building and dedication of a temple in Jerusalem to replace the one destroyed by the Babylonians, and the culmination of the entire program of restoration with the celebration of the Passover. Here, too, the implication is that the festival marks the official inauguration of a new commonwealth following the destruction of the old, with the date — the fourteenth of the first month — carefully noted (Ezra 6:19-22;

cf. Exod 12:2, 6). We are reminded inevitably of the founding of the State of Israel on May 14, 1948, linked historically as it was with the disaster of the Holocaust a few years earlier.

That Ezra 1–6 is an ideological construct rather than an example of archival reporting may be readily accepted. It must seem improbable, for one thing, that Cyrus would address a firman to the Jewish ethnic minority in Babylon urging them to return to their ancestral homeland and rebuild their temple (1:1-4). It is even less likely that some 50,000 Judeo-Babylonians would immediately and enthusiastically take up his invitation, especially in view of the embarrassing fact that more than two decades passed before work on the temple was finished. But we can accept that, at a minimum, some Jews did return from Babylon and elsewhere at different times throughout the first century of Persian rule, no doubt mostly in dribs and drabs, and settle in Judah. This in itself is a situation worthy of comment. With the benefit of hindsight we now see that there was nothing inevitable about this outcome, and that only by assimilating the memory of the disaster of 586 could a new commonwealth come into existence at all. Deported or relocated peoples almost always ended up assimilated to the local population in their new habitat. That is what happened to the inhabitants of Samaria deported by the Assyrians, a fate no different from the hundreds of thousands uprooted from their homelands by the Assyrians and resettled in foreign lands.

A striking feature of this phase of the history is the strong emotional link between diaspora and homeland. We recall the vow of the deported psalmist to remember Jerusalem now in ruins (Ps 137:5). Long afterward Nehemiah, cupbearer to the Persian king in distant Susa, breaks down in tears when he hears a report of the sad state of affairs in Judah (Neh 1:4). At every point of the story we feel the anxiety to preserve or create visible tokens of the past by, for example, building the temple on the site of the destroyed edifice and restoring to use the sacred vessels salvaged from the disaster.

Memory was therefore essential for survival, but the survivors also needed quite a bit of luck. It was fortunate for them that, unlike the Assyrians, the Babylonians did not practice cross-deportation, which would have effectively ruled out a return of the dispersed, or of their descendants, to Judah. Babylonian imperial policy also favored, or at least permitted, for administrative and fiscal rather than humanitarian reasons, displaced ethnic minorities to maintain their own distinct identity, organization, and institutions. Deported Judeans were also fortunate not to have been reduced to slavery, a circumstance due less to Babylonian magnanimity than to the fact that for working the land slave labor was less cost-effective than rent capitalism. In addition, the region in which they and other ethnic minorities (Greeks, Egyptians, Carians, etc.) were settled, the alluvial plain around the city of Nippur in Lower Mesopotamia, was due for redevelopment. Jewish communities were therefore able to maintain common worship, common customs (no doubt diluted with local customs), and therefore links with their past. They may also have built their own place of worship, perhaps at "the place Casiphia" that provided Ezra with temple personnel (Ezra 8:15-20), as the Jewish settlers at Elephantine on the first cataract of the Nile were doing about the same time.

Then, in due course, the province of Judah was granted a fair degree of autonomy by the Achaemenid court, which tended to support local temples and their personnel. While subjection to foreign rule was always basically unacceptable, the Persian Empire protected the emergent Jewish commonwealth from Samaria to the north and the expansive Kedarite Arab kingdom to the south and east. This support, which could not have been taken for granted, was literally a matter of survival. To quote Elias Bickerman: "If Jerusalem had not been a part of a Gentile empire, the nomads would have driven the Jews into the sea or swallowed up Palestine, and the rock of Zion would have been the foundation of an Arabian sanctuary a thousand years before Omar's mosque" (Bickerman 1962: 10).

4

Without a doubt it was important to survive, but the new commonwealth also had to shape an identity and therefore to construct a past that would give that identity body and substance. Comparative studies show that the creation of a past, and therefore of an ethnic memory, tends to take the forms of myths of origin and corresponding rituals, stories about culture heroes, and trade secrets passed on from the first inventors or founders *(prōtoi heurētai)*. All of these elements are to be found in the Pentateuch, which, in its finished form, is the chef d'oeuvre of the Jewish intellectual and religious elite of the late Persian or early Hellenistic period (5th to 4th century B.C.). The ways in which this constructed past reflects back a refracted image of the time of composition is not difficult to detect in these writings.

One example mentioned earlier is the Priestly description of Israel in the wilderness as a well-organized commonwealth under lay and clerical control. Another example is the Abraham story. Abraham is the first to make aliyah. He leaves Mesopotamia (Ur Kasdim), lays claim to the land of Canaan on behalf of his deity, purchases some real estate in the land as an assurance of permanence in it, and keeps his distance from the locals. In these ways he served as a model for diaspora Jews, those of Judeo-Babylonian descent and those who returned with them, who, according to our sources, had the dominant role in forming the new polity in Judah in the early Persian period (the mid-6th to the mid-5th cent. B.C.). Those who belonged to this segment of the population imitated his example by keeping their contacts with the locals to a minimum and avoiding marriage with their women.

In some respects the paradigmatic nature of these narratives comes through even more clearly in the Jacob story. The center of the four-generation history of the ancestors is occupied by Jacob's exile in Mesopotamia and his eventual return accompanied by portentous events and signs. That he merits to bear the name Israel only after his return would have left the reader in the postdestruction period in no doubt as to whose history was being recounted. But, to repeat, the clearest paradigm is the exodus story in its Passover reenactment with whose celebration the new commonwealth was inaugurated.

We will not find it difficult to verify the pervasive presence of this exodus tradition in the literature of the Second Temple period, especially in Isaiah 40–55, which critical scholarship dates to the postdestruction period. But at this point especially we must bear in mind the ambiguities involved in appealing to traditions or, even more insidious, tradition in the singular. Traditions can be cobbled together out of repressed desires or anxieties, a kind of collective false memory syndrome, or simply invented. Historians have quite properly pointed out that, apart from the biblical record, we have no evidence for an Israelite stay in Egypt in the late-second millennium B.C., and therefore none for the Israelites leaving Egypt. Archaeological data once confidently marshaled to establish an Israelite conquest of Canaan at a time consistent with the date conventionally assigned to the exodus have shrunk to the point of disappearance. Scholars now acknowledge that the biblical record's allusion to the store cities of Pithom and Rameses (Exod 1:11) does not necessarily date the record to the Ramesside period. The presence of the ubiquitous ʿapiru in Egypt probably has nothing to do with the biblical ʿibrîm (Hebrews), and appeal to the volcanic eruption in Thera-

Santorini to explain the crossing of the sea and the plagues (a tsunami and volcanic ash blotting out the sun) is too desperate to contemplate.

By now all of this is fairly well known. But we must also take into account that the myth of alien or nonautochthonous origins makes a good fit with the ideology and self-image of the Judeo-Babylonian elite in the Persian province of Judah vis-à-vis the indigenous population. Quite apart from unconscious controls at work in the society as a whole, history provides many examples of the deliberate manipulation of social memory and the imposition of a particular construction on the past by a ruling elite. As Jacques Le Goff puts it: "To make themselves the master of memory and forgetfulness is one of the great preoccupations of the classes, groups, and individuals who have dominated and continue to dominate historical societies. The things forgotten or not mentioned by history reveal these mechanisms for the manipulation of collective memory" (Le Goff 1992: 54). Examples of the deliberate manipulation of collective memory are at hand: the official version of Russian history as presented in the Soviet Encyclopedia during the Stalinist era, for example, or the Whig history of England of the George Macaulay Trevelyan type that was standard fare when I attended grammar school in England those many years ago.

Some historians who hold that the exodus story is an origins myth invented in the Persian period point to the parallel case of the Roman myth of Trojan origins familiar from Virgil's great epic poem. They claim that this is an invented tradition that responds in much the same way as the exodus tradition to the need for ancient foundations, distinctive origins, and a prototypical culture hero, at a time of radical change and new beginnings, namely, the transition from the republic to the principate. The comparison is indeed suggestive. Societies modern as well as ancient seem to need a charter myth, indications are not lacking that the myth-making faculty is especially in evidence in accounts of ethnic origins, and these accounts can be pure inventions. No one, for example, will feel obliged to defend the historical veracity of those medieval chroniclers who supplied London with a founder in the person of Brutus, a Trojan descendant of Aeneas who built a settlement on the Thames known as New Troy. Nor would the critical reader be taken in by the rabbinic fantasy that the Canaanites voluntarily surrendered the land to the incoming Israelites and meekly agreed to move to Africa (*Mekilta Pisha* 18; Philo, *Hypothetica* 6.5).

The comparison between Israelite and Roman origins can be instructive if it sets us thinking in a more nuanced way about the relation be-

14

tween mythography and historiography, the psychology of invention in general, and the inventive faculty as applied to ethnic origins in particular. While we have no more direct access to the historical Aeneas than to the historical Moses, we cannot simply describe him as an invention of Virgil and leave it at that. Virgil was drawing on the account of the First Punic War by Gnaeus Naevius in the course of which the latter describes the vicissitudes of Aeneas, including his sojourn with Dido at Carthage as the cause of the war. By that time, the late third century B.C., the tradition associating Aeneas with Roman origins must have been well known. From an inscription discovered at Tor Tignosa near Rome from the fourth century B.C., we also know that by that time Aeneas had been co-opted into the Roman *lares et penates*. Historians of ancient Rome could no doubt fill out the history of the tradition and draw suitably nuanced conclusions about its antiquity. Speculation about its origins would also take into account the contacts between western Asia Minor and central Italy during the Late Bronze Age. We will not succeed in fully demonstrating the historicity of the tradition, but we will have to reject the idea that the founding of the city by the Trojan Aeneas was a pure invention of the Augustan Age.

It may be advisable to proceed along somewhat the same lines with the exodus story. No critical reader will defend its literal historical truth. Six hundred thousand adult males with wives, children, and other dependents trekking through the wilderness of Sinai (Exod 12:37) present logistical problems of mind-boggling proportions even to the most outré literalist. But we can at least lead off by saying that, if this narrative tradition was invented, the invention must have taken place considerably earlier than the Persian period. It is implausible to maintain that none of the many allusions to the exodus in biblical texts antedates the fall of Jerusalem. In the History just about everybody has heard about it, including such rank outsiders as Jericho prostitutes, Gibeonites, and Philistines (Josh 2:8; 9:9; Judg 6:13; 11:16; 1 Sam 4:8; 15:6). The argument for a Persian period invention would require us to radically postdate *all* those allusions in prophetic books that assume this tradition to be well known and not in need of explanation (e.g., Hos 11:1; 12:9; 13:4; Amos 9:4). Collective memory, including the memory of Egyptian beginnings, also provides motivation for the observance of laws, as we saw earlier. Memory is therefore also a component of the ethical act.

If the weight of evidence is against a pure invention, it may be consistent with the view that what happened in the postdestruction period was a process of selection, incorporation, and adaptation drawing on a common memory bank. Perhaps that invention came much more into play in the process of assimilating contemporary situations and events to a traditional pattern rather than the reverse, a process that we suspect is going on in the account of the refounding of a Judean-Jewish commonwealth in the opening chapters of the book of Ezra.

Our personal experience of remembering provides an analogy to this process of selection of aspects or facets of the past from a potentially infinite number, the selection dictated by the conscious but more often unconscious agenda of the remembering subject. And to return to a point made earlier, the recomposition of these shards of memory into a pattern of some kind represents a quite different and ultimately more satisfying appropriation of the past than that of the historian.

5

As I was finishing writing the first draft of this paper, I came across the deeply moving account, by the great Russian neuropsychologist Alexandr Luria, of a Russian soldier who sustained a terrible brain wound during the Great Patriotic War that left him in a state of profound amnesia and aphasia (Luria 1972). Luria documents the struggle of this Zazetsky, "the man with the shattered world" — the title of the book — to rebuild his devastated life. Over a period of twenty-five years Zazetsky managed to produce, with the help of Luria and with enormous and painful effort, about three thousand pages of writing containing scraps of memory of his life before the disaster, out of which he constructed a sense of personal identity that enabled him to go on living. Without this process of recall, selection, arrangement, and recomposition, we either have the blanked-out past and empty future of the amnesiac or the chaotic excess of Borges's fictional *Funes el Memorioso*. This hard-won truth, that the possibility of a future depends on the past being remembered and reconstructed, applies as much to societies as to individuals like Zazetsky.

At this point we return once again, and finally, to the catastrophe of 586 B.C. The event was recorded by the Historian, and in fact was the reason for the History being written in the first place and the point of reference dictating the way events in it are recorded. The same could be said of much of the biblical literature, beginning with the account of human origins (Genesis 1–11), which replicates the structure of Israel's historical experience as interpreted in the light of the disaster. But none of this would have happened if the event had not been remembered. Remembering is a condition sine qua non of survival.

As a footnote to these reflections, I recall that in Jewish tradition the fast of Tisha b'Av, and therefore the commemoration of the disaster, is linked with the messianic hope. "On the day the temple was destroyed, the Redeemer will be born" (*Bereshit Rabbah* 55). The memory of past disaster is therefore linked with the prospect of future restoration.

II

Old Testament Theology and
the Jewish-Christian Connection

1

To speak, in defiance of the weight of history, of a Jewish-Christian connection can at least claim a measure of justification from the historical fact
that the Christian movement emerged from Judaism and first achieved
historical visibility as a Palestinian Jewish sect. In an obvious sense, therefore, if Christianity is to be understood historically at all, it has to be understood with reference to Judaism. To that extent, and allowing for the
possibility that Christianity may enter in some way into Jewish self-
understanding, there is an element of asymmetry in the relation between
Judaism and Christianity. It is arguable, and some would argue, that Judaism can be understood historically without reference to Christianity, but it
is impossible to understand Christianity historically without reference to
Judaism. On the other hand, both Judaism and Christianity attained their
classical expressions only some three or four centuries after the rise of
Christianity, and certainly not without reciprocal influence, which suggests the possibility of viewing them as juxtaposed but contrasting appro-
priations of the same historical and textual traditions.

One of the aspects of this problematic juxtaposition, the only one
with which I will deal in this paper, is the enterprise of Old Testament Theology. It is possible to speak of an Old Testament Theology (a designation
that is historically precise even if often avoided by contemporary Christian
scholars) only because the first Christian generations chose to retain as essential to Christian self-understanding and self-definition texts that had

been produced, revered, and passed on in Jewish circles. This decision was not an inevitable consequence of the Palestinian-Jewish roots of the first Christian communities, certainly not for those who emphasized the transcendental reality and newness of the formative Christian events. Some of the most sophisticated minds in the first two Christian centuries and many since have opposed this decision. In the second century Marcion opted for a spiritual religion antithetical to what he took to be the religion of the Jewish Scriptures, a religion deriving from an alien deity and characterized (as he thought and as many still think) by narrow-minded nationalism, materialistic cult practices, and obsessive ritualism. The attraction of Marcion's teachings and of the alternative church founded by him, which was still in evidence as late as the fifth century, can be gauged by the volume and violence of the polemic directed against both by mainstream Christians.

The Marcionite option did not therefore win acceptance. On the contrary, the Scriptures of Judaism came to be seen as an essential component of the church's self-understanding. But doubts about the Christian relevance of the Old Testament did not go away. Schleiermacher at the beginning of the nineteenth century, and Harnack at the beginning of the twentieth, argued that the link between the Christian revelation and the Old Testament is an accident of history rather than of the essence. While selectively useful to Christians as a book of edification, consolation, wisdom, and counsel, the Old Testament also exhibited a religion and morality other than Christian and presented the danger of an inferior and obsolete principle forcing its way into Christianity (Harnack 1901: 200-201). For the Christian, therefore, the Jewish Scriptures were basically expendable.

While this view was argued on its own theological merits and no doubt sincerely held, we can now see that it was not unconnected with cultural and religious anti-Jewish sentiment particularly in evidence in German academic circles — Germany being the great heartland of theological and biblical studies — though by no means confined to that country and that environment. If this view of the Christian relation to the Old Testament did not prevail, one reason must have been the need to account for the fact that Jesus himself was Jewish and spoke and acted as a Jew, from which followed the impossibility of severing him from the history and destiny of the Jewish people. Historically worthless as were the attempts, beginning with Friedrich Delitzsch and taken up by Nazi ideologues like Rosenberg, to substitute an Aryan for a Jewish Jesus, they were at least logical in seeing the ideological urgency of detaching Jesus from Judaism. To sever early Christianity from its Jewish matrix is to render unintelligible the agenda of the early church and, to the extent that we have access to it, the agenda of Jesus himself. One is hard put to think of any issues of concern to the first generations of Christians — the nature and location of the true Israel, the authoritative status of the laws, the identity and fate of the Messiah, the kingdom of God, the Gentile mission, the final consummation of history — that were not already issues internal to Judaism in its development during the time of the Second Temple.

This is the point of departure for understanding the genesis of Old Testament Theology as a distinct discipline. Once the Jewish Scriptures had been taken over, they had to be expounded in a way consistent with the view that they were also the Christian Scriptures. Throughout the patristic age this task was discharged in the form of sermon and catechesis. While early Christian exposition had some features in common with contemporaneous Jewish exegesis, the differences are more evident than the similarities. In the first place, Christian teachers and preachers preferred the Greek translation of the Scriptures, the Septuagint (LXX), which differed from the Hebrew Bible as it then existed in the number of books, their arrangement and content, and numerous points of detail. Polemical requirements also favored a shift of emphasis from the Torah to the Prophets and the Psalms, interpreted in oracular fashion according to a theory of inspiration drawn from classical Greek religious thought. Unassimilable elements, the dietary laws, for instance, could be subjected to allegorical interpretation following the lead of the Alexandrian philosopher Philo. The temptation to pick and mix, to opt for what is sometimes called a "canon within the canon," was present from the beginning and remained a distinctive and perhaps inevitable feature of biblical interpretation. One recalls Luther's dismissal of the Epistle of James as "an epistle of straw" and his outburst, recorded in his *Tischreden:* "I so hate Esther and Second Maccabees that I wish they did not exist; there is too much Judaism in them and not a little heathenism" (Bainton 1963: 6-7).

The standard approach to scriptural texts whose Christian relevance was not obvious was by way of typology. So, for example, Rahab's thread could stand for the blood of Jesus, and the serpent lifted up in the wilderness for the cross. If it seemed that Abraham or Jacob lied, a possibility not to be entertained, this could be regarded, as it was by Augustine, not as a lie but a mystery: *non est mendacium sed mysterium.* In contrast to the

Qumran community, the early Christians did not produce biblical commentaries. For these we have to wait until the third century, the earliest being that of Hippolytus on Daniel. With Origen in the same century we have the beginnings of text criticism and a conscious effort to make biblical interpretation philosophically respectable. Naturally, no one as yet thought of biblical interpretation as an activity independent of church life in general.

Before going further, I should make a clarification. It would, I think, be a mistake to assume that in the earliest period Christians or any other group within the intellectual and religious ambit of Judaism had at their disposal a fixed canon of inspired writings to which they owed allegiance. The earliest lists of biblical books are from Christian sources of the second century (Audet 1950: 135-54), and for an official list in a Jewish source we have to wait for the publication of the Babylonian Talmud (*b. Baba Batra* 14b-15a).

Early Christian writings do contain allusions to "the law and the prophets" and, in one instance, "the law of Moses, the prophets, and the psalms" (Luke 24:44), and similar expressions can be found even earlier (e.g., Dan 9:2; 2 Macc 15:9; Prologue to Ecclesiasticus). But such designations did not rule out the promulgation, in the book of *Jubilees* and the *Temple Scroll* from Qumran, of authoritative legal enactments over and above the laws in the Pentateuch, and they did not prevent writers of apocalyptic tracts from assigning their own compositions to authors of greater antiquity and, to that extent, greater authority than Moses. There were those groups within Judaism that revised the laws, that accepted only those promulgated prior to the apostasy of the golden calf, that put "the traditions of the elders" on the same footing as the written laws, and that rejected everything except the Pentateuch. In view of this diversified and fluid situation, it makes better sense to think of early Christians and roughly contemporaneous Jewish groups (e.g., the Qumran community) not as having available a fixed set of authoritative texts awaiting commentary but as themselves existing within a textual, exegetical continuum that would eventuate only later in a fixed canon of sacred writings.

An essential prerequisite for the study of the Bible as an independent activity was the emergence of theology as a distinct science in the medieval schools (Smalley 1952, 1963: 6-7). To schematize and no doubt oversimplify: the first stage in this process was the passage from *lectio,* exposition of the sacred text *(sacra pagina),* to *quaestio,* the formulation of questions arising out of texts that were thought to present theological or moral problems. These then became the subject of disputation involving appeal to philosophical or theological principles and criteria. Originally limited to issues not touching the essence of the Christian faith, the *disputatio* came in the course of time to subsume all doctrine in an organized presentation, resulting in the theological *summae* of which that of Aquinas is the best known. The intellectual revival of the eleventh and twelfth centuries, fostered by the monastic and cathedral schools and, eventually, by the universities (Paris in 1150, Oxford shortly afterward when English students were expelled from Paris), led to specializations in theology, philosophy, the Bible, and profane disciplines. Systematic and critical lectures on the Bible were held, perhaps for the first time, at the Abbey of St. Victor in Paris. While the basic text was Jerome's Vulgate, there were those who mastered Greek — for example, Robert Grosseteste, first-known Chancellor of the University of Oxford — and Hebrew — among whom Andrew of St. Victor was preeminent. Concordances and dictionaries were produced, and the best minds turned from allegory and typology to the task of determining the literal sense of the biblical text. Of these one of the most assiduous was Nicholas of Lyra, a victim of the great plague of 1348-50, whose monumental fifty-tome commentary on the Bible *(Postillae Perpetuae in Universam Sacram Scripturam)* was to have considerable influence on the sixteenth-century Reformers.

Christian scholars can easily overlook the fact that the impetus towards the critical study of biblical texts in the Middle Ages came in considerable measure from the work of Jewish commentators. Nicholas of Lyra quotes Rashi (Solomon ben Isaac of Troyes, 1040-1105) on numerous points of detail. As Beryl Smalley says somewhere, picking the brains of rabbis was the medieval equivalent of excavating a biblical site. Increasing concentration on the literal sense *(pěšaṭ)*, from Saadya Gaon in the tenth to David Kimchi in the thirteenth century, helped to bring about the prevalence of the *sensus litteralis* in the work of the best Christian exegetes. At the same time the study of Biblical Hebrew, essential for scientific exegesis, was being put on a solid basis by Menahem ben Saruk, Dunash ibn Labrat, and their students. Since most biblical scholars today are not too familiar with these pioneers, they will from time to time come up with "original" meanings and derivations that are in fact anything up to a thousand years old. Some of the work of these Jewish lexicographers and grammarians did, at any rate, percolate through to Christian circles, setting the stage for the Hebrew scholarship of Johann Reuchlin, Sebastian Münster, and others in the early sixteenth century.

It would be natural to suppose that the Reformers' principle of the sufficiency of Holy Writ and the right of private judgment in interpreting it would favor the study of the Bible as an independent discipline, and to a certain extent this is the case. But the initial impetus had already been imparted to the independent status of biblical study by the work of linguistic pioneers like Erasmus and Reuchlin, supported by the enthusiasm of scholar-printers like Daniel Bomberg and Aldus Manutius. The study of the Bible, however, was soon harnessed to the requirements of denominational polemics. It is no accident that the division into verses dates from this epoch, given the need for biblical ammunition in Protestant-Catholic and intradenominational polemics.[1] On the Catholic side, emphasis on tradition as an authoritative source of doctrine independent of but theoretically connected with Scripture, together with the reaffirmation of the privileged status of the Vulgate over against the many vernacular versions then appearing, discouraged independent critical inquiry. While there were some excellent Catholic commentaries between the sixteenth and nineteenth centuries, a deterrent attitude continued to prevail, as certain independent spirits like Richard Simon and Alexander Geddes were to discover to their cost. The result was that Catholics played a negligible role in the rise and development of critical biblical study, and were further marginalized by the Modernist controversy in the late nineteenth and early twentieth centuries. Catholics began to enter the critical mainstream only after the Second World War, about the same time that Jewish biblical scholarship was making the same move, the latter especially in the United States and Israel.

2

As a distinct academic discipline, Biblical Studies saw the light of day as a child of the Enlightenment and was nurtured into maturity by the

---

1. The system now in use has been traced back to the French Reformer Robert Estienne, who is said to have divided the Greek New Testament into verses on a coach trip from Paris to Geneva in 1550. Three years later the verse division was extended to his French translation of the entire Bible.

historiographical revolution of the nineteenth century. The essential condition for its emergence was independence of church dogmatics, a point made forcibly by Hermann Schultz, author of one of the better nineteenth-century theologies: "In a description of this progress [of Old Testament Theology], the one really instructive fact is this, that it was only through the gradual giving up of the conviction as to the perfect harmony between the teaching of the Bible and the Church that this science of ours could obtain a start and acquire a position of growing authority" (Schultz 1892: 79).

One of the first to affirm the need for free inquiry according to the dictates of reason was Johann Salomo Semler, who had exchanged the Lutheran Pietism of his early years for a liberal and rationalist theology, and whose *Treatise on the Free Investigation of the Canon* appeared in 1771. The following statement from that work may serve to illustrate the problematic implications of biblical theology for Christian relations with Judaism: "For the most part the canon of the Old Testament consists of a collection of crude Jewish prejudices which are diametrically opposed to Christianity, and only a small proportion of this canon contains divine and inspired writings in which useful and serviceable truths can be found also for Christians" (Semler 3:28).

Following along much the same lines, Johann Philipp Gabler, in his inaugural lecture delivered at the University of Altdorf on March 30, 1787, argued the need to distinguish between biblical thought and systematic theology or, in the lecturer's own words, between the simplicity and perspicacity of biblical ideas and the subtlety and severity of dogmatic theology. Biblical theology, he maintained, is historical, consisting in the sum of what biblical writers thought about divine things. Dogmatic theology, on the other hand, draws on philosophy and nonbiblical history in addition to the Bible. One should therefore proceed by gathering together and comparing all the biblical "testimonies" with a view to producing a synthesis, in much the same way that one might make a synthesis of the teaching of the Stoics. Only then would it be possible to decide to what uses, if any, the results could be put by the dogmatic theologian (Gabler and Gabler 1831: 179-98).

Once these foundations were laid, the way was clear for the composition of an Old Testament Theology according to current *wissenschaftliche* methods based on the canons of reason. The first and possibly the worst of these theologies, that of Georg Lorenz Bauer, was published in 1796 (Bauer

1838). If it is worth recalling today, it will be only in order to illustrate the rationalist thought of that epoch at its most intransigent. While incorporating the latest critical advances, including the breakdown of the Pentateuch into sources introduced half a century earlier by Jean Astruc, physician to Louis XIV, and the late date of Isaiah 40–66, Bauer went through the Old Testament book by book with a view to describing its religious ideas. The results were not exactly encouraging. The Pentateuch was found to contain a mix of primitive ideas and the crudest kind of nationalism and chauvinism. Far from possessing any religious or moral value, the book of Joshua was "calculated to produce an injurious effect on the mind of its readers" (p. 43). The book of Judges is the product of a barbarous age, and the other historical books are full of crude and unworthy notions about God. The preexilic prophets were a bit better, but still too judaical. That there is anything to praise in the postexilic prophets is due to the fact that, in the meantime, the religious notions of the Jews had been purified and elevated by contact with the Persians. The book of Daniel, finally, manifested "all the illiberality which characterized the opinions of the later Jews" (p. 142), and much the same could be said of other postexilic compositions.

Practically the only Old Testament compositions to escape Bauer's censure were the sapiential books, including Proverbs with its excellent religious views, Job, the most sublime work of the Hebrews, and Ecclesiastes, second only to Job. The point is made forcibly in his summing up, where he asserts that in Israel the torch of religious enlightenment was carried not by priests and prophets but by sages: "The purest and most elevated conceptions of God are to be found in those books composed by private individuals, who either disregarded the peculiar national ideas and prejudices of their countrymen, or had raised themselves above them" (p. 167).

Bauer's *Theology* illustrates not only eighteenth-century rationalism at its most intransigent but also the unsympathetic attitude of Gentile, and even some Jewish, *maśkîlîm* to Judaism as an illiberal form of religious expression reflected in its canonical scriptures. This attitude was pervasive in that culture, but there were exceptions. Gotthold Lessing read the Old Testament as the first stage in the moral education of the human race, leading to the teachings of Jesus and, eventually, to the point where the human race could dispense with both the Old and the New Testaments.[2] Lessing

---

2. See his "The Education of the Human Race," in *Lessing's Theological Writings,* ed. Henry Chadwick (Stanford: Stanford University, 1956), pp. 82-98.

was also an advocate for Jewish emancipation and civil rights postulated on Enlightenment principles, and this open-minded approach was illustrated by his drama *Nathan the Wise,* inspired by his friend Moses Mendelsohn. Johann Gottfried Herder, whose *Vom Geist der hebräischen Poesie (On the Spirit of Hebrew Poetry)* was published in 1782, three years after Lessing's drama appeared, is also a name to recall because of his enthusiasm for early Israelite poetry and the culture that produced it. But the Romantic reaction, as it bore on the study of the Bible, also unfortunately served to highlight the contrast between Herder's "Hebrew humanism" and the legalistic and ritualistic system that supplanted and stifled it.

This dichotomy between Hebrew religion characterized by spontaneity and feeling *(Gefühl)* and a religion dominated by law and ritual then became a *locus communis* in most theologies written during the late eighteenth- and early- to mid-nineteenth century. Not uncharacteristically for that time, Wilhelm de Wette spoke of Judaism as a hybrid intellectual system lacking that inner quality of sentiment — *Gefühl* once again (Kraus 1956: 160-82; Rogerson 1985: 28-49). De Wette, appointed as the first Professor of Bible at the newly founded University of Berlin where Hegel was later to teach, was a close friend of Schleiermacher and was no doubt influenced by him. Schleiermacher rejected not only the legalism and ritualism that he deemed characteristic of Judaism but also any intrinsic theological link between the Old and the New Testaments. His approach was to be echoed about a century later by Adolf Harnack: whatever the situation may have been in the first or in the sixteenth century, there was no longer any justification for the Christian church in the modern world to retain the Jewish Scriptures.

3

Bauer's *Theology* illustrates another problem that all authors of an Old Testament Theology have had to face, that of identifying a theme or principle according to which the diverse points of view contained in the biblical texts can be organized and brought together into a coherent system (Smend 1970). In this respect it is ironic that Bauer gave pride of place to those more discursive and sapiential perspectives that subsequent practitioners have found most difficult to integrate into their syntheses. Gustav Friedrich Oehler, author of a Theology popular throughout the nineteenth century, dealt with Wisdom last, after what he called Mosaism and Propheticism. His idea was to use the so-called wisdom writings to highlight the failure of Israel to solve the deeper problems of human existence, thus proving the need for a new and definitive revelation. The point is made on the last page of his book, indeed in the last footnote, in which he quoted from Franz Delitzsch's commentary on Ecclesiastes to the effect that "Ecclesiastes, upon its heap of rubbish, shows how needful it is that heaven should now open above the earth" (Oehler 1883: 569).

Somewhat less forced was the position taken by Hermann Schultz, author of what is generally taken to be the best of the nineteenth-century Theologies of the Old Testament, one that at any rate went through five editions. Schultz put the speculative wisdom writings outside the scope of his inquiry, dedicating only four or five pages to practical wisdom and reading Ecclesiastes (Qoheleth) as symptomatic of the spiritual decline and disorientation characteristic of *Spätjudentum* (Schultz 1882: 1:434, 437-38; 2:83-86).

Most of the twentieth-century essays have followed a similar pattern and have encountered similar difficulties. The most comprehensive of them, that of Walther Eichrodt, restricts itself to wisdom as a divine attribute and notes that the work of the sages came, like everything else, to be dominated by Torah-piety, a development Eichrodt regarded as problematic if not deplorable (Eichrodt 1967: 2:80-98, 374-79). In most other essays the teachings of the sages fall for brief discussion under the heading of ethics (Vriezen 1970: 377-404) when they are not simply omitted (Clements 1978). Only in recent years have Old Testament theologians begun to integrate these writings into their syntheses, generally under the rubric of ethics or natural theology (e.g., Barr 1993: 146-71; 1999: 468-96).

At any rate, the history of the enterprise since Bauer suggests that it is not easy, and perhaps not possible, to come up with a theme or principle around which the biblical material can be organized in a satisfactory manner. Emphasis on the narrative content of the Bible, much in evidence in recent writing, leaves questions about the theological significance of the non-narrative parts unanswered. It is now generally acknowledged that one of the more important factors in the collapse of the Biblical Theology Movement in the postwar years (the 1950s to 1970s) was its uncritical and unanalyzed allegiance to the idea of history as the arena of divine activity and the medium of divine revelation. We encounter a similar problem in the *Old Testament Theology* of Gerhard von Rad. The division of this work

into the historical and prophetic traditions of Israel is dictated by two ruling ideas. The first is the proposal to organize the theology around the acts
of God on Israel's behalf and Israel's response, sometimes in confession and
praise, more often in unresponsiveness and covenant violation. Now whatever may be the advantages of this strategy, it makes it difficult to integrate
those writings that evince little or no interest in *Heilsgeschichte* or, a fortiori,
deny its possibility (see, e.g., Qoh 1:3-11 and 3:11). The second idea arises
from von Rad's conviction that the Prophets proclaimed the end of the
salvific history, and that that history actually came to an end once the Law
came into the picture as a suprahistorical reality (von Rad 1962: 1:91, 126).

Leaving aside this curious idea of a *Heilsgeschichte* that comes to an
end at a certain point or — even more curious — stops and starts again,
we note the irony involved in a Theology of the Old Testament unable to
accommodate those writings that most closely approximate theology as we
recognize it today. The sages of Israel dealt discursively and sometimes in-
cisively with issues such as free will, divine providence, and theodicy, they
appropriated mythology as a way of thinking theologically, and the concept of wisdom itself came to serve as an interpretative principle for eluci-
dating history, for example, in the Wisdom of Solomon (Sheppard 1980).
Another not unimportant point is that lines of continuity exist between
the writings of Israel's sages and both classical Judaism and early Christianity. The earliest attributions in the Mishnaic treatise *'Avot* ("The Sayings of the Fathers") take us back into the biblical period, and the Christian Alexandrian school has links with the same scribal-sapiential tradition
through the work of Jewish scholars active in that city, Philo in particular.

4

The contrast between the more aphoristic, didactic, and discursive writings subsumed under the rubric "wisdom" and writings dedicated to history, prophecy, and law illustrates the many contrarieties and aporias facing the person who aspires to write an integrative and systematic theology.
Prior decisions have to be made as to what is more or less important, and it
goes without saying that the decision making will be controlled either con-
sciously or unconsciously by the commitments and presuppositions of the
author, the author's social class, denomination, or other interest group.
Here, as elsewhere, there is no such thing as an *innocent* or neutral inter-

pretation. This brings us back to our starting point with the issues involved in writing a *Christian* theology of the Old Testament. The author of such a theology must account not only for the fact that the Christian canon includes the New Testament but that what he or she calls the Old Testament (or the Former Testament, or the Hebrew Bible) is held in common with those of Jewish faith, and that therefore — to return to the title of this paper — the connection with Judaism as a theological issue cannot be set aside.

At one time it was common to express the connection in terms of a continuous providential history that reached its goal in Christ and the Christian movement. First proposed by Eusebius, though adumbrated in Luke's Gospel, this deceptively simple schema entered the theological mainstream through the work of German Pietists of the early eighteenth century. Rejecting what they regarded as the arid scholasticism of their own Lutheran tradition, theologians like Haymann and Bengel emphasized the concrete, historical record of God's dealings with Israel and humanity as recorded in the Bible. This brand of salvation history was then systematically developed by conservative Lutheran theologians in the following century, conspicuously by J. C. K. von Hofmann, for whom the history recorded in the Old Testament follows an ascending, preordained parabola leading to Christ. As Hofmann saw it, it follows for the understanding of the place of the Old Testament that "the things recorded therein are to be interpreted teleologically . . . and thus as being of the same nature as the goal, yet modified by their respective place in the history" (Hofmann 1959: 135).

So stated, von Hofmann's understanding of history in the Bible raises all kinds of questions. In what ways, if at all, does this allow for the Old Testament to be intelligible from the perspective of Jewish faith? Is Christ within the history or does he, so to speak, stand outside the continuum? Does the history proceed along a line from lower to higher forms of religious life, eventuating in the Christian instantiation, understood to be the highest of them all? Is it a continuous or a broken line? A further and particularly grievous problem for salvation history, either in the older forms elaborated by the federal theologians of the seventeenth century, or in that of the conservative theologians of the nineteenth, or in the updated form in which it was presented in the twentieth century by von Rad and Cullmann, is its vulnerability to critical historiography. If *Heilsgeschichte* implies that God was active in the events of Israel's history as they really happened, and not just as Israel believed and confessed them to have happened, it must come to terms with the critical reconstruction of the history that was already well advanced by the time von Hofmann was writing. It has since become abundantly clear that this coming to terms happens only at the price of abandoning the naive idea that biblical narrative affords clear and unobstructed access to situations and events during the biblical period.

The salvation-history theologians, therefore, read the Old Testament as the record of a progressive revelation of divine deeds and disclosures that had the purpose of educating humanity, through Israel, for the coming of Christ. The Old Testament was, therefore, a *praeparatio evangelica*. If the biblical record from the beginnings of humanity and Israel to its consummation in Christ is thought of as a continuous and uninterrupted line, the question what to do with the later period of biblical history, the part that overlaps with the early history of Judaism, is unavoidable. Wellhausen was aware of this problem, and at the beginning of his *Prolegomena* remarked how, for this species of salvation-history theology, which of course he rejected, early Judaism was "a mere empty chasm over which one springs from the Old Testament to the New" (Wellhausen 1957: 1).

What was crucial for many who shared Wellhausen's aversion for the theocratic system expounded in the Priestly source and Chronicles was to link early Christianity with Israel before the rise of Judaism or, in other words, to sever the history of Israel and of God's dealings with Israel from the history of Judaism in its earliest phase in the biblical period. For Von Rad, the classical prophets proclaimed the end of Israel, and he seems to be saying that, as a result of the discontinuity between preexilic and postexilic Israel, God's dealings with Israel did in some real sense come to an end with the fall of Jerusalem in 586 B.C. (von Rad 1962: vii; 1965: 2:176-87). All the important elements in his theology were therefore based either on the earliest period of Israel's history as reflected in the Hexateuch, that is, the first six books of the Bible, or on preexilic prophecy. Prophetic and historical texts continued to appear after the fall of Jerusalem, but once the law took over, the forward movement of the history stalled (von Rad 1962: 1:85-92; 1965: 2:388-409).

Much can be learned about the intent or basic tendency of Theologies of the Old Testament published in the modern period by observing how the authors periodize the history. One of the major advances in the critical study of the Old Testament was the demonstration that the prophetic movement was well underway before the law codes were put together. This was taken to imply that the prophets could not be viewed, in the traditional Jewish manner, as primarily preachers, interpreters, and tradents of the laws. First proposed by Wilhelm Vatke in his *Biblische Theologie* of 1835, this chronological reversal was confirmed by Karl Heinrich Graf's demonstration that the Priestly Code (P), formerly known as the basic document or *Grundschrift* (G), came not at the beginning but at the end of the history of Israel, in the transitional period between Israel and early Judaism. These conclusions provided the basis for Wellhausen's reconstruction of the religious history of Israel in his *Prolegomena* of 1883. According to Wellhausen's schematic presentation, the old nature religion based on kinship was dealt a fatal blow by the Deuteronomic centralization of worship, and the process of "denaturing" *(Entnaturierung)* was capped by the authors of the Priestly Code, who gave to Judaism its essential features of legalism and heteronomy, characteristics that Wellhausen did not admire. This was the religious worldview against which Jesus reacted. As Wellhausen put it in his article on Israel in the *Encyclopaedia Britannica,* "Jesus casts ridicule on the works of the law, the washing of hands and vessels, the tithing of mint and cummin, the abstinence from even doing good on the Sabbath. Against unfruitful self-sanctification He sets up another principle of morality, that of the service of one's neighbour" (Wellhausen 1957: 510).

Another aspect of the schema that was beginning to dominate Old Testament Theology in the late nineteenth century can already be detected in Vatke's *Biblische Theologie,* which divided the history into preprophetic, prophetic, and postprophetic. (Tripartite arrangements, practically de rigueur in nineteenth-century and early-twentieth-century Theologies, may be taken to testify to the pervasive influence of Hegel.) The profile of the prophet as embodying the supreme religious ideal was already present in the pioneering work of Heinrich Ewald, with whom Wellhausen had studied at Göttingen. In his *Propheten des alten Bundes* (The Prophets of the Old Covenant), published in 1840, Ewald described the prophet as the interpreter of the thoughts of God, which were destined to prevail in history and which it was the prophet's duty to proclaim in the political arena. To his credit, Ewald practiced what he preached, and to such effect as to be removed from his university post and to spend some time in one of Bismarck's prisons for his refusal to take the oath of loyalty.

The implications of Ewald's work were spelled out by another of his students, Bernhard Duhm, whose *Theologie der Propheten* (The Theology of the Prophets) appeared in 1875. The full title of this work is significant: *The Theology of the Prophets as Foundation for the Inner Historical Development of Israelite Religion.* The tripartite divisioning of the history follows Ewald but is more fully set out as Mosaism, Propheticism, and Judaism. For Duhm, the prophet is the exponent of ethical individualism, an approach to God that dispenses with the mediation of priests and sacrifice; in brief, it is a religion in which personal experience counts for more than institutional forms of religious life. On this view, prophecy marked the high point of "inner historical development," after which the historical process had nowhere to go but down.

The outcome of this view of prophecy in relation to law, and the periodization of history to which it led, was to drive a wedge between Israel and early Judaism. Prophecy, the high point of religious developments in the history of Israel, comes to an end with the rise of Judaism and the dominance of law. The same pattern can be observed — to take a final example — in the *Theology of the Old Testament* of Walther Eichrodt, no doubt the most comprehensive and certainly one of the most influential written in this century (Eichrodt 1960, 1967). This is not the place for a critical review of Eichrodt's impressive achievement, but one or two remarks relevant to the point under discussion are in order. Eichrodt set himself against the dominant genetic and historicist approach, proposing instead to concentrate on the structural and thematic unity of Old Testament thought by starting out with the idea of "covenant" as the central theme, *die Mitte,* and then taking a cross-sectional approach to different themes. Hence the different kind of tripartite sectioning, inherited from his teacher Otto Procksch, which gives his work a decidedly systematic though at times repetitious look: God and the people, God and the world, God and man. Each theme within this structure is worked through developmentally. If we concentrate on the last phase in each section — the post-exilic period and *Spätjudentum* (late Judaism, though really early Judaism!) — we shall see that nothing has changed. It is a period dominated by legalism, heteronomy, and vain observances that leave the heart empty. What continually confronts us is "the inner disintegration of the structure of the Jewish faith," "the inner schizophrenia of Jewish piety," and more of the same. The conclusion to which these judgments lead can be predicted. This situation could be overcome only when early Christianity broke free from its Jewish roots to rediscover in the Old Testament, in the Israel prior to its Jewish deformation, the pattern of true religion (Eichrodt 1967: 315, 464).

At this point someone will object that in the atmosphere in which the discipline of Biblical Studies is conducted today, all of this is really *vieux jeu,* regrettable indeed, but a matter of historical rather than current interest. It is fortunately true that in academic circles the situation is, in several important respects, quite different from what it was during the heyday of the discipline when von Rad and Eichrodt were publishing. Those churches that have been most responsible for what has been called "the teaching of contempt" have formally renounced, if not always without reservations, this sad and scandalous aspect of their history. Jewish and Christian scholars work together harmoniously in the biblical associations and departments of Religious Studies, and chairs have been established in Judaica at many institutions of theological and biblical learning, not least in Germany, still the heartland of Biblical Studies. The often contentious history of research on the Qumran scrolls provides a good example of cooperation between Jewish and Christian scholars, with the occasional flare-up confined to the periphery.

While all this is undoubtedly the case, there are still abundant indications that Christian students preparing to teach Old Testament and New Testament are not on the whole well acquainted with the Jewish religious and intellectual tradition. And in spite of what one would expect to be the case in the post-Holocaust epoch, it cannot be said that these changes in attitude have made much of a difference to the theological understanding of the Scriptures (Fackenheim 1990). The sobering fact is that, in the absence of an adequate theological understanding of Judaism, most people's attitudes will tend to be controlled by the Zeitgeist, the prevailing climate of opinion, and Zeitgeists are notoriously fickle. In the most recent period we see indications that the Israeli-Palestinian conflict has impacted opinion in academic institutions in this respect, primarily but by no means exclusively in Europe.

Perhaps the most significant factor in bringing about change in the academic study of Judaism in institutions formerly or currently affiliated with Christian churches is the detailed attention that the period of the Second Commonwealth, which is the period of early Judaism, has been receiving over the last few decades. Study of the emergent Judaism of the Persian (Achaemenid) period is now one of the growth areas in the discipline, and the publication of the Qumran material has revitalized the study of Judaism (or Judaisms) in the Roman period. Prejudicial generalizations about the law have in most quarters given way to careful study of individual collections of legal material in the social and political context of the period, including, most recently, the issue of imperial authorization as a possible external factor in the compilation of laws during the Persian period. Engagement with sociological and anthropological theory has dispelled the negative aura that for many Old Testament scholars of a former generation surrounded ritual activity. As a result, a quite different interpretation of the religious history of the Second Temple period is emerging, and of course the Second Temple period includes in its final phase the emergence of the Christian movement.

This leads to a final consideration, the possibility of a repositioning and revisioning of early Christianity within the greatly improved understanding of Second Temple history now available. This is a vast and complex project, rendered more difficult by the division of competence imposed by the distinct disciplines of Old Testament Studies and New Testament Studies inherited from the traditional seminary curriculum. The first and easiest step would be to restate the standard and by now admittedly *depassé* antitheses — Christian universalism over against Jewish particularism, Christian freedom from the law over against Jewish legalism, and so on — as issues *internal to Judaism* on which different positions could be adopted, and were adopted, during the entire period during which the Second Temple stood (literally, from 515 B.C. to A.D. 70). The universalism-particularism issue has generally taken the form of pitting one text against another, for example, Jonah and Ruth against Ezra and Nehemiah (Smend 1962: 169-79). Few, however, bothered to clarify these slippery terms of reference. Does religious universalism imply belief in the universal salvific will of God irrespective of religious affiliation? Is conversion an essential condition for salvation or not? Do the efforts of a religious or ethnic-religious group to control recruitment or discourage intermarriage with nonadherents brand it as particularistic or integrationist? These issues were being contested within Jewish communities in the homeland and the diaspora from the beginning of the Second Temple period. An example would be Isa 56:1-8, which affirms the good standing within the community of foreigners and the sexually mutilated in direct contradiction with the law governing community membership in Deut 23:2-9 (23:1-8) which excludes both the sexually mutilated and several ethnic categories from membership in the Israelite community.

34

Something along the same lines can be said about attitudes to law in early Christianity. Paul's exegetically elaborate and often paradoxical reflections on the subject are not antithetic to normative Jewish teaching, since we know of no orthodox doctrine of law from that time against which such reflections could be measured and found wanting. He speaks as a Jew ("we Jews," Rom 3:9; 9:3; 11:1), though hardly a typical Jew if such existed at that time, he affirms the holiness and preeminence of Torah (Rom 7:12, 14; 9:4-5), and he can speak of the Christian message as enabling the fulfilment of the law according to what he took to be its ultimate purpose (Rom 8:4). And since he speaks as a spokesman for a messianic branch of Judaism (the metaphor is his, Rom 11:16-24), his observations should be placed in the context of contemporary speculation on the place of Torah in the messianic age.

We could look at other issues in earliest Christianity from this perspective, not least of which would be the identity and mission of Jesus himself. It is in fact difficult to think of any issue on which early Christian communities were divided that was not a divisive issue within Judaism much earlier. This kind of repositioning and revisioning should also, incidentally, lead to caution in speaking of anti-Semitism in the New Testament. Unfortunately, people have quoted texts from the New Testament abusively in support of attitudes and actions hostile to the Jewish people. But the historical context of most of these problematic texts is in fact that of inner-Jewish polemic, comparable to sectarian polemic in Qumran texts and, for that matter, the contentious and often much more virulent diatribe in prophetic books.

The challenge, then, would be to come up with a more adequate cognitive map of the Jewish environment in which the Christian movement emerged and developed. This, in its turn, could lead us back into a Christian understanding of the Scriptures flowing from the tradition of biblical interpretation that developed as an important constituent element in early Christian self-understanding. Since, in spite of the much improved environment for the theological study of the Scriptures, it has proved to be extraordinarily difficult to find a way to put together a theology of the Old Testament, that is, a *Christian* theology of the Old Testament, this rather different perspective or angle on early Christianity may provide a new way of thinking about the task, perhaps even a new point of departure for undertaking it.

III

Creation, the Body, and
Care for a Damaged World

1

Sooner or later talk about the ecological crisis turns to biblical texts, and more often than not to what the Bible has to say about the creation of the world and our place in it. I must say at once that for me discussions about "the Bible and ecology" convey an impression of remoteness and unreality. Factors that have nothing to do with the Bible, or indeed with religious matters at all, are quite often simply left out of account. The environment was being devastated and species rendered extinct long before Judaism, Christianity, and their Scriptures appeared on the scene. The destruction of the Lebanon cedar forests was well under way by the second millennium B.C., and the Syrian elephant had been hunted to extinction by the seventh century B.C. If the Assyrians, mighty hunters before the Lord, had been more technologically advanced, they would no doubt have done even more damage than they did to the flora and fauna of the Near East. Ecological disaster has also more often than not been the result of stupid and thoughtless policies pursued by rulers and governments. The deforestation of Palestine, to remedy which strenuous efforts have been made, was due not to its Bible-reading Jewish and Christian residents or its Koran-reading Muslims but to the policy pursued during the three centuries of Turkish rule of taxing property according to the number of trees on it, with predictable results. And where religious influences *are* detectable, deforestation is generally an unforeseen side effect rather than a direct consequence of religious attitudes. So, for example, centuries of practicing

36

cremation, required by Hinduism and Buddhism, contributed to the deforestation of India, which, in turn, has contributed to endemic flooding in neighboring Bangladesh.

From the beginning of the latest phase of environmental crisis literature, it has nevertheless been the practice to blame the biblical heritage of Judaism and Christianity, and especially the biblical doctrine of creation, for our present ecological woes. In 1967 a prominent exponent of this view, Lynn White Jr., published an article in the journal *Science* under the title "The Historical Roots of Our Ecological Crisis." In this curiously influential article he argued that Western Christianity and the biblical doctrines that sustained it were mainly responsible for the development of science and technology, which in turn led to the exploitation of natural resources and the degradation of the environment. Lynn White's point was that the Christian doctrine of creation sets humanity over against nature, thereby objectifying the latter and encouraging the idea that nature is at the disposal of humanity. From this flows an ethic unsympathetic to or uncaring of the natural world. This he took to be encapsulated in the creation command to subdue and have dominion over the earth (Gen 1:26-28)(Lynn White 1967: 1203-7).

Though this kind of writing seems thoroughly *depassé* by now, one still comes across it in journal articles and TV specials. It is, of course, true that the creation text has served as justification for exploitative attitudes to nature. To take a well-known example, it provided New England divines of the early settlement period with the biblical warranty they needed to justify the domination and exploitation of the new world, including its indigenous inhabitants. It also provided them with the first of several biblical texts they needed in order to preach their gospel of godly wealth; in this respect the contrast with Native American religions based on a friendly symbiosis with the natural environment could hardly have been greater. Lynn White also appealed to the idea of creation as the desacralization of nature, a thesis expounded with breathless excitement by Harvey Cox in his bestselling book *The Secular City*, published a couple of years earlier. Cox's thesis was that the "de-divinizing" or "disenchantment" of nature implicit in the biblical idea of creation provided the basis for the development of the sciences and technology, and therefore for the secular urban world that most of his readers inhabited and that Cox invited his readers to celebrate. On this showing, the nature-culture dualism, which many writers on ecology now see as the root of our present troubles, was definitely a Good

Thing (Cox 1965). Lynn White could also find support for his thesis in the writings of Max Weber *(Wirtschaft und Gesellschaft)* and R. H. Tawney *(Religion and the Rise of Capitalism)* relating a particular form of worldly and individualistic asceticism to the rise and consolidation of capitalism, though of course neither of these authors addressed directly the ecological issue. And the Reformation could always be blamed for shifting the locus of divine activity from nature to the introspective self. Other theologians around that time came out with one variation or another of these same lines of argument (e.g., Metz 1969).

Lynn White's thesis was for a while a principal focus of debate and was reprinted several times, but by the time it appeared in *Ecology and Religion in History* in 1974 it was beginning to look a bit threadbare. James Barr, one of the contributors to that volume, pointed out that the biblical texts to which Lynn White appealed cannot bear the weight placed on them, that in fact the Bible has little to say about technology, and that if we must look to antiquity for the source of our problems it would make better sense to look to Greece than to Israel. He concluded: "As far as one must speak of responsibility and guilt, I would say that the great modern exploitation of nature has taken place under the reign of a liberal humanism in which man no longer conceives of himself as being under a creator, and in which therefore his place of dominance in the universe and his right to dispose of nature for his own ends is, unlike the situation in the Bible, unlimited" (Barr 1974: 73). This is the point that must be emphasized. The problem lies with us, with the world of diminished moral purposefulness that we inhabit rather than with the ancient world of Israelites or Greeks. We can explain to some extent how the ecological crisis came about, but we should not use the Bible as an alibi.

The first point to make, therefore, is that it does not make sense to blame the Bible for the mess we are in. The answers we get from the Bible depend on the questions we put to it, and they in their turn are determined by our own agenda, presuppositions, and ideology, including the ideology of the social class, religious denomination, or other interest group to which we belong. We know only too well that an uncritical reading of the Bible can provide warranty for almost any position on which we have already made up our minds, whether it be race relations, sexual ethics, the death penalty, or the date of the Second Coming. But for those of us who are Jews or Christians, and who believe we are called on to use our God-given critical faculties when reading the Bible as in other respects, there is no other recourse than to keep returning to the Bible if we are to review critically and within a context of faith our own opinions and those of others on such a basic issue as our relation to the environment. Biblical interpretation has always been a constitutive element of the tradition in which Jews and Christians in their different ways understand themselves and their place in the world.

The trouble is that appeal to the Bible is rarely easy or unproblematic. Biblical texts reflect a conceptual universe very different from the one we inhabit. Unlike ourselves, the people of the biblical period had no idea that they could modify or have a significant impact on the natural world, except perhaps exceptionally through miraculous divine intervention solicited by congregational prayer or the intercession of a prophet. Nature, the phenomenal world in all its beauty, strangeness, and power, was just *there*, to be admired, occasionally feared, to elicit the praise of God, and to provide, in the aphoristic literature, analogies and lessons for human behavior. We might recall God's answer to Job in the whirlwind consisting in a vast display of natural phenomena and forces — constellations, seas, clouds, precipitation, flora, and fauna — with no human being in sight. Together with certain psalms of praise and thanksgiving, this response is the closest we come to a comprehensive presentation of nature. But there is no evidence that the biblical writers and their publics were concerned either theoretically or practically with nature as such — for which, incidentally, there is no word in Biblical Hebrew. If we are to find anything relevant to our theme, we must therefore work by way of indirection, occasionally on but more often between the lines in search of clues to the rediscovery of a sense of responsibility with respect to the physical environment in which we have to live out our lives.

It is hardly surprising that the New Testament has not had much of a role in this task of rediscovery. Most of the writings from the early Christian period are either of an ad hoc nature — the epistles of Paul and of other church leaders, reading that is rather like listening to one end of a telephone conversation — or are dominated by the sense of an imminent ending and therefore not much concerned with attitudes to the physical environment. But even here we note how the dominant eschatological perspective, taken over from biblical and postbiblical apocalyptic, envisages the reversal of the ancient curse on the earth (Gen 3:17-19) and the transformation rather than the destruction of heaven and earth in a final "singularity" or *apokatastasis,* a decisive turning point. In a remarkable passage Paul comes close to our theme in speaking of creation in its totality *(ktisis)* as dependent on human transformation and waiting eagerly for it as a woman anxiously awaits the birth of the child she is carrying (Rom 8:19-22). The analogy may have been suggested by the prophetic figure of the emergence of the new age represented as pregnancy followed by birth (e.g., Isa 66:7-9). There is also the prophetic theme linking the natural environment in a relationship of dependence with human attitudes and behavior. But neither Paul nor his readers would have thought to draw from this observation consequences of a practical nature of the kind that press on us today.

2

Biblical scholars are fortunately not called upon to address the technical matters of environmental degradation, sustainable world population, and related issues on the agenda of numerous conferences in recent years.[1] But since there is a crisis calling for fundamental changes of attitude vis-à-vis the physical environment, and since the Bible is still a factor in the thinking of many people, we are justified in taking another look at these ancient texts, and in the first instance at the creation narrative in Genesis, from this perspective. Let the reader be warned that this will be a different kind of exercise from the many essays in postmodernist or ecofeminist environmental theology currently on the market, and will certainly not attempt to compete, keep up with, or even document them. My aim is, so to speak, to fly close to the ground with an eye for some hint or clue in the details of the text to a different way of thinking about these important issues. More specifically, I want to propose a reading that will provide an alternative to the idea of the creation command as dominion and in the direction of what I will call an ethic of limitation. I invite readers to read the texts with me and test the ideas for themselves.

1. The first draft of this paper was occasioned by the United Nations International Conference on Population and Development held in Cairo in September 1994. The agenda document of the conference called for "a healthy and productive life in harmony with nature for every man, woman, and child on the planet." Few would wish to argue with such praiseworthy aims expressed at that level of generalization, and it was no doubt to be expected that there were no arguments of a philosophical or religious nature why people should want to live longer or favor a global community rather than one of more modest proportions.

Let us start on a safe note with those interpreters who have been pointing out for a long time that the work of creation in Gen 1:1–2:4 consists essentially in ordering, separating, and delimiting. This work begins with the primordial, amorphous chaos, the dark abyss — whether itself created or there *in situ* from the outset we may for the moment leave undecided. On each of the first four days God was occupied in creating distinct entities by a cumulative process of separation: light from darkness, the upper waters from the lower waters, water from dry land, and, finally, day from night. This process ended on the fourth day, thus before the emergence of living beings, including human beings. I take the implication to be that from this point on the task begun by God of delimiting and making distinctions is to be continued by humanity. *How* this is to be done remains to be seen. Consider, then, how God assigned a name, and therefore a distinct identity, to light and darkness on the first day, the firmament as distinct from the circumfluent waters on the second, and the dry land and large bodies of water on the third. Here, too, we have the impression that this work of identification, taxonomy, and distinction is to be continued by humanity. In the following episode, in fact, it is the First Man in Eden, the *'ādām*, who names the different species of animals, made from the same stuff as himself, as they parade unspecifically before him (Gen 2:19-20). In the creation recital we are reminded redundantly — ten times — how plants and living creatures were created "according to their kind," thus emphasizing the need to acknowledge and preserve distinctions. These distinctions prepare for and lead up to the creation of humanity, male and female yet one and undivided, and here, too, we are asked to understand that making and preserving distinctions is a human task.

To the emergence of order out of chaos in space corresponds the creation of order, or the potential for order, along the temporal axis. The sun, moon, and stars are placed in the dome of the sky for signs, seasons, days, and years or, in other words, to make it possible to establish a liturgical calendar. This takes place on the fourth day, the Wednesday of the creation week. The sequence of events is logical since dry land is required as the platform from which the heavenly bodies can be observed and their movements calculated. It is important for our theme to note that the image is one of conjuring into existence an integrated world of harmony and order, a *cosmos,* rather than just setting up scenery for the stage on which human beings were to appear and act out their roles as the crown of creation.

That human beings are commissioned to continue the work begun by God suggests a way of thinking about the "image and likeness" qualification quite different from the idea of dominion and subjection often associated with it. The idea would be that human beings not only represent God on earth, as an image or statue re-presents, that is, makes present or serves as a surrogate for the one represented, but that they also carry further the work of creation. One indication that this is so is that the image is reproduced through *human* procreation (Gen 5:1). Human cooperation with the initial creative impulse is to be in the form of making due distinctions, specifying, and naming taxonomically. This idea suggests a link with science and technology, but of a quite different kind from the one proposed by Lynn White. In the ancient Near East, distinguishing and naming were aspects of practical wisdom, a first run at what we might call a science of nature. The classic example is Solomon, master of onomastic wisdom and list making. He discoursed about trees from the cedar that is in Lebanon to the hyssop that grows out of the wall, as also of animals, birds, reptiles, and fish — a precursor of Linnaeus, therefore (1 Kgs 4:33). The author of the Wisdom of Solomon, writing in the late first century B.C., would expand the list of achievements to take in all branches of knowledge, including astronomy and meteorology (Wis 7:15-22); and, later still, cabbalists would regard Solomon as the fountainhead of magical lore. This is a formidable set of achievements indeed, but the biblical authors were also conscious of the ambiguous nature of a wisdom that easily generates a sense of boundlessness, of freedom from moral restraint. We get an early clue to this ambiguity in the way the first technological advances — working in bronze and iron — are attributed to the tainted line of Cain (Gen 4:22). On this showing, technological progress is neither an absolute nor an unmixed blessing.

The command to subdue the earth and exercise dominion is frequently linked with the naming theme as licensing a proprietary attitude to nature. In the biblical context naming can certainly be a proprietary act, as when one or other of the imperial overlords imposed a new name on a Judean vassal (2 Kgs 23:34; 24:17). But it is also an essential element in ordering and making distinctions, in individuating and drawing thoughtful and careful attention to the variety and distinctness of life forms and other specific features in the physical environment. This may be the place to add, parenthetically, that the metaphor of *imperium*, of the exercise of kingly power, still so much in evidence in the language of prayer and worship (King of Glory, Prince of Peace, begging for mercy, etc.), is a relic or left-over from the long subjection of Israel and early Judaism to a succession of great empires. In addressing their God, both the psalmists and the prophets often reproduce the protocol language used by subordinates in speaking to their overlord, as, for example, in the Amarna correspondence from the early fourteenth century B.C. (Moran 1992: 326, 335, and passim). Feminist theologians have been among the first to point out that this language of absolute, arbitrary royal power used of the deity has influenced our thinking on a range of issues, including the one that is our present concern. But even for those who insist on retaining the metaphor, authority does not have to be exercised in an absolute and arbitrary fashion. Rulers used to be known as shepherds, and their primary responsibility was the establishment and preservation of justice and righteousness, perspectives that, as we know only too well, routinely give way to political expediency. Our experience is that authoritarianism and loving care for the physical world do not seem to go well together.

3

We move on to explore one approach to what I have called an ethic of limitation by inviting reflection on the Jewish laws of clean and unclean, inclusive of the dietary laws. This particular avenue of inquiry may not seem very promising, but the reason for attempting it can be simply stated, though following through may turn out to be more difficult. We shall see. The focus, the point of reference, of these laws is *the body*. They take seriously bodily integrity. They are concerned with the boundaries and orifices of the body, with what it ingests, its contacts and interactions with its environment. An ethic of limitation would mean that I start from where I am in my world, with my body, the only one I shall ever have, as that part of the world for which I am more directly responsible. My body is a layered deposit of millions of years of organic development. The tail and gills of the foetus, the saline content of the amniotic fluid, identical with the saline content of the oceans of the world, the reptilian brain, testify that my body is part of nature while, at the same time, individuating me within nature. I am deeply, irrevocably, inescapably part of nature, and it will never be otherwise.

The learned priests and scribes who drew up the laws of clean and unclean and the dietary laws refer everything back to the primordial creation. To the work of distinction and separation during the creation week corresponds the requirement to distinguish between clean and unclean and therefore between what may and may not be eaten ("You are to distinguish between the holy and the common, between the unclean and the clean," Lev 10:10). God made living things "according to their kind," hence living species must be distinguished in the same way. In listing clean and unclean creatures, Leviticus 11 uses the same categories or kinds *(mînîm)* as Genesis 1, dividing them according to habitat in the order of creation — air, water, and land creatures, with insects in a distinct category. (They never seemed to be quite sure what to do about insects.) The same language is used in the ritual laws as in the creation narrative. Scholars have discussed the rationale for the dietary laws endlessly since late antiquity. We need not add to the discussion except to observe that, whatever their original impulse, these prohibitions at least help to inculcate a discriminating ethical attitude toward killing for food and a degree of respect for life forms in general. In the first creation no animal or human being kills or is killed for food (Gen 1:29-30), but in the second creation, the damaged world we inhabit, killing for food is permitted. However, the ritualization of the process known as kashrut, including the requirement of draining the blood, that is, the life fluid, inhibits the kind of indiscriminate, thoughtless, and cruel slaughter of animals for their flesh, pelt, tusks, or whatever that has been a characteristic human activity from early times (Gen 9:3-4). Ritualizing, in other words, provides a symbolic context for our interaction with other living forms. It delimits and channels options.

Understood as a form of symbolic interaction with the physical world, the laws of clean and unclean align the observer of the laws with the forces and energies of life pitted against death. They serve to head off the penetration of death into the realm of the living. We miss the point badly if we think of them as *only* symbolic. To accept the symbolism and to live within a system of symbolic meanings is not to retreat from reality into illusion but to embrace a meaning-conferring reality, to disclose and at the same time create a conceptual world and a way to inhabit it that is livable. The biblical (and Mishnaic) schema is filled out by referring to certain skin diseases, discolorations of various kinds, and, by analogy, fungus and mildew in buildings and clothing, as suggestive of death and decay and therefore to be treated with caution (Leviticus 13–14). Contact with carcasses and cadavers is to be avoided (Lev 11:24-40). Great care is to be taken with both normal and pathological loss of blood and semen, the bodily fluids most indicative of life and most intimately associated with the integrity of the body (Leviticus 15). These are elements of a code, we might say clues to a code, the decryption of which progressively reveals the interconnections and interdependencies between the body and the world.

We realize, of course, that these prescriptions are incumbent only on those of Jewish faith, and not even on all of them. But it is arguable that the biblical authors, and especially the priest-author in Genesis 1–11 (conventionally identified with the siglum P), saw these laws as a special application of a more general *human* obligation. In other words, it is possible to detect a rational connection between the laws of clean and unclean and limitations and constraints imposed by the demands of a life that aspires to be truly human. In biblical and rabbinic terms, the connection is expressed in the Noachic covenant and laws based on the prescriptions in Gen 9:1-7 addressed to Noah and his sons after the deluge. In the original creation animals and humans know only a vegetarian diet. There exists therefore a realm of peace and the absence of violence. Only in the damaged world after the deluge, *our* world, is permission given to kill for food, but there is the restriction, previously unnecessary, that the blood must first be drained away (Gen 9:3-4). This is presented as a universal prescription, just as the covenant that follows is made with all humanity, in fact with all living creatures (9:8-17). All this happened long before the Creator God had any transactions with Israel, indeed long before Israel appeared on the scene. We might say that these are emergency measures, a kind of damage control or, in the language of the Hasidim, a form of fixing or mending the world (*tiqqûn hā'ôlām*), a task that is not confined to those of Jewish faith. Whether we observe these purity rules or simply read them with reverend attention, they insinuate a way of looking at our interaction with the physical environment of a very different kind from the dominating and exploitative model frequently justified with reference to the creation narrative.

Parenthetically, it is interesting to observe that the Priestly source in the Pentateuch or Hexateuch, from which the creation story and the laws of clean and unclean derive, was repeatedly criticized in the modern period for its illiberal and sclerotic approach to religious life and experience. For Wellhausen it embodied "a petty scheme of salvation," and for many of the most prominent biblical scholars of the nineteenth and early twentieth centuries it represented a decline into ritualism and formalism after the high point of prophetic religion. This is not the place for a thorough refutation of this prejudicial assessment. It will suffice to state the thesis that these "Priestly" writings are theologically among the most innovative in the Hebrew Bible. They boldly challenge the received covenant theology — expressed most comprehensively in Deuteronomy — according to which God is tied to the world by obligation, and they therefore question the idea that it is possible to win God's benevolent attention by moral performance. They show an interest in the details of ordinary, physical existence and a conviction that our existence in time and in space can be hallowed without the need for continual divine intervention. For these learned priests holiness is a rational concept, and it is to be realized in day-to-day living.

Though pockets of Judaic Christians continued to observe the ritual laws for centuries, the requirement of draining the blood and the prohibition of eating what had been strangled were the only prescriptions to be officially maintained, and that only for a relatively short time, in early Palestinian Christianity (Acts 15:29). We may regard this as inevitable, but the result was that the symbolic system of interconnections with the physical world of which they were a part soon became alien and unintelligible. It seems, in general, that without some sense of a symbolic and meaning-conferring universe the ecological issue will always remain somewhat peripheral, forced on our attention from outside by a succession of crises. We have also inherited impulses from our religious past that are not conducive to active concern for the physical environment. The parade example is the tendency in some Christian denominations, perhaps in most, to undervalue the sexual function and to regard the material world as an obstacle to salvation. This attitude is still more than residually present and does not easily mesh with a positive attitude to bodily existence and the possibility of hallowing both the body and the earth from which it comes, on which it depends, and to which it returns. But for all the mainline religions the environmental crisis will call for a reexamination of attitudes toward care of the body and of the physical world in general.

4

The ritual laws focus our attention on corporeality, on the body both in itself and in its social and ecological context, that is, as the medium of interaction with the physical environment, including other bodies. But the physical body with its interconnections and its orifices is also mapped on to the social body and serves as an image or replica of the social environment. In several of her publications Mary Douglas has developed this idea of the body-society homology (Douglas 1966, 1970). The point is that the body can serve as model for any bounded system. To quote: "Bodily orifices seem to represent points of entry or exit to social units, or bodily perfection can symbolise an ideal theocracy" (Douglas 1966: 4). The homology is not limited to bodily orifices. The metaphor of society as a body with interconnected and interdependent parts, *the body politic,* has been in use from antiquity (e.g., in Aristotle's *Politics* 1:1.11). It suggests that each part of society must perform its task for the good of the whole (e.g., Plato's *Timaeus* 45B). For the Stoics, the body was the microcosm to which corresponds the macrocosm held together in all of its parts by the world soul. Influenced by this rich vein of analogy, early Christian writers described the community in its collective, social, interdependent existence as the body of Christ, a topos richly developed in the Pauline corpus (e.g., 1 Cor 12:27; Col 1:18). The physical body is therefore a metaphor for the social-political body of which the ecclesial body is part.

The corporeal metaphor suggests that we think of our place in the world in terms of functionality, interdependence, and interconnectedness. It can therefore act as a deterrent to the utilitarian individualism to which our contemporary culture beckons us in so many ways. It can also lead us to think of care of bodies, our own to begin with, at a deeper and more authentic level than the current "wellness" culture that seems to function in some of the developed countries as a surrogate moral system. Individualism tends to induce a sense of boundlessness that effectively rules out appreciation for body symbolism and ritual in general. It will therefore not be easy to appreciate any kind of ritualized approach to bodily existence, of which the purity laws of Judaism are one instantiation, and thus our technology operates directly and without inhibition on the environment, including other life forms with which we share the planet. Perhaps, then, relearning the point and purpose of ritual might be one way to a saner and more responsible relationship with our environment.

5

An important environmental concern has to do with the earth on which we depend in one way or another for our sustenance, the visible, vehement earth, the ground of our being in a quite literal sense, from which we come, on which we depend for life and sustenance, and to which we return. The specific, practical concerns are well known and have often been analyzed — erosion of topsoil, deforestation, strip mining, toxic wastes seeping into the soil, the rapidly diminishing water table. Here, too, if we take the trouble, we might rediscover in the biblical record clues to a different way of thinking about the issues.

We might start, once again, on the first page of the Bible. An important structural feature of the creation narrative is the correspondence between different life forms and habitats. The work of creation, carried out over a period of six days, is arranged in parallel triads as follows:

I	IV
light	sun, moon, stars
separation of light	separation of day and
from darkness (vv. 3-5)	night (vv. 14-19)

II	V
firmament	water and air creatures
separation of upper	(vv. 20-23)
and lower waters (vv. 6-8)	

IIIA	VIA
dry land	land creatures
separation of water	humans (vv. 24-28)
from dry land (vv. 9-10)	

IIIB	VIB
vegetation (vv. 11-13)	vegetation as food
	(vv. 29-31)

VII
the sabbath of God (2:1-3)

After the correspondence between the creation of light on the first day and the stars and constellations on the fourth, the firmament was created on the second day in order to provide distinct habitats for aquatic creatures and birds on the fifth day. Then, finally, dry land emerged out of the primeval waters on the third day to make life possible for land creatures, including human beings on the sixth. And it was all very good (Blenkinsopp 1992: 58-63).

This particular and deliberate way of organizing the activities of the six days of creation (1-4, 2-5, 3-6) insinuates a close connaturality between the soil and human beings, between the *'ădāmâ* and the *'ādām,* between humus and humanity. The point is made more clearly as the story proceeds. We come from the earth and return to it. "Naked I came from my mother's womb, and naked I shall return to it" (Job 1:21). In the logic of the Eden story, putting on clothes is a prelude to leaving the paradise of nature, a concession and adjustment to a new and lesser reality. To be naked, on the contrary, is to be close to the earth and the natural order of things. The earth is, quite unsentimentally, the mother of us all. The first man was put in the garden to care for the earth and its produce (Gen 2:15). As we now realize only too well, and hope that the realization has not come too late, the well-being of the earth depends in important ways on what happens in human society. Physical order and moral order go together. Societal dysfunction, beginning with the first couple and spreading out with the spread of the gene pool, results in the ground producing scrub, thorns, and thistles and requiring unremitting labor, the backbreaking work of the Palestinian subsistence farmer.

The interaction between human society and the physical environment, and therefore between human and environmental degradation, also keeps on cropping up in the prophetic writings. Sickness and death in the animal world are brought on by social transgression, and above all by the shedding of blood. An anonymous seer makes the point in summary fashion in proclaiming that "the earth lies polluted under its inhabitants" (Isa 24:5). One of the more disquieting motifs in the book of Isaiah is the return of civilized life to nature, with great cities like Babylon becoming the haunt of wild animals, of satyrs and demons, creatures of corrupt and malevolent intelligence, with Lilith, the female demon of Jewish folklore, presiding over them — a salutary reminder of our own impermanence. For us, the garden of paradise remains only as a nostalgic myth, a memory evoked by poets like Milton and Wordsworth or painters like Gaughin and Rousseau.

Responsiveness to the needs of the earth is not, in biblical terms, a matter of moral indifference. The biblical authors make this point in their own nondiscursive ways, for example, by personification. The land can be rendered unclean, polluted by the conduct of those who live on it. No less than human beings, it needs rest, restoration, and recreation. Hence the sabbatical year when the land must be left fallow (Exod 23:10-11; Lev 25:1-7), corresponding to the sabbath rest enjoined in the Decalogue for both theological and humanitarian reasons (Exod 20:8-11; Deut 5:12-15). The human right to exploit the land is not unlimited. The festivals, corresponding to the important points of the agrarian year (Unleavened Bread–Passover, Weeks or Pentecost, Booths or Tabernacles), serve as a reminder of these moral constraints. Our residual blessing of crops, rogation days, and harvest festivals, for most of us now only a memory, could, if we cared enough, serve the same purpose. But even in the absence of appropriate ritual, we must know that limitless and thoughtless exploitation of natural resources is not an option if we are to survive, let alone flourish.

The need for restraint is also implicit in the biblical legislation about the possession, use, and usufruct of land. The common theology of the ancient Near East held that land was the property of the local or national deity. There was therefore no such thing as human sovereignty over land; it was held in fief by those to whom the deity leased it out. Those who lived on the land did so in the capacity of stewards, a status that excluded a proprietary way of relating to the land. This idea of *leasehold* provided the basis for the inalienability of patrimonial domain, the ancestral plot of land (Lev 25:23), and therefore theoretically excluded expropriation, enclosure, or even mutually advantageous exchange of real estate. King Ahab offered to give Naboth a good price or even a better vineyard in exchange for his own vineyard, which happened to be contiguous to the royal enclosure, but Naboth did not feel able to accept the offer: "The LORD forbid that I should give you my ancestral inheritance" (1 Kgs 21:3). One had to care for the plot of land belonging to the household and pass it on in good condition to the next generation. Ownership by the deity was reinforced by the practices of tithing, offering of the first fruits, the fallow year, and the year of release, which, again theoretically, excluded the granting of leasehold for a period in excess of fifty years (Lev 25:8-55). Stipulations about the gleaning rights of the poor (Lev 19:9-10; 23:22; Deut 24:19-21) were a reminder of the link between self-restraint and distributive justice. Also relevant are laws forbidding the removal of boundary markers, chopping down fruit trees, and even robbing birds' nests (Deut 19:14; 20:19-20; 22:6-7).

To labor the point that legal theory is not an infallible guide to actual behavior will not be necessary. The very fact that these laws were, so to speak, on the books, and the frequency of prophetic protests against such abuses as joining house to house and field to field, reveal that practice could be, and generally was (and is), quite different from theory. The discrepancy was particularly in evidence in Israel of the biblical period with the consolidation of the state and its insatiable need for land. But the laws at least reflect a special relationship to land, one that created obligations and discouraged unlimited exploitation. They might also help us to imagine the difference it would make if we could think of ourselves as stewards and custodians rather than as proprietors of natural resources including land.

6

The agenda document for the United Nations Conference on Population and Development held in Cairo in 1994 stressed the need for limitation in the use of natural, nonrenewable resources, though of course it did not look for support to the scriptures of Judaism and Christianity or of any other religion. The document issued warnings about unsustainable production and consumption patterns as factors contributing to environmental degradation and social inequality, and it contrasted lack of resources in some regions with excessive and wasteful patterns of consumption in others. But it stopped short of saying that most of the consumption, and most of the damage to the ecosphere, takes place in the wealthiest and the industrially and technologically most advanced countries.

This point hardly needs documenting, but we are told (for example), and do in part believe it, that the top 20 percent of the world's population dispose of 80 percent of its resources, the bottom 20 percent of only 1.4 percent, and that the United States with 4 percent of the world's population uses 25 percent of its nonrenewable energy resources. This situation calls for scaling down needs and limiting acquisitive and incorporative appetites. The gap between wealthy and poor nations, and between the wealthy and poor in general, and not least in the United States, draws our attention to the close linkage between environmental issues and social justice. Here, too, the biblical tradition and its ongoing interpretation can provide resources for reflection and action.

The rediscovery in the nineteenth century of the prophet as the bearer of a distinctive social message was one of the most important contributions of Biblical Studies to the churches and to public life in general. The impact of this critical achievement was felt in different ways, for example, by the Social Gospel Movement, and it provided powerful ammunition in the struggle against economic injustice by influential public theologians of the caliber of Reinhold Niebuhr and Martin Luther King. While churchmen and theologians do not always practice what they preach, especially in the matter of material possessions, the harmful potential of excess is a recurring theme in the history of Christian moral thought. For Aquinas, greed or avarice, defined as an inordinate love of possessing *(immoderatus amor habendi),* is not only disorderly in itself but constitutes a violation of social justice since "one person cannot abound beyond measure *(superabundare)* without causing others to go without" (*Summa Theologiae* 2.2 qu. 118, art. 1). This way of thinking would not go down well with the neoconservative apologists for capitalism, and we can only imagine what would happen if we took it seriously and tried to implement it as a principle of social policy. At least we know what happened to those radicals who tried to do it during the Middle Ages and the Reformation. In early Christian writings, especially the Pauline epistles, inordinate love of possessing *(pleonexia)* is one of the qualities most corrosive of the Christian life (e.g., Rom 1:28-29; 1 Cor 5:9-10; Eph 4:19). In the Gospels, finally, the same point is made in the parable of the rich fool who discovered the hard way that "one's life does not consist in the abundance of possessions" (Luke 12:13-21).

We are under no illusion that ethical values alone, whether drawing their inspiration from the Jewish and Christian Scriptures or from some other source, will provide solutions to the environmental crisis. For some solutions it is probably too late any way, much is beyond our control, and we soon develop immunity to exhortation, however well intentioned. But we are not entirely at the mercy of impersonal social and economic forces either. We can begin with ourselves, where we are, in this business known in the Hasidic tradition as *tiqqûn hā'ôlām,* mending the damaged world. We can begin by getting the point, circumscribing our natural and endemic acquisitive and incorporative instincts, and redirecting our moral energies toward responsible use of the resources at our disposal.

IV

Sacrifice and Social Maintenance
in Ancient Israel

1

This essay will not deal with sacrificial techniques, procedures, categories, and materials in Israel during the biblical period as set out in the manual for sacrificial practitioners in Leviticus 1–7. For information on these matters one can consult the exhaustive commentary by Jacob Milgrom or, more briefly, standard treatments in dictionaries and encyclopedias (Milgrom 1991: 131-489; de Vaux 1964; Anderson 1992: 5:870-86). The official cult, as described in Leviticus 1–7 and related texts, has been systematized and streamlined in keeping with a particular priestly theology, and to that extent it is less revealing of the social coordinates of sacrifice in general than the nonofficial practice associated with clan and household.

Since the early days of William Robertson Smith and Emile Durkheim, comparativists have tended to focus on explaining why people sacrifice: whether to feed the deity, propitiate, expiate, ward off danger, present a gift in the expectation of obtaining benefits in return, create bonds of mutual obligation, keep the cosmos in good working order, redirect the violence and aggression endemic to human nature, or even supply for a deficiency in protein.[1] These varied rationales of sacrificial practice have often been accom-

---

1. A sampling of recent writing, with emphasis on psychocultural explanations, can be found in the review essays of Richard Hecht, "Studies on Sacrifice 1970-1980," *Religious Studies Review* 8 (1982): 253-59; Ivan Strenski, "Between Theory and Specialty: Sacrifice in the 90s," *Religious Studies Review* 22 (1996): 10-20.

panied by theories about origins. Some of these have focused on the guilt induced by the slaughter of defenseless domesticated animals (Burkert 1983)
or, in more general terms, on the justification for killing animals (Hallo 1987:
3-13), or as a means of reducing or redirecting internecine violence in prehis-
toric human groups (Girard 1976). I do not intend to engage these issues and
debates on a broad front. What I would like to do instead is offer some reflections on features of non-official sacrifice as recorded in the Hebrew Bible,
and this with the idea of drawing attention to the ways in which it both reflects and reinforces aspects of social structure and hierarchy. I want to argue
that in a society like that of the Israel described in the biblical texts, in which
patrilineal and agnatic descent is an important organizing feature, sacrifice
functions to reinforce hierarchical structures, in the first place by defining
certain classes of people in and others out of the dominant social networks.
The hierarchy of functions allotted to the sacrificial adepts and the uneven
distribution of cuts of the sacrificed animal also reinforce rank and prescriptive role performance within the group. We will then see how ideas about
sacrifice may still be functioning residually in contemporary Judaism and
Christianity, if in very different ways.

In social structures that maintain and perpetuate themselves by
patrilineal descent, active participation in sacrifice is, with few exceptions,
limited to adult males. In this way gender hierarchy and gender-specific
role performance are visibly reinforced. The ritually unclean, and therefore
by implication the physically disadvantaged, are also, typically, excluded
from participation. This is true of all types of sacrifice in ancient Israel.
The congregational law of Deut 23:2-9, for example, excludes the sexually
mutilated and certain ethnic categories of people from membership in the
qāhāl (community, congregation), and therefore from participation in its
central religious activities, among which sacrifice is the most important.
Robertson Smith traced the origin of sacrifice to a ceremony in which the
tribe reaffirmed its unity and its union with its deity in a communal meal
in which the flesh of the totemic animal was consumed. Together with
Emile Durkheim, he was among the first to emphasize sacrifice as a powerful means of bonding within the agnatic group, thus as essentially conjunctive (Robertson Smith 1972: 213-352; Durkheim 1995: 340-55). That sacrifice can function in this way is surely correct, but it will be evident from
what has been said so far, and will become more evident as we proceed,
that it can also have a disjunctive function, manifested in its concern for
social boundaries and traditional hierarchies.

I also want to draw attention to some neglected links in the biblical texts between sacrificing and covenanting, which typically includes commensality, taking a meal together. This too is inspired by what Robertson Smith had to say, on the basis of his pre-Islamic Arabian data, about sacrifice as creating mutual social obligations.

2

Let us consider as a first test case the covenantal sacrifice between Jacob and Laban, representing two distinct but related kinship groups (Gen 31:43-54). Laban takes the initiative in proposing a covenant whose purpose is to protect the interests of his daughters, Leah and Rachel, as they prepare for departure from Mesopotamia with Jacob. Though both women are already married to Jacob and have children, Laban opens negotiations by affirming his right over them, their children, and Jacob's livestock: "The daughters are my daughters, the children are my children, the flocks are my flocks" (31:43). This sounds like a formal juridical statement intended as a preamble to any negotiations that might follow. The legal basis for this surprising claim, at one time explained with reference to Nuzi customary law from the fifteenth century B.C.(Speiser 1964: 250-51), can be more readily understood in the light of Israelite law governing treatment of the Hebrew slave who has been obliged to sell himself into indentured service. The law states that this unfortunate person serves for six years and goes free in the seventh year; if he entered into service married, his wife can leave with him; but if his master gives him a wife, the wife and eventual children remain the property of the master. In that case, the only recourse for the husband unwilling to be separated from his wife and children would be to accept perpetual slavery (Exod 21:2-6). So it seems that, at the outset, Laban wants to occupy the moral high ground in generously allowing Leah and Rachel to leave with Jacob and thus waiving his legal rights. We can be sure that this interpretation would not have been shared by his daughters; in fact, they make the counterclaim that Laban has accepted payment for them and that therefore they are no longer members of his household (Gen 31:14-16). At any rate, from Laban's point of view the *běrît* was intended to provide assurance that Jacob would treat his wives well.

One feature of the story that is obvious even on a casual reading is duplication. This is not so surprising since many biblical narratives dealing

55

with religious matters are palimpsests, having been worked over from the perspective of the state cult and its associated theology. In this case there are two of everything: two issues (daughters, boundaries), two witnesses (the cultic stele and the cairn on the one hand, the běrît itself on the other), and two meals. Both parties set up stones, and two sets of deities are invoked (YHVH/Elohim and the respective ancestral deities). There are, in fact, two distinct covenants: the one unilateral, in which Jacob agrees to take good care of Laban's daughters (31:43-50); the other bilateral, in which both parties agree to what is in effect a nonaggression pact (vv. 51-54). This rather obvious feature of the narrative has elicited many attempts at source division, which need not detain us.

As the story now stands, what happens is that, after Laban has taken the initiative in proposing a covenant, Jacob sets up a stone as a ritual monolith and then instructs his kinsmen ('aḥîm, not to be translated "brothers and sisters") to collect stones and make a cairn on which, or beside which, they proceed to partake of a meal. Since commensality is a regular feature of covenant making, it seems likely, though it is not stated, that both parties share in the meal, which would have consisted in sacrificial meat. Laban gives the cairn a name in Aramaic, and Jacob gives it one in Hebrew. Laban then explains the names with reference to the function of the cairn as a witness to the terms of the agreement, the assumption being that both the cairn and the ritual monolith represent the deity. The one stipulation incumbent on Jacob is then stated and presumably accepted (31:50). The parties agree further not to enter each other's territory with hostile intent, the cairn now serving as a boundary marker, and this bilaterial agreement is sealed with oaths pronounced in the name of their respective ancestral deities, followed by a sacrifice and a meal that continues on through the night (vv. 51-54).

This interesting and complex narrative illustrates some significant features of nonofficial sacrifice. First, sacrifice, together with sacrificial commensality, acts as a powerful means of reinforcing solidarity among the male members of the descent group. Where a covenant is involved, we would expect both parties to partake of the sacrificial meal, but the narrator explicitly mentions only Jacob and his kinsmen ('aḥîm) as sharing in both the meal on or beside the cairn and the all-night meal on the mountain (31:46, 54). In this and similar contexts the term 'aḥîm must be understood literally as adult male members of the kinship group or phratry, just as covenant partners are elsewhere referred to as 'anšê běrît, "men of the covenant" (Obad 7). Disputes and negotiated agreements between related kinship groups will often deal with marriage, the treatment of women and inheritance, but they are invariably conducted by fathers and husbands.

An incident with similar features is the encounter on "the mountain of God" between the Midianite priest Jethro and Moses, accompanied we assume by their respective kin (Exod 18:10-12). Here, too, there is a sacrifice and a meal, reflecting a Midianite-Hebrew alliance comparable to the Aramean-Hebrew covenant in Genesis 31. Jethro's "confession of faith" (Exod 18:11) might also suggest some kind of Midianite incorporation into the Moses group, perhaps sending back a faint echo of Israelite (and Yahvistic) origins in the southern Transjordanian region but also reflecting the practice of accepting proselytes during the time of the Second Temple.[2] In an ostensibly different but in one important respect quite similar incident, the Israelites on their way through the wilderness were enticed sexually by Moabite women to take part in their ancestral rites, including a sacrificial meal, and then "yoked themselves" to these foreigners by marriage (Num 25:1-9).

A second point about the narrative as paradigmatic is that it presupposes an association between sacrifice and covenant. Covenant signifies primarily the making of a pact or agreement, as in the classic Deuteronomic formulations, but it also connotes incorporation into a group, or reinforcement of group identity, almost invariably accompanied by sacrifice. This association between covenant and sacrifice, familiar to churchgoing Christians from the words of eucharistic institution ("the blood of the new covenant"), can be easily overlooked. We find it in what appears to be the oldest of the conflated Sinai covenant ceremonies, one carried out at the foot of the mountain and involving a blood ritual and sacrifices performed by young Israelites (Exod 24:3-8), an utterly unpermissible procedure according to priestly orthopraxy. It is this tradition that is referred to in allusions to "the blood of my covenant" in Zech 9:11 and making a covenant with sacrifice in Ps 50:5. The same association appears in the Shechem covenant tradition (Deut 11:26-30; 27:1-26; Josh 8:31). The linkage will appear in a more developed and abstruse form with the Priestly theology of the sacrificial blood of circumcision by which the Israelite enters the covenant — an aspect that will call for comment later.

A third and final point about the Jacob-Laban covenant is that sacri-

---

2. Statements beginning "Now I know" (*'attâ yāda'tî*) appear to be formulaic and confessional; cf. Rahab of Jericho (Josh 2:9, 11) and Naaman of Damascus (2 Kgs 5:15).

ficing within the kinship group generally has a mortuary character. That is to say, the gathering is thought to bring together both living and dead members of the kinship group in a strengthened bond. The dead are those who, in the familiar phrase, have been "gathered to the ancestors" or, less succinctly, aggregated to the totality of the clan. The dead are not mentioned in the present narrative, but the appeal to ancestral deities — the deities associated with Abraham and Nahor on the one hand and the "Fearsome One of Isaac" on the other — is suggestive in this respect. It is well attested that ancestors, especially remote ancestors, were closely related to the sphere of the divine and that sacrifices were offered with them and perhaps also to them. While the cairn *(gal)*, referred to nine times in this short narrative, is not explicitly designated a burial mound, burial *gallîm* are mentioned elsewhere (Josh 7:26; 8:29; 2 Sam 18:17) in general conformity with analogous rites from other cultures.

3

Unfortunately, we hear of the Israelite *zebaḥ hayāmmîm*, literally "the sacrifice of days," less literally "the annual sacrifice," only incidentally, in the narrative about Saul's hostility to David (1 Sam 20:5-29), and in a densely edited form in the story of Hannah's vow at Shiloh (1:3-28). The alternative designation of *zebaḥ mišpāḥâ*, "clan sacrifice" (20:29), provides the essential clue to its function. In order to justify his absence from the new moon festival meal at Saul's court, David persuaded Jonathan to explain to Saul that he, David, was required by his *'aḥîm*, his fellow clansmen, to attend the annual clan sacrifice in Bethlehem. We learn from this incident (whether historically true or not is beside the point) that this annual sacrifice coincided with the new moon and lasted three days, and that attendance was mandatory for adult males belonging to the *mišpāḥâ*. Saul's anger on hearing the excuse can be explained by the *political* significance of these "gatherings of the clan" as providing a convenient occasion for conspiracy and revolt (20:30-34). David himself was to discover this on the occasion of Absalom's raising the flag of revolt at Hebron (2 Sam 15:7-12). The allusion in this incident to invited guests (15:11) confirms the point about limited incorporation. The attempted coup of Adonijah, no more successful than that of Absalom, also featured sacrifice to which some were invited and others were not (1 Kgs 1:9-10).

With its focus on fertility and the birth of a child, 1 Sam 1:3-28 perhaps gives an unrepresentative impression of the annual sacrifice as celebrated at Shiloh for the clans of the Ephraimite hill country, though there were no doubt local variations. It lasted at least two days (1:19), involved the sacrifice and consumption of a bull (1:24-25), and probably involved a significant amount of imbibing (1:12-16). The "annual festival of Yahveh at Shiloh" (Judg 21:19), during which the women performed a dance routine, illustrates another aspect of the same festive occasion.

Given this rather slender documentation, Robertson Smith was right to caution that the existence of an annual clan sacrifice in ancient Israel is a matter of inference rather than proof (Robertson Smith 1972: 275). But these rather by-the-way bits of information are supported by analogy with similar observances elsewhere. Robertson Smith, who so often drew upon pre-Islamic customs, in this instance adduced the analogy of the Roman *sacra gentilicia,* the annual sacrifice of the *gens* in which the ancestors were represented as participants and *commensales* (Robertson Smith 1972: 275-76). Participation in this celebration established one's social status as a member of the *gens* and one's rank within it. Somewhat similar was the *apatouria* festival of the Greeks "at which the fathers and kinsmen meet together" (Xenophon, *Hellenika* 1.7.8). This three-day celebration, which took place toward the end of the autumn, was important for establishing and confirming membership in the kinship group. Children were admitted into the phratry, the initiates shaved their hair and offered it to a god, sacrifices were made to Hephaestus, god of fire, and all of this conspired to reinforce the phratry's sense of identity and solidarity.

For both Robertson Smith and Durkheim the basic feature of this clan observance was commensality, what Durkheim called "alimentary communion." But both authors caution that solidarity was more a matter of adherence to the group ethos than of physical, biological descent from the same patronym. It was also, as noted earlier, at least primarily a matter of solidarity among the adult males of the group, who alone were active participants in these sacrifices. At Shiloh Elkanah did the sacrificing and gave cuts to the women, even though it was Hannah who provided the sacrificial material on the occasion of the second visit (1 Sam 1:3-5, 24-25). In due course the state priesthood, also organized according to fictive descent, would reinforce the same exclusionary access to sacrificing with a formidable system of purity rules and genealogical bookkeeping (e.g., Ezra 2:59-63).

Along the same theoretical trajectory as Robertson Smith and Durk-heim, Victor Turner presented a somewhat different perspective on the conjunctive-disjunctive issue by distinguishing between the prophylactic, expiatory, and piacular type of sacrifice and what he called the sacrifice of abandonment to good (Turner 1977: 189-215). The prophylactic type aims to ward off danger and get rid of disorder, and is therefore concerned with boundaries and restrictions. The purpose of the other kind is, for Turner, encapsulated in the word *communitas;* not so much thrusting away evil as unclogging channels of communication in the society, restoring the flow, collapsing hierarchical and segmentary differentiations. While the one tends toward separation and social stratification, the other is conjunctive and integrative, bringing together the living and dead members of the de-scent group in a strengthened social bond. Turner was at pains to point out that the distinction is rarely if ever clear-cut. The way a particular society conceives of what it is doing when it is sacrificing will be situated at a point, or successively at several points, on the prophylaxis-abandonment spectrum, and there will generally be elements of both types in any given instance.

4

The social and political importance of sacrifice comes through loud and clear in the religious legislation of the Deuteronomists. It will not be nec-essary to decide whether the Deuteronomic law book (Deuteronomy 12–26) was composed under the Judean monarchy and intended for immedi-ate implementation, or was drafted as a utopian document for a possible future after the fall of Jerusalem, or underwent successive editions both be-fore and after 586 B.C. In any case, it presents what is in effect a state consti-tution including guidelines for the ruler, the judiciary, priests, and other cult officials. Deuteronomy is what we might anachronistically call the first canonical document, the first consistent attempt to impose an orthodoxy and orthopraxy. It features the "canonical" requirement that nothing must be added to it or subtracted from it (4:2), it must be read from in public as-sembly at stated intervals (31:10-13) and deposited in a designated place in the sanctuary (v. 26), and the ruler must have a copy near him at all times (17:18-19). It is, in other words, intended to be definitive, but experience shows that such attempts to draw the line, to make final and irreformable statements, are not invariably successful. We shall see that this is the case with what Deuteronomy has to say about sacrificing.

The centrality of the state cult in the political program of this document is apparent from the beginning in the abolition of regional sanctuaries as the normal loci for sacrifice. Max Weber enunciated the general principle that the gradual consolidation of a civil and religious bureaucracy, together with the concentration of power and wealth in cities and the growth of international trade, inevitably combines to diminish the social significance of a descent system and undermine its ethos (Weber 1978: 1:370-84). It seems that in its formative period a state must, if it is to succeed, work to undermine a descent system with its sustaining ceremonies, among which communal sacrifice is the most important. The point would be to transfer allegiance to itself, an essential precondition for the effective exercise of its authority (Cohen 1969: 658-87; Steinberg 1991: 161-70).

Several stipulations in the Deuteronomic law point in this direction. Among these are the restriction of the discretionary power of heads of households and tribal elders by the state judiciary (Deut 16:18-20; 17:8-13) and the establishment of a class of officers *(šōtĕrîm)* to keep the peasants in line, in function not unlike Soviet commissars (16:18; 31:28). Blood vengeance, a basic component of tribal justice, is to be phased out in favor of a state-mandated law of sanctuary (19:1-13). Requiring a member of a household in which non-Yahvistic cults were being practiced to denounce the offending party to the authorities (13:6-11) can be read as a blatant attempt to undermine the traditional household from within. Less obvious, but no less insidious, is the Deuteronomic polemic against mortuary cults involving the recently and not so recently dead of the household and clan. These cults were an essential prop of the ritual and emotional life of the descent group, attaching it more firmly to the land where the ancestors were buried. It is therefore not surprising that they are denounced toward the beginning, at the end, and at the precise midpoint of the law (14:1; 18:9-14; 26:14).

For the present purpose, however, the most significant of these stipulations is the requirement restricting sacrifice to the one, central sanctuary (Deut 12:5-7, 11-14). How radical and drastic this requirement was will be apparent once we recall that, in Judah as in contemporary Greece, all slaughter of animals for food was considered sacrificial. Sacrifice was therefore an essential aspect of everyday religious practice. From this requirement there followed, as a necessary corollary, the secularization of butchering (12:15-16, 20-25), a very drastic "modernizing" measure. More directly aimed at neutralizing the annual sacrifice as the focus of clan affiliation would appear to be the requirement that all adult males present themselves three times a year at the central sanctuary (16:16). The same demand for males to "appear before YHVH" is made in the so-called Covenant Code (Exod 23:17; cf. 34:23), but without the requirement that this must be at the place YHVH will choose, that is, the state sanctuary in Jerusalem.

This aspect of Deuteronomic ideology is consistent with the political and contractual construal of covenant *(běrît)* in Deuteronomic writings. Covenant implies obligation, and specifically the assiduous observance of certain stipulations *(děbārîm,* Deut 28:69; 29:8), in the first place the Decalogue (4:13) written on the tablets (9:9-15) and deposited in a special box called "the ark of the covenant" (10:8; 31:9, 25-26).

Comparison with the articulation of the covenant idea in learned priestly circles is instructive, though in this context the society whose maintenance is at stake is not the state but the priesthood. In the first place, the authors of the Priestly corpus put covenant making back into the archaic period, which is a way of universalizing and dehistoricizing it. This earliest covenant is entered into with the second creation, the damaged postdiluvian world represented by Noah and his family (Genesis 9). There is also a covenant with Abraham (chap. 17), but none at Sinai. According to this theology, covenant is a once-for-all divine dispensation; therefore, unlike the political model of the Deuteronomists, it does not have to be renewed and revalidated from time to time; hence the designation "everlasting covenant." More importantly, the Priestly covenant is not contractual in the sense that what God commits to is contingent on the moral performance of the human party. The covenant of circumcision in Genesis 17 *(běrît mîlâ)* is a covenant of incorporation rather than of contractual obligation, since fulfilling the command to circumcise is not a condition contingent on the performance of which God commits to certain actions but a sign of membership in a group that, on account of the very nature of the act, it marks as male-dominant — a point to which we shall return.

5

Sacrifice, therefore, is an essential feature of patrilineal-descent groups. In that type of social arrangement the crucial factors are intergenerational continuity between males and the preservation and transmission through time of the material resources of the lineage, especially patrimonial domain. Participation in the sacrificial cult of the group defines and delimits membership and controls recruitment into it. Sacrifice is the emotional focus of the group's existence and collective consciousness. Sacrifice was *the* way of giving people a sense of belonging, sustaining a traditional way of life, and infusing it with the emotional charge without which it would quickly disintegrate.

In societies organized in this way sacrifice was almost invariably a male affair. The few instances of societies in which, in addition to adult males, postmenopausal women were allowed to participate provide illustrations of the widespread belief that menstrual and postpartum blood is defiling and disqualifies the woman from being part of the central religious acts of the group. Women, therefore, did not function as priests in Israel of the biblical period or later since, quite apart from menstruation, the laws of clean and unclean excluded them from the sanctuary for forty days after childbirth, eighty if the child was female (Lev 12:1-5). We can explain the exclusion of women along these lines, but to explain why certain societies felt the need to generate such laws would be a different and more complicated task.

In addition, the ritual marginalization of women in societies like that of ancient Israel is not just a matter of ritual purity laws but rather a feature of social organization in general. A patrilineal system works by importing women into a household to bear children for its adult males, one of whom will in time become the paterfamilias and perpetuate the system. In that respect women are always imperfectly integrated into the social system as honorary members of the household of destination and as such excluded from the most significant cultic events except as spectators. This would be more or less the case whether we are speaking of Israel, Greece, Rome, or traditional patrilineal societies in sub-Saharan Africa. Women contributed their reproductive capacities, but the contribution was to a system over which they exercised no direct control.

In our disgregated postindustrial societies the closest thing to a sacrificial ceremony like the annual clan get-together, the *sacra gentilicia* or the *apatouria*, would be something like the annual office party or the block barbecue. But sacrificial symbolism and its associated social ethos still exert their influence, and do so most directly through certain Jewish and Christian rituals. Two examples come to mind.

First, in Judaism. In a provocative study published a few years ago, Lawrence A. Hoffman argued that, as a basic feature of normative Judaism, circumcision came to express and perpetuate the distinction not only between Jews and Gentiles but also between men and women (Hoffman 1996). According to rabbinic teaching, circumcision presupposes a theory of sacrifice that sets up an iconic binary opposition between the sacrificial blood of circumcision that purifies and saves, and menstrual blood that pollutes. Understood as a covenant, which is how it is described biblically (Genesis 17), circumcision marks and effects incorporation into Judaism understood as a lineage, a patrilineal descent group. But given the nature of the rite, it does so directly only for males, and only indirectly and secondarily for females as mothers, wives, or daughters. Hence circumcision functions as the ritualization and validation of male status, as entry into a male bloodline. In this way, the male body becomes the signifier of gender dichotomy.

Hoffman traces this rabbinic teaching back to the Priestly innovation referred to earlier, an innovation consisting in the combination of covenant and circumcision, *běrît* and *mîlâ*. He notes that a covenant of circumcision is unattested before the composition of the Priestly source, and that the prophetic books prior to Ezekiel know nothing of it. We might add that Deuteronomy, for which the covenant idea is so central, speaks of circumcision only in metaphorical terms (Deut 4:4; 9:25-26), never as a ritual requirement. To take another example, sabbath and moral conduct rather than circumcision appear as the main criteria for Judean status in Isaiah 56-66. On the whole, we have the impression that circumcision was not diagnostically and religiously very important before the ascendancy of the Zadokite-Aaronide priesthood in the later Persian period.

Hoffman's point is that circumcision is the functional equivalent of piacular and disjunctive sacrifice projected into the modern period. Toward the conclusion of his study, he notes how, since the beginnings of Reform Judaism, opposition to circumcision has been, and continues to be, argued on medical, ritual, and moral grounds. If nevertheless there is no great call to abandon it, it will continue on account of the anxious knowledge that to do so would threaten an established social order. It would call into question established social hierarchies, not least gender hierarchy, inherited from the rabbinic and, ultimately, the biblical past.

So much for Judaism. For a Christian instantiation, we might start with the apostolic letter *Ordinatio Sacerdotalis* of John Paul II published

May 22, 1994, by coincidence the anniversary of the burning of Joan of Arc at the stake. This document not only rejected the possibility that women might be admitted to ordination as priests in the Roman Catholic Church but insisted that the issue was not even subject to debate. Such a peremptory closure on discussion and argument may be taken to imply that something very important was at stake for the redactors of the document, something not fully manifest in the arguments from the Bible and church tradition presented in support of this position.

What is basically at issue in this document may be stated as follows. In the post–Vatican II Roman Catholic situation, the revised edition of canon law permits women to do many church-related things previously denied to them, but the one thing they may not do is preside over the Eucharist. The basic theological reason for drawing the line at this point is the strongly sacrificial understanding of the Eucharist that has been traditional in official Roman Catholic teaching. Church councils defined the sacrificial character of the Eucharist and stipulated that only a validly ordained priest might preside over it, adding that the Eucharist, the Mass, retained this character even if the presiding priest was the only one present (Denzinger 1955: 200, 334).

For Christians of the first generations the Eucharist inevitably had sacrificial associations (Christ as Passover sacrifice in 1 Cor 5:7, for example), but it was only much later that the presbyter began to be viewed as a sacrificing priest in more than a symbolic or metaphorical sense. Thus, in the third century, Cyprian of Carthage insisted that Christian ministers undertake no other service than that of the altar and sacrifices (*Epistula* 1.1). The first Christian communities were not organized according to the Jewish ritual system, and in early Christian writings we note the same purely metaphorical use of the vocabulary of sacrifice as in Qumran and Philo. The theological development from presbyter to sacrificing priest cannot be detached from certain historical and social determinants, in the first place the need to sustain intergenerational continuity in a male descent group. In this respect a celibate, sacrificing priesthood is, from the social-scientific point of view, analogous to a descent group in a traditional patrilineal society. To admit females to the ranks of sacrificial adepts is seen, correctly, to pose a threat to the social organization and the distribution of power that sacrificial ritual functions to maintain and perpetuate.

A further point is that sacrifice as prophylaxis, in the sense explained by Victor Turner, entails the need to exclude ritual taint. Women did not function as priests in ancient Israel since menstrual and postpartum blood was considered ritually defiling. This is naturally not presented as an argument in *Ordinatio Sacerdotalis*, but the same fears and anxieties still linger around the Christian Eucharist to the extent that it is thought of in terms of traditional Roman Catholic sacrificial theology.

This issue of ritual taint was dealt with in a brilliant and intuitive study by Nancy Jay that appeared posthumously (Jay 1991). Nancy Jay drew on a wealth of data from ancient and traditional societies to show how uniformly women of childbearing years are excluded from active participation in sacrificial rites. In societies based on male descent, sacrifice makes amends for having to have recourse to the reproductive faculties of women. Sacrifice, she says, is a remedy for having been born of women; it is birth done better. There is therefore the same iconic and symbolic contrast that we noted in Hoffman's study between sacrificial, circumcisional blood that purifies and protects and menstrual and postpartum blood that threatens danger and defilement. Nancy Jay went on to note that, if this is so, it is hardly surprising that there still linger around the Eucharist, when understood as a sacrifice in more than a symbolic and metaphorical sense, anxieties and fears associated with the sexual function, childbirth, and the menstrual cycle. I would agree with this, but I would argue that there is even more at stake. As long as social maintenance is considered the principal function of sacrifice, admitting women on an equal basis with men will be perceived as a threat to existing social arrangements including access to power and privilege within specific social groups.

· V ·

YHVH and Other Deities: Conflict and Accommodation in the Religion of Israel

1

In speaking about "the religion of Israel" it is important to distinguish, on the one hand, between what people in the ancient kingdoms of Israel and Judah were doing and how they were thinking in the religious sphere of their lives, and, on the other hand, what the priests, prophets, scribes, and other religious specialists who wrote the biblical texts thought they ought to have been doing and thinking. The Hebrew-Aramaic Bible is, in fact, for the most part, *against* the religion of Israel understood in the former sense. These texts were put together and edited from the point of view of an un-challenged Yahvistic orthodoxy, with the result that we do not know how much has been airbrushed out of the record and how much has been de-liberately altered (e.g., changing *'ăšērâ* from a proper to a common noun, from Asherah the goddess to a cult object called an asherah). All serious investigators therefore acknowledge that the task of reconstructing the re-ligious history of the kingdoms and of emergent Judaism has to be done as it were against the grain of the texts.

While these texts do occasionally, directly or indirectly, acknowledge a polytheistic past (e.g., Josh 24:2; Jer 2:28; 44:17), use of the biblical texts for reconstructing the religion or religions of Israel has to rely on indirect evidence culled from such sources as prophetic diatribe and accounts of religious reforms. The results must then be checked against the by-now considerable amount of contemporaneous or near-contemporaneous arti-factual, inscriptional, and onomastic data. The historian will have to allow

67

for regional variations, differences of type and emphasis at different social levels (family and clan, professional and artisan classes, temple and court), and developments over time, especially after the emergence of an effective state system no earlier than the ninth century in Israel and the eighth century in Judah. And so many gaps will remain that the results will inevitably be provisional.

In this essay I wish to offer some reflections on the process that resulted in the emergence of a dominant monotheistic Yahvism during the two centuries (6th to 4th B.C.) of Persian control of Judah and other centers of Jewish population in the Near East and Levant. To speak of relations between different competing cults involving both conflict and accommodation raises unavoidably the old issue of religious universalism and its antonym, particularism or integrationism. It is sometimes maintained that the triumph of the monotheistic "YHVH alone" party (Smith 1971: 347), reflected in Isaiah 40–55 and other texts from the Neo-Babylonian and Persian periods, was accompanied by the emergence of Yahvism as a genuinely universal religion. This claim calls for scrutiny, quite apart from the need to clarify what meanings can properly be attached to the notoriously elusive term "universalism." At no time in history has the triumph and persistence of a monotheistic faith had as a *necessary* corollary a universalistic perspective in religious matters.

Coming to the matter at hand, the reader is assured that this is not intended as another well-documented study of religious cults and practices in their development throughout the biblical period, a topic on which the bibliography is huge and expanding exponentially all the time. The aim is rather to identify, within the biblical period, some of the points on the uneven line of development that led eventually to the emergence of Judaism (and therefore also Christianity and Islam) as a monotheistic faith. It will be less important to come up with definite answers than to raise questions for further discussion, questions that may have some interest for those of us today for whom religion is still important.

2

We begin by taking the biblical authors' account of national origins at face value. Biblical traditions are unanimous in affirming that the entity that came to be known as Israel was not indigenous to Canaan. If this is assumed, the relation between the cult of YHVH and the cult of other deities must have emerged as a problem once Israel settled in the land of Canaan. The story begins with the family of Terah, including Abraham, which served other gods beyond the Euphrates (Josh 24:2). There follows Abraham's journey from "Ur of the Chaldees" to the land of Canaan (Gen 11:31–12:4). Sometime after his arrival, he sent his servant back to find a wife for his son Isaac (Gen 24:10). Jacob also returned to the same region in search of a wife (chap. 29), and all but one of his twelve sons, progenitors of the tribes, were born there (29:31–30:24). Northern Mesopotamia was the homeland of the Arameans, and Israelite tradition retained the memory of northern-Mesopotamian, Aramean origins (Deut 26:5-9).

Other traditions, however, point in the opposite direction, to the south, the "great and terrible wilderness" in which Israelites wandered, at times aimlessly, for a generation (Deut 1:19). Some biblical texts give the impression that this southern region was a place of permanent or at any rate long-term residence rather than just wandering (Hos 2:14-15; 9:10; 13:5; Jer 2:2, 6-7). Other traditions reported in the Pentateuch speak of close relations in the earliest period between the Israelites and other ethnic groups in those parts, including Edomites, Kenites, Kenizzites, and Midianites. Hymns that purport to be ancient locate the original home of YHVH in the same region, variously described as the Sinai wilderness, Seir, and Paran (Deut 32:2; Judg 5:5; Ps 68:9, 18; Hab 3:3). In one way or another, therefore, the tradition that achieved dominance regarded Israel as originally nonautochthonous. Since, consequently, the Israelite settlement in Canaan involved the introduction of a new deity into the territorial jurisdiction of other deities whose writ had run there for centuries, the problem of competing religious claims was bound to arise. How was this problem resolved?

The least complicated, and therefore the most common, solution was to attribute a change in the status quo to the direct intervention of the incoming deity. This was common practice in the Near East. Thutmoses III conducted his successful campaigns in Syria and Palestine by direct command of Amon-Re. Assyrian kings routinely justified their annexation of territory with reference to an oracle of Ashur. The Zoroastrian Xerxes ascribed his campaigns, including presumably the less successful ones against the Greeks, to an oracle of Ahura-Mazda (Kent 1953: 147-53). This resolution of the jurisdictional issue by force majeure is well illustrated by the inscription of Mesha, king of Moab, from the ninth century B.C., which speaks of the capture and destruction of Israelite towns by direct command of the Moabite national deity Chemosh (Gibson 1971: 71-83). Though they did not like it, the Israelites of that time could hardly have complained since one of their own heroes, Jephthah, had justified the Israelite conquest of Canaan to an Ammonite king in the same way: "Will you not possess what Chemosh your god gives you to possess? And all that YHVH our god has dispossessed before us we will possess" (Judg 11:24; the writer has overlooked the fact that Chemosh is the national deity of Moab, not Ammon).

The same unsophisticated form of justification appears in the attempt of the Assyrian generalissimo to intimidate the besieged Jerusalemites to surrender during Sennacherib's campaign of 701 (2 Kings 18). At one point he takes a straight line of attack by asking rhetorically whether YHVH was any different from the gods of the other western states crushed by the Assyrian juggernaut (vv. 33-35). But he also argues, somewhat inconsistently, that YHVH had himself commissioned the operation to punish Hezekiah for his impiety in abolishing the regional sanctuaries (vv. 22, 25). This appeal to the anger of the native deity could serve as an *apologia,* or at least an explanation, either before or after the event, from the side of the conquered. Hence Assyria can serve as the rod of YHVH's anger (Isa 10:5), and it was YHVH not Marduk, who handed over the western states, including Judah, to Nebuchadrezzar, "his servant," presumably for the same reason (Jer 27:1-7). One of the clearest examples is the famous cylinder inscription of Cyrus in which he claims that Babylon fell to him because Nabonidus had incurred the wrath of Marduk by neglecting his rituals (Pritchard 1955: 315-16).

In keeping with the theory of conquest by divine decree, the standard way of affirming a territorial claim was the establishment of a new cult in occupied territory. So, for example, Saul set up his first altar to YHVH in territory newly won from the Philistines (1 Sam 14:31-35). Albrecht Alt argued many years ago that the rebuilding of the YHVH altar on Mount Carmel by Elijah and the contest with the Baal prophets were inspired by the Israelite claim to possess this disputed piece of real estate (1 Kgs 18:30-31) (Alt 1966: 2:135-49). It is probably along these lines that we are to understand the otherwise bewildering movements of Abraham after arriving in Canaan, and his setting up altars or other cultic installations at Shechem, Bethel, Mamre, and Beer-sheba (Gen 12:7-8; 13:3-4, 18; 21:33). The phrase "he invoked the name of YHVH" *(vayyiqrā' běšēm YHVH),* which occurs frequently at these points in the narrative, may be understood as the establishment of the YHVH cult at the location in question. In the kind of society envisaged by these texts, territory and cult are indissolubly linked. Cain was driven out "from the face of YHVH," a technical term implying expulsion from the cult community, to become a *na vanadnik,* a wanderer without status (Gen 4:14). Hunted by Saul, David cursed those who had driven him out from YHVH's inheritance "to serve other gods" (1 Sam 26:19). Compelled to return to his own land, but wishing to worship the God of Israel there, Naaman the Syrian general took a cartload of Israelite soil back to Damascus with him (2 Kgs 5:17). Exiled Judeans ask how they can continue to sing their hymns in a foreign land (Ps 137:4).

This territorial dimension is obviously a restrictive and inhibiting factor, and it is difficult to see how any positive evaluation of other religions could be expected as long as it remained operative. The anger of native deities is not adduced as justification for the Israelite conquest of Canaan, no doubt because this would detract from YHVH's sole sponsorship of the operation. What we find is that the destruction of native cults together with their devotees is justified on the grounds of their assumed moral turpitude, beginning with the eponymous Canaan (Gen 9:20-27) and reaching a climax in the systematic program of extermination sponsored by Deuteronomy (Deut 7:1-5, 23-26).[1]

3

Not all ancient Near Eastern religions evince such a negative attitude to other peoples and their different forms of worship. According to the hymns to Aton from early fourteenth-century-B.C. Amarna in the Nile delta, for example, the high god assumes responsibility for the well-being of all peoples:

> You set every man in his place,
> you supply their necessities;
> everyone has his food, and his time of life is reckoned.

1. Jon Levenson has shown how the demonization of those who opposed the Israelite conquest of Canaan is reflected with particular clarity in the hatred of Amalek carried over into the book of Esther and the festival of Purim and concentrated in the arch-villain Haman; see his article "Is there a Counterpart in the Hebrew Bible to New Testament Antisemitism?" *Journal of Ecumenical Studies* 22 (1985): 242-60.

Their tongues are separate in speech,
and their natures as well;
their skins are distinguished,
as you distinguish the foreign peoples. (Pritchard 1955: 370)

Some scholars have nevertheless claimed to find a kind of religious universalism in the Pentateuch (e.g., Martin-Achard 1959: 32-35). Attention has focused especially on the promise that Abraham will be a blessing for all nations or, alternatively, that all nations will bless themselves with reference to Abraham's blessing (Gen 12:1-3). These narratives do indeed evince considerable interest in neighboring peoples, but it remains to be seen to what extent the interest is benign. The eponymous ancestor of the Canaanites is cursed (9:25), Moab and Ammon are tainted in their origins (19:30-38), Edom is destined to servitude (25:23; 27:27-29, 40), and the Arabian tribes are not to inherit the promise (chaps. 16 and 21). We may therefore ask if Abraham is to be a source of blessing for the nations or an example of beatitude to which they can only vainly aspire.

The syncretistic option provided a more benign solution to competing jurisdictional claims than conquest by divine decree. In this context "syncretism" refers to a fusion of deities based on the perception of shared characteristics. This is something quite different from the idea that an originally pure, monotheistic YHVH cult was later contaminated by the incorporation of foreign and especially Canaanite elements, a thesis espoused by Yehezkel Kaufman and, residually, by some Jewish scholars who follow in his footsteps (Kaufman 1960; Tigay 1986). The evidence for YHVH-El and YHVH-Baal syncretism so defined is, however, overwhelming. Israel's original allegiance to El, supreme deity of the Canaanite pantheon, is inscribed in its name, and El Shaddai is one of several El hypostases explicitly identified with YHVH (Exod 6:2-3). Baal imagery is applied to YHVH in poems and psalms, and personal names compounded with Baal are attested in biblical texts and inscriptions. It is telling that none of the ancestors or "judges," and no king prior to Jehoshaphat in the ninth century, bears a name compounded with the theophoric element YHVH or one of its variants.

A particularly interesting example is the encounter between Abraham and Melchizedek as described in Gen 14:17-23. Abraham returns from defeating the coalition of kings, and the ruler of Sodom goes out to meet him. The text continues as follows (my translation):

Malchi-zedek king of Shalem, priest of El Elyon, brought out bread and wine and pronounced a blessing as follows:

> Blessed be Abraham by El Elyon,
> Creator of the sky and the earth;
> and a blessing on El Elyon,
> who delivered your foes into your hand.

Then Abraham gave him a tithe of everything. The king of Sodom said to Abraham, "Give me the people, and you take the goods." But Abraham replied to the king of Sodom, "I have raised my hand in a solemn oath to YHVH El Elyon, creator of the sky and the earth, that I would not take from what belongs to you as much as a thread or a shoelace, so that you could not say that you had enriched Abraham."

Melchizedek pronounces a blessing on Abraham in the name of the creator-deity El Elyon (*theos hypsistos,* "the most high god," in the LXX), whom Abraham immediately identifies as YHVH El Elyon. Reference elsewhere to Shalem in parallelism with Zion (Ps 76:3) and to Melchizedek in a psalm extolling Zion (110:4), locate Melchizedek in Jerusalem. The name of another king of Jerusalem, Adonizedek, has the same theophoric element (Josh 10:1), as does Zadok, David's priest. These names complicate the situation, since the priest-king's name is compounded with that of the northwest Semitic deity *ṣdq* (Ṣidqu?), while the name of his city derives from that of the lower-status god *šlm,* in the Ugaritic texts an offspring of El (Batto 1999: 929-34; Huffmon 1999: 755-57). The theophoric element *šlm* also appears in the names Solomon and Absalom, which of course strengthens the Jerusalem connection.

An interesting variation on the syncretistic option, embodying a kind of theological subordinationism, is reflected in a remarkable passage in the Song of Moses (Deut 32:8-9, my translation):

> When Elyon gave the nations their inheritance,
> when he established the divisions of humanity,
> he fixed the boundaries of peoples
> according to the number of divinities.[2]

---

2. Literally, "sons of god," reading *běnê 'ēl,* or *běnê 'ēlîm* or *běnê 'ĕlohîm* for MT *běnê yiśrā'ēl;* cf. Qumran *bny 'l* (4QDeut^q); LXX has *kata arithmon angelōn theou,* "according to the number of the angels of God."

> Surely, YHVH's portion is his people,
> Jacob is his allotted heritage!

Elyon is certainly an epithet of El, whatever else it is, and El is the supreme god in the Canaanite pantheon, which, according to the Ugaritic Baal text (2.6.44-46), comprised seventy divine beings. The point would then be that YHVH has been co-opted by El into the Canaanite pantheon and assigned as guardian deity to Israel.

4

That Israel was distinctive and distinctively nonautochthonous from the beginning cannot be sustained in the terms in which the normative tradition states it. Practically all critical students of Israelite origins now see the systematic contrast between Israelite and Canaanite, a fundamental point of interpretation for scholars of an earlier generation like Albright and Alt, to be misconceived. The criteria pointing to a distinctive culture that emerged in the central highlands toward the beginning of the Iron Age (terrace farming, the four-room house, collar-rim storage jars, rock-hewn plastered cisterns) do not cash out in terms of a distinctive ethnic identity, and in any case appear not to be exclusive to that region. What indications we possess bearing on religious practice among early Israelites suggests rather that "the religion of Israel" was a subset of the religion of Canaan. The Israelites observed the same agrarian festivals, worshiped the same gods and goddesses (see, e.g., Judg 2:11-13; 3:7; 8:33), and were named after them (Shamgar ben Anat, Jerubbaal, Samson, etc.). Of the personal names on the ostraca discovered during the excavation of Samaria, dating from the late ninth or early eighth century B.C., eleven contain a variation on the divine name YHVH, eight are formed with Baal, and others with the names of other deities (Gibson 1972: 1:5-20, 71-83).

A further indication is that marriage with non-Israelite women, presumably not YHVH-worshipers, passed without comment even in such distinguished cases as Judah, Joseph, Moses, David, and Solomon.

Any account of Israelite origins has to accommodate those poetic compositions that have every appearance of being among the oldest biblical texts and that place YHVH's origins in the southern Transjordanian region — variously described as Sinai, Seir, Edom, the wilderness or mountain of Paran, and Teman (Deut 33:2; Judg 5:4-5; Ps 68:8-10; Hab 3:3-6, to which we can add one of the Kuntillet ʿAjrud graffiti recording a blessing in the name of YHVH of Teman). Like the ancient Semitic god Hadad (Adad, Haddu), YHVH is represented as both a warrior-deity and a storm-deity, who rides the storm cloud like a charioteer (Ps 68:5a; cf. Deut 33:26a; Ps 68:18; Hab 3:8). When he marches out to do battle, the ground shakes, the mountains tremble and are shattered, the skies pour rain, and his enemies are blinded by his effulgence. "He of Sinai" (*zeh sînay,* Judg 5:5; cf. Deut 33:16) is accompanied by myriads of holy ones (Deut 33:2b-3a), including Pestilence *(deber)* and Plague *(rešep)* (Hab 3:5a), and the stars join battle from the sky (Judg 5:20; cf. Ps 68:18).

If the expression *YHVH ṣĕbāʾôt,* first encountered during the Philistine wars, may be translated "YHVH of the (heavenly) hosts," a linking of these allusions to YHVH's origins and original character would be indicated. This, in its turn, would suggest that, initially and for some time to come, the preeminence of YHVH among the gods had much to do with his sponsorship of "the wars of YHVH" (Num 21:14; cf. Josh 10:13; 2 Sam 1:18) in which, according to the biblical record, the Israelites were engaged practically without a break. Total and exclusive devotion to YHVH the warrior-god was promoted by such extreme groups as the Rechabites (2 Kgs 10:15-17; Jer 35:1-19), the Nazirites (Judges 13–16; 1 Samuel 1–3; Amos 2:11-12), and those dervish-like conventicles known as "sons of the prophets" (1 Kgs 20:35-43; 2 Kgs 2:1-25; 4:1-7, 38-41; 6:1-7; 9:1-13) during the constant warfare against Philistines, Syrians, and other neighboring and hostile peoples. It was probably from such groups that commanding figures such as Elijah and Elisha emerged. Both were closely associated with these "prophetic" coenobia, and both were addressed as "father" (*ʾāv,* 2 Kgs 2:12; 13:14) comparable to the abbot in a monastic establishment or to the sheik *(muḥaddam)* who presided over the Sufi brotherhood.

In the Kingdom of Samaria religious allegiances were further polarized by political opposition to the pro-Phoenician policies pursued by the Omri dynasty. This was especially the case after Ahab's wife, Jezebel, daughter of the Tyrian ruler Ittobaal, and clearly a remarkable woman, began to actively promote the cult of the Phoenician Baal at the court in Samaria and throughout the Northern Kingdom. Elijah was commissioned to eliminate the pro-Phoenician faction by anointing the usurper Jehu as king (1 Kgs 19:16), though the actual anointing was consigned to a prophetic acolyte of Elisha (2 Kgs 9:1-13). With the support of the fanatical

Rechabites (10:15-17) and no doubt similar marginal groups, Jehu carried out a thorough purge of the Omrides and massacred their Baalist supporters (chaps. 9–10). While it was by no means as final and definitive as the biblical history would have us believe, Jehu's coup (ca. 842 B.C.) marked a significant stage in the movement away from accommodation and compromise in the direction of conflict between irreconcilable religious allegiances. The issue came to a head with the contest on Mount Carmel between Elijah and the *nĕbî'îm* (1 Kgs 18:20-40).

Although in several respects very different from the conventicles of the "sons of the prophets" in the Kingdom of Samaria, the demilitarized prophecy of the following century inherited the same struggle for exclusive attachment to YHVH. Though both Hosea and Amos denounced the dynasty of Jehu (Hos 1:4-5; Amos 7:9-17), Hosea continued the polemic against the Baals and the bull cult at Bethel and other sanctuaries in the Northern Kingdom (Hos 2:15, 18-19; 8:5-6; 10:5; 13:2). After the fall of Samaria (722 B.C.), the focus of the Historian's animus was directed at state-sponsored syncretism. We are told that Hezekiah, the first Judean king to rule without a counterpart in the Kingdom of Samaria, closed the regional sanctuaries (*bāmôt*, "high places"), destroyed monuments to Baal and Asherah, and removed Nehushtan, the bronze serpent worshiped in the temple (2 Kgs 18:1-4). His successor Manasseh reversed Hezekiah's Yahvistic monism: the *bāmôt* flourished once again, Baal and Asherah were installed once again in the Jerusalem temple, the court sponsored the Assyrian cult of sun, moon, and stars, and necromantic rituals flourished, including the ritual burning of children in honor of the chthonic deity Molech (21:1-9).

After the death of Manasseh, a movement in the Judean countryside against the syncretistic and pro-Assyrian court in Jerusalem seems to have set in. Under the leadership of provincial elders, these "people of the land" (*'am-hā'āreṣ*) put their candidate Josiah, an eight-year-old child, on the throne (2 Kgs 21:24). Encouraged by the prospect of political emancipation with the rapid decline of Assyria, Josiah and his sponsors outdid Hezekiah in their zeal for unadulterated Yahvism, even extending their activity into the territory of the former Kingdom of Samaria (2 Kgs 23:4-20). But Josiah died, inexplicably at an early age according to current ideas on divine retribution, and his reforms died with him. At that point (609 B.C.), it appears, state-sponsored syncretism was still the norm but advocacy of exclusive Yahvism, though still a minority position, was a force to be reckoned with.

It enjoyed the support not only of prophets like Jeremiah but also of prominent Levitical and lay families, conspicuously the family of Shaphan, a high official under Josiah.

The origins of Deuteronomy continue to be debated, but it was probably during this final half-century of Judah's independent existence that the Deuteronomic movement began to consolidate around the prophetic-Levitical coalition referred to a moment ago and to achieve social visibility. While it is possible that a first draft of the book of Deuteronomy and the associated History were produced at that time, the party survived the Babylonian conquest, finding its own ways to cope with the experience of disaster. In the Deuteronomic law the centralization of worship was an essential aspect of political centralization, the creation at least on paper of a unified state system, a program for a future commonwealth. We see it in the polemic against regional sanctuaries, in emphasis on participation in and support of the Jerusalem temple, in the creation of a central judiciary, and other measures of this kind. State centrism brought about religious centralization as a corollary together with the exclusive cult of one national deity. This is not to say that specifically religious considerations were unimportant, but the exclusive worship of YHVH was a *political* necessity if the restored commonwealth was to survive in a decidedly unfriendly environment.

It is obviously impossible to trace the history of Israelite and early Jewish monotheism throughout the Second Temple period in a short essay. The syncretistic cult survived the disaster and even appears to have been dominant during the half-century preceding the missions of Ezra and Nehemiah (see, e.g., Isa 57:3-13; 65:1-7; 66:17). At the same time, the loss of political independence and of royal patronage, together with the deportations, helped to undermine the idea of allegiance to a locative deity.[3] The Zoroastrian cult of Ahuramazda in the Persian Empire would also have tended to reinforce a broader and more cosmic view of deity. The title "God of heaven," attributed to YHVH in texts from the Persian period, points in this direction. The praise of Ahuramazda that features in several contemporaneous Persian inscriptions brings to mind certain passages in Isaiah 40–55: "A great god is Ahuramazda, who created this earth, who cre-

---

3. The abandonment of the idea of the deity's exclusively territorial jurisdiction is expressed symbolically in Ezekiel's mobile chariot throne and the mobile wilderness sanctuary in the Priestly history.

ated yonder sky, who created humanity, who created happiness for humanity" (Kent 1953: 138 and passim).

In his masterful and controversial survey of the vicissitudes of the "YHVH alone" party during the Second Temple period, Morton Smith emphasized the decisive contributions of Nehemiah and, about three centuries later, the Maccabees. But he also noted that it was Nehemiah in the first place who secured the triumph of the "YHVH alone" party, but did so at the cost of endowing the deity once again with the territorial character it seemed to have lost forever after the Babylonian conquest — a development Morton Smith considered regrettable. He concluded as follows: "The national, political, territorial side of Judaism, by which it differed from the other Hellenistic forms of oriental religions, was, as a practical matter, the work of Nehemiah. He secured to the religion that double character — local as well as universal — which was to endure, in fact, for five hundred years and, in its terrible consequences, yet endures" (Smith: 147).

5

Morton Smith's view of the dual nature of Judaism as it emerged during the two centuries of Persian rule induces reflection on the relation between monotheism and religious universalism. "Universalism," with its antonym "particularism," is one of those slippery words generally left vague and undefined. The concept of religious universalism goes back to the Enlightenment with its postulate that true religion must be in conformity with the universally valid laws of reason and a universally accessible moral law derived from them. On this view, the least authentic religious expressions are those that are most distinctive and peculiar to one form of belief — whether creeds, rituals, or regulative norms. The ideal was that the great religious traditions would converge toward a higher consciousness and, in doing so, would shed what was most distinctive, prejudicial, and divisive in each of them.

A good example of this way of thinking is Lessing's dramatic poem in five acts entitled *Nathan the Wise* (1779), mentioned earlier.[4] The drama brought together Christianity, Islam, and Judaism, represented respectively by the Knight Templar, Saladin, and the Jew Nathan (modeled on Moses

---

4. See above, pp. 25-26.

Mendelsohn) in a rather contrived harmony against the background of the religious politics of Palestine at the time of the Crusades. Lessing was, by any reckoning, an extraordinary figure, not least in his struggle against prejudice and his defense of the civil rights of Jews in Germany. But what was much more common, both at that time and later, was the practice of contrasting Jewish observances with the more accessible and universal aspects of religion as embodied in Christianity. It was in this prejudicial form that the universalism-particularism discussion was generally presented in the new discipline of Biblical Theology, itself a product of the Enlightenment.

It will not be necessary to elaborate in any detail on the ways in which this discussion unfolded. The general drift can be illustrated from Johann Salomo Semler's programmatic *Essay on the Free Investigation of the Canon*, published in 1771. According to Semler, the New Testament reflects the essence of universal religion transparent to reason, while the Old Testament is marked by much that is narrow, nationalistic, and time-conditioned, not least in what it has to say about the character of the Godhead. A generation later, Wilhelm de Wette, a friend of Schleiermacher, saw Israel's basic error as fixing on the particularities themselves — that is, legal and ritual stipulations — rather than viewing them as a complex symbolization of the inner religious life. Then Wellhausen, in his famous *Prolegomena*, concluded that the external observances that set Judaism apart from other religions did indeed secure its survival, but at the same time prevented it from evolving into a genuinely universal religion (Wellhausen 1957: 499-513).

Enlightenment thinkers and those liberal theologians of the nineteenth century who followed their lead were, in general, too optimistic about the human prospect to give much weight to the need for salvation. Today it would seem natural to use the term "universalism" in the sense defined in the *Oxford English Dictionary* as "the doctrine of universal salvation or redemption," a usage first attested in 1805. But here, too, clarification is in order. A doctrine of universal salvation would presumably exclude ethnic or physical disqualifications for entrance into the company of the saved or saveable, such as we find in the community law of Deut 23:2-9 or in the Qumran sect that adopted that law. A religion that extends the possibility of salvation to all on condition of conversion to, or some form of association with, the "true religion" could perhaps be said to be universalistic. One could also argue, a fortiori, that salvation is accessible in any religion, or in none, on certain conditions short of adhesion to or incorporation into, say, Judaism or Christianity. But it would then remain to be determined whether in that case salvation would be considered attainable on conditions laid down in Judaism (the Noachic laws) or Christianity (the unique mediatorial role of Christ). One could also contend that to insist on such conditions or to say, for example, that if a Buddhist attains salvation it will be on account of Christ, not the Buddha, is to forfeit the claim to universality, and in a sense that must be acknowledged. But it is characteristic of religions to define the redemptive process according to their own terms of reference, and it is difficult to see how this claim could be surrendered without loss of identity.

To return to our main theme: scholars have often observed that universalism, in the sense of the universal availability of salvation, is a corollary of monotheism and developed historically as a consequence of monotheistic faith that came to clear and unambiguous expression for the first time in Isaiah 40–55 (e.g., May 1948: 100-107; Rowley 1950: 62). Here, too, some clarification is called for. It is surely possible to maintain belief in one God while accepting a plurality of manifestations, hypostases, or names under which the one God is known and acknowledged. We saw earlier that the Priestly writer (P) identified El Shaddai, god of the ancestors, with the YHVH who appeared to Moses (Exod 6:2). During the Hellenistic period those Jews who recognized in Zeus Olympios an alternative manifestation of their traditional deity may have been misguided, but they would not have thought of themselves, and could hardly be called, polytheists (Hengel 1974: 1:261-67). In some respects, in fact, a syncretistic approach to religious belief might seem more likely to lead in the direction of universalism than monotheism. But religion is a matter of socially embodied practices and behaviors, not just of believing, and therefore it is not surprising that the Jewish mainstream rejected this option on the grounds that it constituted a threat to its own identity.

6

During the heyday of Old Testament theology one of the most common assumptions was that the author of Isaiah 40–55, commonly referred to as Deutero-Isaiah, active in the decade preceding the fall of Babylon to the Persians (539 B.C.), proclaimed for the first time that the revelation of the one, true God made to Israel was to be shared with the nations of the world. This was often accompanied by the further claim that Deutero-

Isaianic universalism anticipated the missionary drive of early Christianity, which eventually took it out of its Jewish matrix; hence the frequency with which early Christian writings cited from these chapters. The tragedy of Second Temple Judaism could then be seen as a failure to grasp and exploit the message of Deutero-Isaiah. As Harold Rowley, one of the proponents of this approach, put it, "Judaism became exclusive instead of aggressive, a little garden walled around instead of a great missionary force" (Rowley 1956: 65). Fortunately, most Christian scholars no longer read the Hebrew Bible from such an uncompromisingly one-sided Christian perspective, but the position taken by Rowley is still heard and therefore still calls for comment.

The latter part of the book of Isaiah falls into three parts of unequal length: chapters 40–48, 49–55, and 56–66. The principal theme of chapters 40–48 is the expectation of a revived national life and return from the diaspora following the anticipated conquest of Babylon by Cyrus, which actually happened in 539 B.C. It is this perspective that explains the frequency of polemic and satire directed against Babylonian intellectual and religious traditions and practice in these chapters — one aspect of Isaiah that is admittedly anything but universalistic (see especially 40:19-20; 41:6-7; 44:9-20; 47:1-15). In this section and the one following, much that might appear at first reading to be sympathetic to foreigners is more in the line of what has been called "the fantasy of the oppressed," seasoned with a good dose of *Schadenfreude*. In general, the attitude toward other peoples in these chapters is not particularly benign. They are destined to be subject to the Israelites (49:7; 54:3) and to lick the dust of their feet (49:23). They will perform menial labor for them, and one of their assigned tasks will be to see to the repatriation of diaspora Jews (49:22). The same attitude carries over into the third section, especially in its eschatological core (chaps. 60–62): Gentiles will witness rather than participate in the event of salvation; they are to bring tribute and will serve as *Gastarbeiter* in the future Jewish commonwealth (61:5-7). If this is an offer of salvation for the Gentiles, we would have to characterize it as an offer they cannot refuse.

All of this is in contrast to certain passages in the first section of the book remarkable for their irenic tone; one thinks especially of 19:16-25, which ends with a blessing on traditional enemies: "Blessed be my people Egypt, Assyria the work of my hands, Israel my possession" (19:25).

What might be called the negative side of religious universalism is the alliance between triumphant monotheistic faith and political domination, limited to the realm of fantasy fueled by resentment in these passages in Second Isaiah, too often translated into harsh and intolerant reality in the course of the history of all three great monotheistic faiths. Thus far, Second Isaiah has not moved beyond the perspective of the earlier prophets in their attitude to foreign peoples. But in one important respect the situation is now different: Israel is no longer a nation state but a community to which adherence can come about by free choice. The consequences are not worked out in these chapters, but the implications are there. Take the following passage:

> I will pour out water on the thirsty ground,
>> streams of water on the parched land;
> I will pour our my spirit on your descendants,
>> my blessing on your offspring.
> They will flourish like well-watered grass,
>> like willows by the runnels of water.
> This one will say, "I belong to YHVH,"
>> another will take the name Jacob,
> yet another will write YHVH's name on the hand,
>> and add the name Israel to his own. (44:3-5)

The subtext for this passage is the Abrahamic blessing (Gen 12:1-3), interpreted as a blessing bestowed on outsiders by reason of their adherence to the community of Israel. Judaism is therefore *in principle* a confessional community that welcomes proselytes. Adherence is sealed by certain symbolic acts, including the taking of a new name, as in Christian baptism. Later in the same section we read:

> Turn to me and accept salvation,
>> all the ends of the earth!
>> For I am God, and there is none other.
> I have sworn an oath by my life;
>> the word that overcomes has gone forth from my mouth,
>> a word that will not be made void:
> "To me every knee will bend,
>> by me every tongue shall swear an oath."
> About me it will be said, . . .
>> "Victory and strength come only from YHVH." (45:22-24)

What does this "turning to YHVH" as the necessary condition for salvation mean? One could invoke a deity who had conferred some benefit on the petitioner (e.g., by healing or deliverance from danger) without severing the link with one's original cult. But in this Isaianic passage the bending of the knee *(proskynēsis)* and the confession of faith seem to imply adhesion to the cult of YHVH together with abandonment of other gods; a new element, therefore, and one of the greatest importance for the future.

Rather than contrasting Jewish particularism with early Christian universalism, we should say that the tension between the advocates of these two tendencies was characteristic of the entire Second Temple period. If Second Temple Judaism had been entirely integrationist and particularist, and consequently had rejected proselytism, it would be impossible to explain the enormous demographic expansion of the Jewish ethnos between the Persian and the Roman periods.

The tension can be illustrated with reference to the beginning and end of the last section of the book of Isaiah. In Isa 56:1-8 resident foreigners and the sexually mutilated, threatened by the application of the law excluding certain ethnic categories and the sexually mutilated from membership in the *qāhāl* (Deut 23:2-9), are assured of their good standing in the community. Incorporation, membership, and full participation in worship are to be determined not on ethnic or physical considerations but on a profession of faith and a level of moral performance compatible with it. The passage therefore advocates an open admissions policy of remarkable liberality. Toward the end of the book (Isa 66:18-21) we find a remarkable prediction of a mission to Gentiles as a necessary prelude to the final, decisive intervention of God in human affairs. The final sentence ("I will take some of them to be priests and Levites") even contemplates the admission of proselytes to the priestly and Levitical offices. It would not be surprising if moves of such bold liberality met with resistance, and indeed it appears that a nervous interpolator has, by adding a sentence (v. 20), reinterpreted the purpose of the mission as the repatriation of diaspora Jews.

7

The conflict between advocates of the exclusive worship of YHVH and syncretists was essentially solved by the time the Pentateuch was compiled in the late Persian period, but on the related issue of relations with outsiders, including outsiders who wished to become insiders, no one position prevailed. In this respect as in others, the Pentateuch is a compromise document. In spite of the xenophobia evident in certain passages in Deuteronomy, extreme positions were repudiated by those who drafted the laws. Ezra's program of coercive divorce of foreign wives (Ezra 9–10), which one suspects was doomed to failure from the outset, has no counterpart in the legislation and is implicitly repudiated in Pentateuchal narrative. Abraham married two Arab women (Gen 16:2; 25:1), Joseph married an Egyptian (41:45), Judah a Canaanite (38:2), and Moses two foreign women, namely, Zipporah a Midianite (Exod 2:21) and an unnamed Cushite woman (Num 12:1). Only the last gave rise to comment, and the comment did not receive a sympathetic hearing.

The Pentateuch displays numerous other examples of inconsistencies both within the legal compilations and between laws and customary ways of acting illustrated in its narrative content. Of these the most significant for the future were the ones bearing on relations between Israel and those outside of its confines. Deuteronomy's attitude to the devotees of foreign cults and to non-Israelites in general is decidedly negative, yet resident aliens *(gērîm)* are listed with orphans, widows, and unemployed clergy as in need of assistance, and judges were especially charged to see that their legal rights were protected (Deut 1:16; 14:29; 24:17, 19; 26:12-13; 27:19). The juridical status of the *gēr* was underpinned with the historical memory of the Egyptian bondage, a memory that runs like a symphonic theme throughout the legal sections of the Pentateuch: "When a *gēr* lives with you in your land, you shall do him no wrong. The *gēr* who lives with you shall be to you like the native-born among you, and you must love him as yourself; for you were *gērîm* in the land of Egypt" (Lev 19:33-34).

Compared with practice elsewhere in the Near East and the Levant, Deuteronomy's injunction to love the alien is remarkable. As Elias Bickerman put it, an Athenian contemporary of Ezra would have been astonished to hear that he had to love the metics (Bickerman 1962: 19). In this respect the Pentateuch, taken as a whole, can offer a model for an age that seems to be increasingly intolerant of religious and cultural differences.

VI

Gilgamesh and Adam: Wisdom through Experience in *Gilgamesh* and in the Biblical Story of the Man, the Woman, and the Snake

1

According to a widely accepted critical reading of Genesis 1–11, the history of early humanity from creation to the first Hebrews contained in these chapters is a relatively late version of a Mesopotamian mythic narrative tradition. The sequence of episodes in the biblical version is to a considerable extent parallel to that of the Mesopotamian *Atraḫasis* myth assembled from fragments some of which date to the early second millennium B.C. The narrative sequence in *Atraḫasis* is as follows: after the begetting of the gods, human beings are created, seven male and seven female, to take over the service of the high gods that the lesser gods, the Igigi, are reluctant to perform. In due course, however, the noise and tumult of humanity on the overcrowded earth lead the gods to decide to reduce the population by a series of natural disasters at intervals of 1,200 years. When these Malthusian measures proved to be unsuccessful, the decision was taken to destroy humanity by means of a great flood. Forewarned by the god Enki, the sage Atrahasis built a boat, took aboard animals and birds, and rode out the deluge, which lasted seven days and nights. When the floodwater subsided, Atrahasis (Utnapishtim, Noah) offered sacrifice on the purified earth, and the mother goddess produced a lapis object to remind her that this must not happen again. The conclusion is unclear, but it seems that measures were taken to avoid a recurrence of the disaster (Lambert and Millard 1999).

In both Genesis 1–11 and *Atraḫasis* the deluge is the great divide in early history. In the biblical version, as in the Sumerian King List (Pritchard 1955: 265-66) and the *Babyloniaka* (History of Babylon) written by the Babylonian priest Berossus in the Hellenistic period (Burstein 1978), the deluge is preceded and followed by the genealogies of individuals of extraordinary longevity. The Akkadian story of the deluge was incorporated into the *Gilgamesh* poem, where it occupies most of the eleventh and originally final tablet. The biblical version reproduces numerous features of this well-preserved Mesopotamian text, including such details as the reconnaissance of the birds and the use of pitch or bitumen in the making of the ark.[1] What this means is that the biblical account of the history of early humanity can be read as one version of an already well-established narrative tradition. Reading it in this way may help to bring out its individual features and unique point of view.

In all these versions, nonbiblical and biblical alike, the primary intent is not to provide information of a historical nature but to present paradigms of the possibilities, limitations, and complexities of human existence. Genesis 1–11 (J) in particular is the work of an author who writes out of deep reflection on the history of his own people and on the human situation in general. To use Plato's language, both *Gilgamesh* and Genesis 1–11 (J) express a form of philosophizing by means of myth. In the Near East, inclusive of ancient Palestine, the path of wisdom leads back to the archaic period, and it is there that the narrative paradigms and the philosophizing are located. The name of the hero Atrahasis means "the exceedingly wise one," and commentators on *Gilgamesh* have noted many sayings of a didactic and reflective nature in the poem, some of them attributed to Utnapishtim, also known as Atrahasis, about the transitory nature of human life and the inevitability of death. The title of the work known as the *Gilgamesh* epic — "He Who Saw Everything" *(ša nagba imuru)*, or perhaps "He Who Looked into the Deep" (an alternative meaning of the Akkadian *nagbu*), taken from the opening words of the proem — hints at an interpretation of the hero's journey as more than a discovery of new worlds, as a progressive self-discovery, a quest for a kind of wisdom obtainable only through experience and suffering — the *tō pathē mathos* ("learning by suffering") of the Greeks. In biblical terms, both *Gilgamesh* and the J version in Genesis 1–11 would more properly be characterized as wisdom literature than as history.

---

1. *kōper*, Gen 6:14, a hapax legomenon but the equivalent of Akkadian *kūprū* occurring at the same point in *Gilgamesh* 11.54, 65.

This brings me to the point of this paper, which is to propose a reading of the first episode in the J narrative, namely, the story of the Man, the Woman, and the Snake or, more conventionally, the Garden of Eden story, in the light of *Gilgamesh*. The texts are of course very different in length (about 3,000 verses as against 46 biblical verses), incident, and dramatis personae, but for over a century now specialists in the ancient Near East and the Hebrew Scriptures have noted a preoccupation in both texts with certain fundamental themes. My idea is that by comparing the parallel or divergent development of themes, incidents, and characters in these two texts we might be helped to appreciate the rich narrative texture of Genesis 2–3 and uncover further layers of meaning in it. I would go further and propose that the parallels between *Gilgamesh* and Genesis 2–3 (more precisely 2:4b–3:24) are close enough to permit the suggestion that the author of the Genesis story was familiar with, and had reflected on, *Gilgamesh*, probably in the standard, canonical version eventually deposited in the library of Ashurbanipal in Nineveh where most of it was discovered. The suggestion is neither original nor particularly far-fetched since stories about this legendary Sumerian god-king were translated into several languages, including Hittite and Hurrian, and fragments have been discovered in Syria (Emar) and Palestine (Megiddo). Parallel claims have been made for the influence of *Gilgamesh* on ancient Greek literature, especially *The Odyssey* (Burkert 1992: 88-124).

2

While there is no substitute for reading this great poem, it will be helpful to preface our discussion with a summary of its narrative line (set out by tablets) and a brief account of its formation. The text summarized is the standard version of the epic composed in Akkadian, according to tradition by the incantation priest Sin-leqe-unninni, an expanded version of the Old Babylonian version from the early- to mid-second millennium B.C. More than two hundred fragments of the standard version have come to light, and more are still being discovered, some of considerable length. Whichever of the numerous modern translations one reads, it will be important to bear in mind that there are many gaps in the text, some of which can be tentatively filled with the help of fragments surviving in Sumerian and Hittite, and that considerable uncertainty remains about the location of several of the fragments. We now possess about two-thirds of the original poem, but its recovery and editing is still a work in progress.

I. In the proem the poet announces and summarizes his theme: Gilgamesh, whose wisdom is the product of experience, completed a long journey, suffered much, and brought back hidden knowledge from before the deluge (cf. the opening of the *Odyssey*). The reader is invited to share this experience by reading the story of his adventures. The account is at hand, written on a lapis tablet deposited in Uruk, the city whose foundations were laid by the primordial Seven Sages. Gilgamesh, son of Lugalbanda and the goddess Ninsun, is two-thirds divine and one-third human. He rules in Uruk, but his heart is restless; he exacts the *ius primae noctis* from brides and harasses the population in general. Complaints addressed to the gods lead to the creation by Aruru, the birth goddess, of Enkidu, a beast-man who will be the counterpart to Gilgamesh the god-man and neutralize his unfocussed energy. Enkidu, created out of a lump of clay, is covered in hair, roams the steppe, cohabits with the animals, and frustrates the hunter. He is the prototypical Wild Man. The hunter appeals to his father, who proposes that Enkidu be seduced and tamed by Shamhat, a cult prostitute and devotee of Ishtar. The ruse works spectacularly well, but after a weeklong sexual encounter Enkidu discovers that the animals avoid him, he cannot keep up with them, and he is no longer part of their world. In the meantime, Gilgamesh has anticipated his arrival in a dream interpreted by his mother Ninsun.

II. This tablet has many gaps, but the main narrative line can be picked out. The prostitute cleans Enkidu up, clothes him with part of her own garment, and introduces him to the amenities of city life, including the consumption of bread and beer. Enkidu enters the city, and after a wrestling match with Gilgamesh the two become inseparable friends. Anxious to make a name for himself, and thus to inflict an at-least-provisional defeat on death, Gilgamesh proposes an expedition to the Cedar Forest in Lebanon to kill its guardian, Humbaba, appointee of the god Enlil, and thus rid the land of evil. The expedition involves cutting down a giant cedar. Enkidu's attempt to dissuade Gilgamesh on account of the danger is unsuccessful.

III. The city elders also attempt to persuade the hero to give up the idea, or at least to let Enkidu take the lead and thus risk losing his life, but Gilgamesh, fortified by the blessing of Ninsun and the sponsorship of Shamash, the sun god and his tutelary deity, is adamant. According to the Old Babylonian version, omens are consulted that, it seems, are unfavorable, but Gilgamesh and Enkidu depart anyway, cheered on by the people of Uruk.

IV. The heroes proceed on their way to the Cedar Forest of Lebanon. On three successive nights Enkidu prepares a cultic enclosure and magic circle within which his friend solicits dreams about the outcome of their enterprise. The dreams are full of foreboding — a mountain that falls on him, then pins him down, and finally erupts in smoke and fire — but Enkidu nevertheless gives them a favorable interpretation. There may have been other dreams — the number is uncertain — but eventually they reach the edge of the Cedar Forest and hear Humbaba's roar. For some reason Enkidu's arm has been paralyzed, but Gilgamesh urges him on.

V. The heroes enter the Cedar Forest, the dwelling of gods, where Humbaba is on the prowl. They make ready their weapons and urge each other on. After many dangers intercalated with ominous dreams, the battle is engaged. Humbaba taunts them and Gilgamesh loses heart, but encouraged by Enkidu he prays to Shamash, who plays a decisive role in the defeat of Humbaba. The monster pleads for his life, Gilgamesh is inclined to spare him but Enkidu insists on his death, and he is beheaded. The heroes then cut down the Great Cedar, out of which Enkidu makes a door and floats it down the Euphrates to the sanctuary of Enlil in Nippur.

VI. After Gilgamesh has washed, changed his clothes, and put on his royal diadem, Ishtar, dazzled by his beauty, attempts to seduce him into marriage. Gilgamesh demurs, tactlessly reminding her of the sad fate of previous lovers. Outraged, Ishtar complains to Anu and his consort Antu, demanding that they call down the Bull of Heaven (represented by the constellation Taurus) upon Uruk, which would result in seven years of famine. After threatening to (literally) raise the dead, Ishtar gets her way, but to no purpose since the two heroes slaughter the bull, Gilgamesh sets up its horns as a trophy in his bedroom, and Enkidu insults the goddess by throwing a haunch of the slaughtered animal at her. The tablet ends with a parade and celebration in the streets of Uruk.

VII. The slaying of the Bull of Heaven is the climax of the first half of the poem, the *peripateia* or turning point after which the tone and mood change. The gods convene in assembly to punish Enkidu for his hubris. Over the objections of Shamash his death is decreed, Enkidu becomes sick and, close to death, curses the cedar door (on account of Enlil, who voted for the death penalty), and in yet stronger terms the hunter and the prostitute as the agents of his enlightenment and therefore indirectly responsible for his death. After Shamash remonstrates with him, however, he withdraws the curse, and Gilgamesh attempts to console him. Enkidu has an ominous and premonitory dream of the Underworld, reminiscent of *Ishtar's Descent to the Underworld,* a text also preserved in the Nineveh library (Pritchard 1955: 106-9, cf. 52-57). After twelve days he dies.

VIII. In this very defective tablet Gilgamesh laments his dead friend, proposes to set up a statue of gold and lapis in his honor, carries out the obsequies including offerings to chthonic deities, puts on a lion skin, and roams the steppe as Enkidu previously had done.[2]

IX. Although Gilgamesh was already aware that death is the fate of humanity, and had seen dead bodies in the city and others floating down the river, the death of his friend brings home to him the prospect of his own death and leads him to the decision to go on a long, hazardous journey to seek out Utnapishtim, the only mortal to have escaped death by being transferred into the realm of the gods. He negotiates mountain passes, kills lions, and reaches the mountain named Mashu, into which the sun passes between its setting and rising. This mountain is guarded by Scorpion-Man, whose glance is lethal, but Gilgamesh enters into the mountain and traverses its length in total darkness. He comes out ahead of the sun into the Garden of Jewels with fruit-bearing trees delightful to view.

X. Gilgamesh approaches the tavern of Shiduri ("the pub at the end of the world"), who is frightened by his disheveled appearance, clad in skins as he is, and bolts her door. He explains that his condition is the result of grief at the death of his friend, asks directions to Utnapishtim, and is told that there is no way to cross the Waters of Death. (At this point the Old Babylonian Version has the often-quoted speech of Shiduri reminding Gilgamesh that he will not find the life he is seeking and should rather enjoy the lot of mortals as best he can, 10.3). She refers him nevertheless to Urshanabi the Ferryman, who questions him in the same terms as Shiduri. For some unstated reason Gilgamesh smashes the Stone Charms used to cross the water; however, he is instructed to cut punting poles that will enable him to make the crossing without touching the lethal water with his body. He does so, and repeats the conversation he had with Shiduri and Urshanabi with Utnapishtim the Far-Distant, who muses on death and the fragile and transitory nature of life.

---

2. Recently a fragment of some sixty lines describing Enkidu's funeral has been discovered (George 1999: 62-69).

XI. Having at last reached his destination, Gilgamesh is unimpressed with the far from heroic appearance of Utnapishtim and the *otium cum dignitate* that he is enjoying, stretched out on the ground and doing nothing in particular. The "All-Wise One" goes on to explain how he achieved immunity from mortality, and he does so by giving Gilgamesh a detailed account of the great deluge. Utnapishtim explains how his privileged status came about by direct grant of the gods after he had survived the great deluge. Gilgamesh cannot expect to receive the same privilege, but he nevertheless submits to the ordeal of attempting to stay awake for a week. His failure to do so drives him to despair, and with the help of Urshanabi the Ferryman he is cleaned up and given new clothes for the return journey. But before departure, at the insistence of his wife Utnapishtim gives him a parting gift — a normal feature of oriental hospitality — which is also his last chance. He points out the location of a magical prickly plant in the depths of the Apsu (the Great Deep) that rejuvenates the one who eats it, and Gilgamesh secures it by diving into the Apsu through a shaft in the ground. On the return journey, however, the plant is stolen by a snake, which sheds its skin before disappearing in the ground, thus demonstrating to Gilgamesh that the plant did indeed rejuvenate. The hero and his companion return empty-handed to Uruk, and the poem ends with Gilgamesh inviting Urshanabi to admire the city that he himself had built, using the same words as appeared in the proem (1.1.16-19 = 11.303-5).

The standard, canonical version of *Gilgamesh* is a carefully constructed poem, but it is also as much a composite work, the result of the creative assembling and editing of existing material, as any biblical text. In the first place, the twelfth tablet has no organic connection with the narrative in the preceding eleven. This is clear not only from the lack of any thematic linkage but from the *inclusio* referred to a moment ago:

> Climb upon the wall of Uruk and walk about;
> inspect the foundation terrace and examine the brickwork,
> if its brickwork be not of burnt bricks,
> and if the Seven Wise Men did not lay its foundations. (11.303-5)[3]

---

3. Unless otherwise indicated, the translations are those of Alexander Heidel, *The Gilgamesh Epic and Old Testament Parallels*, 2nd ed. (Chicago: University of Chicago, 1949). While Heidel's translation is in several respects understandably out of date, it has the practical advantage for the reader unfamiliar with Akkadian that the lines are numbered and can therefore be more easily referred to. It can now be compared with the recent translation of Andrew George.

This verbatim repetition of the invitation addressed to the reader in the proem (1.1.16-19) signals the intent to write a unified composition. It also encourages the reader to reflect how Gilgamesh's situation at the completion of the journey is different from what it was at the outset.

Gilgamesh was apparently a historical figure, ruler of the city-state of Uruk (Warka) in southern Iraq in the early third millennium B.C. In the Sumerian King List he is the second ruler after the deluge and reigned for 127 years. By the end of the millennium, the period of the third dynasty of Ur, he had achieved divine status associated with the Underworld, and was the subject of many mythic and legendary episodes several of which have survived and some of which were eventually incorporated into the standard version. Several Gilgamesh tablets from the early second millennium, written in Akkadian, may have belonged to a single, continuous composition (the Old Babylonian Version), providing the basic raw material for the standard version, probably compiled in the Kassite period (16th to 12th cent. B.C.).

Little more need be said about the formation of *Gilgamesh* (on which see Tigay 1982, George 1999). The author-editor utilized one Sumerian poem of some 175 lines, referred to as either "Gilgamesh and the Land of the Living" or "Gilgamesh, Huwawa, and the Cedar Forest" (Pritchard 1955: 47-50; Foster 2001: 104-20) in the first part of his work (cols. 2-4). It tells of the hero's exploit in cutting down the giant cedar and killing the monster Huwawa (Akk. Humbaba), guardian of the Cedar Forest, whose head is offered to the god Enki. The exploit was sponsored by the sun god Utu (Akkadian, Shamash) and supported by fifty volunteers from Uruk, seven theriomorphic beings, and his servant Enkidu. The motivation for the deed was Gilgamesh's resolve to inflict an at-least-partial defeat on death by creating a name for himself — incidentally, a notable theme in Genesis 1–11, especially in the Tower of Babel episode (11:1-9).

Another poorly preserved Sumerian poem has for its theme "Gilgamesh and the Bull of Heaven." The author of the Akkadian epic has worked it into the next episode in the first part of his work (col. 6). It tells of the attempted seduction of the hero by the goddess Ishtar (Sumerian Inanna), her calling down the Bull of Heaven on the city with disastrous consequences, and the slaying of the Bull by Gilgamesh, assisted by Enkidu. Part of another Sumerian text entitled "Gilgamesh, Enkidu and the Netherworld" (Foster 2001: 129-43) was incorporated practically unchanged into the twelfth tablet, which, it is generally accepted, has no organic connection with the preceding narrative. The publication in 1914 of a fragmentary Sumerian account of the great deluge (Pritchard 1955: 42-44) was the first indication that this narrative tradition was also originally unconnected with the *Gilgamesh* epic. It belongs to a different narrative context beginning with creation and ending with the deification of Ziusudra (Akkadian, Utnapishtim, the Noah of Genesis), the one survivor of the flood. It now appears that the author of the standard version took Utnapishtim's account of the deluge directly from *Atraḥasis* rather than from the Sumerian version.

3

We can now return to Genesis 2–3 with a view to reading it in the light of characters, incidents, and themes in *Gilgamesh*. We begin with Enkidu, since Enkidu rather than Gilgamesh is more immediately and obviously the counterpart of Adam ("the Man") in Genesis 2–3.

Together with Gilgamesh, Enkidu is the principal human actor in the first seven tablets, and his death at the end of the seventh tablet sets in motion everything that follows. In the earliest Sumerian accounts (*Gilgamesh and Agga* and *Gilgamesh and the Land of the Living*) he is merely Gilgamesh's servant. Like Odysseus, he visits the Underworld in the odd story incorporated into the added-on twelfth tablet. But in the Old Babylonian Version he is promoted to the status of the hero's companion and friend, and in the Standard Akkadian Version his role is expanded even further. It seems, then, that in the process of formation of the epic Enkidu has moved from the periphery to the center of the story.

Like Adam in the Genesis version, Enkidu was created out of clay in the image of the supreme deity, the deity responsible being the birth-goddess Aruru (1.2.30-35; cf. Gen 2:7). The brief account of his creation appears to have been based on an independent creation story. At any rate, in *Gilgamesh* (1.4.6, 13, 19) Enkidu is described as *lullû amēlu* (primitive man, beast-man), as are the first human beings in the sixth tablet of *enuma elish*, the standard Babylonian creation myth (6.6-8). Enkidu is the earliest example of the Wild Man or Savage Innocent, a figure that keeps on recurring in folklore and literature. Naked, covered in hair, incapable of human speech, cohabiting with wild animals, he is the prototype of humanity in its earliest and most primitive stage. Adam, on the other hand, makes his appearance in a world at a more developed stage. He is an agriculturalist, and his task is to till and maintain the Garden of Eden, Yahveh's own preserve. After his expulsion from the Garden he continues to work the land, if under changed circumstances. We notice, too, a speculative interest in the culture and way of life of early human societies in both texts.

Enkidu's transition from the steppe to the city, from nature to culture, comes about through the sexual ministrations of the woman Shamhat. As in most transitions, there are ambiguities; there is both loss and gain. The Wild Man loses some of his physical strength and is shunned by the wild animals, but he gains reason and understanding (1.4.29). The Woman assures him of this: "You are wise, Enkidu, you have become like a god" (1.4.34). She then clothes him and leads him by the hand, like a child, to the intermediate stage of the sheepfold where the shepherds initiate him to civilized food and drink (bread and beer). He is then ready to leave his old life behind, a step sealed by his turning on his previous associates. He hunts and kills wolves and lions on behalf of his new benefactors, the shepherds (2.3.28-34).

In the Genesis story the primitive man, representative of early humanity, also passes through two stages. In the first he lives with wild animals, with whom he shares a common origin since all come from the earth (*'ădāmâ*). Due to the way the story is told, one might think that the transition from animal to human company takes place almost instantaneously, a matter of minutes or at most hours. But a reading of the first part of *Gilgamesh* would lead us to think rather of two stages of indeterminate length corresponding to two phases in the development of early humanity.

The Genesis story is concerned more with the function than with the physical appearance of Adam, a deficiency supplied for in full measure in the midrash that has much to say about his surpassing beauty and enormous size. During the first phase he is naked like Enkidu, and remains naked until after eating of the forbidden tree at the invitation of the Woman. He has the knowledge and wisdom necessary for naming the animals, somewhat in the manner of Solomon, the paradigm of onomastic wisdom (1 Kgs 4:33). According to a different version of the Eden myth (Ezek 28:12), the first man in Eden the Garden of God was both wise and beautiful. In the case of Enkidu, these characteristics remained in abeyance until his encounter with the prostitute; then they were acknowledged, though perhaps not without a note of irony.

The animals with whom Adam cohabited were intended to serve as "a helper fit for him" (*'ēzer kĕnegdô*, Gen 2:20) as a kind of mirror image of himself, but this did not work out too well. As with Enkidu, Adam's transference into another stage of development came about through the ministrations of a Woman. The seduction scene with Shamhat, graphically narrated in *Gilgamesh* (1.4.8-22), is, in the biblical story, transferred to the Snake, whose approach to the Woman is described by the Woman herself as seduction (Gen 3:13: *hannāḥāš hiššî'anî*). Genesis presents the sexual element only obliquely, in the allusion to nakedness and shame, perhaps also in the metaphor of eating forbidden fruit since eating is a common euphemism for sexual activity (cf. Prov 6:30; 9:17). It also contains the motif of clothing, an essential aspect of civilized life. In Genesis, Adam and his wife first clothe themselves inadequately in fig leaves, and then are clothed more fittingly by YHVH in leather tunics, products manufactured out of animal skins, in preparation for their departure from Eden (Gen 3:7, 21). Toward the beginning of *Gilgamesh* Enkidu is clothed by the prostitute (2.2.27-30) with part of her own clothing — perhaps another indication of sexual ambiguity — and toward the end Gilgamesh must cast off his inadequate covering of skins and be clothed anew for the return journey (11.241-45). We recall that washing and clothing often feature in rites of initiation and passage.

If we take Enkidu's transition as a guide to reading this section of Genesis 3, we would conclude that, though the primal couple in Genesis did not become like gods as the Snake promised, their experience did indeed win them new wisdom and understanding, a fact acknowledged by YHVH (3:22). By offering the Man the forbidden fruit, the Woman initiated a process of humanization and drew the Man away from the immortality of ego consciousness into civilized life as surely as Shamhat with Enkidu, though her intervention took on a quite different form. Comparison with Enkidu's transition would, above all, lead us to highlight the ambiguities involved in Adam's passage from one stage to the next rather than thinking of it in a straightforward way in terms of the Augustinian (and ultimately Gnostic) doctrine of a fall. After Enkidu was led from the steppe into the city, he was to experience much struggle, shed many tears, and eventually get sick and die, but at least he experienced all of this in the context of an achieved human existence. The same can be said of Adam and his wife, in which connection we note that the sentences pronounced on the Snake, the Woman, and the Man simply describe the conditions of life as we experience it (Gen 3:14-19).

95

In the context of the poem, Enkidu is the counterpart, the mirror image, of Gilgamesh. Gilgamesh is two-thirds divine and one-third human (1.2.1; 11.2.16). In the case of Enkidu the proportions are not specified, but he appears on the scene as more animal than human. After Enkidu's death, Gilgamesh reverts to the primitive condition of the uninitiated Enkidu: he abandons the city and wanders in the steppe, filthy and covered in animal skins (8.3; 9.1.1-2). The relation between them can be represented somewhat as follows:

subhumanity	humanity	superhumanity
steppe	city	"mouth of the rivers"
immortality	mortality	immortality

ENKIDU – – – →   ← – – – GILGAMESH

The two characters are the recto and verso of the same image. They are held together in tension between centripetal and centrifugal forces, so that when Enkidu dies Gilgamesh loses his precarious centeredness and spins off to the boundaries of space and time. Their proper place is the city, where alone one can live a truly human life, but while Gilgamesh covets the immortality of the gods, Enkidu looks back with regret to the lost world of timeless animality.

Enkidu's transfer from the steppe to the city is effected by the agency of the woman Shamhat, whereas the function of the woman Havva (Eve) is to be not only the agent of the transition but the counterpart, the mirror image or *alter ego* of Adam, and therefore to that extent functionally similar to Gilgamesh. This is not so remarkable since gender shifts are as common in myths as they are in dreams. There are also intimations in the epic of an erotic relationship between Enkidu and Gilgamesh. After the wrestling match they kiss and form a friendship (3.1.19-20) whose closeness and intimacy is poignantly manifest in the lament following on Enkidu's death (8.11-111), a lament reminiscent of David's lament over Jonathan, whose love was "wonderful, passing the love of women" (2 Sam 1:26).

There is also a Snake that has a small but crucial walk-on, or slither-on, part in *Gilgamesh*. While the hero, on his return journey to Uruk, is bathing, the Snake comes out of the earth attracted by the scent of the magical plant, snatches the plant, presumably eats it, and sheds its skin as it disappears back into the earth (11.287-89). The incident is etiological, purporting to explain a peculiar feature of snakes. But more importantly it makes the point once again that immortality, living in a timeless world, belongs to gods and animals but not to human beings, even one that is only one-third human. The Snake in Genesis 3 also has its part to play in the change of status of the Man and the Woman. There is nothing diabolical about it. It is one of the creatures that YHVH God created, but it is cunning beyond the other animals and possessed of magical powers.[4] Ancient myth and iconography suggest some kind of close connection between the Snake and the Woman that is not transparent in the text. The Snake may be articulating the unexpressed aspirations and velleities of the Man and the Woman, but it is at least clear that, objectively, the Snake functions with the Woman to effect the transition from one state to another.

4

The deities who feature as dramatis personae in *Gilgamesh* and contribute most to the action are Ishtar, Shamash, and Enlil. Ishtar, the great Mesopotamian goddess, shared a sanctuary with Anu, the high god, in Uruk. If her attempt to seduce Gilgamesh into marriage and his rather brutal rejection of the offer reflect in some way the ritual of sacred marriage, the *hieros gamos,* the rejection could imply the hero's refusal to take his rightful place in the liturgies that sustained the city, and therefore his failure to assume the responsibilities of kingship. It was Ishtar, spurned by the hero, who brought destruction on her city in the form of the Bull of Heaven and who was the first to regret her voting in the divine council for destruction by deluge (11.116-23).

Shamash the sun god, whose passage across the sky Gilgamesh, like Herakles, follows in his journey to the ends of the earth, is the tutelary deity and protector of Gilgamesh. After Ninsun intercedes with Shamash on behalf of Gilgamesh and Enkidu, he intervenes decisively in the struggle with the monster Humbaba, but is unsuccessful in opposing the decision in the divine council to bring about the death of Enkidu. Though he is the only one who can cross the Waters of Death (10.2.23), he does not assist

---

4. Note the clever pun in Gen 2:25–3:1: the Man and the Woman were both naked (*'ărûmmîm*); the Snake was the most cunning (*'ārûm*), read also "naked," among animals. Magical powers are perhaps hinted at in the word itself — *nāḥāš* (snake) — cf. the verbal stem *nḥš*, meaning to practice divination or sorcery.

Gilgamesh in his search for immortality since he knows that the quest is futile and assures Gilgamesh that he will not succeed.

The deity whose character and functions most closely approximate those of YHVH in the so-called Yahvist source that, with the Priestly narrative, comprises the so-called primeval history (i.e., Gen 2:4–11:26), is Enlil. Enlil, son of the high god Anu, but unlike Anu an active, interventionist deity, similar to Baal in relation to El in the Canaanite pantheon, is described as wise and understanding, has a special concern for agriculture, and is known as "king of populated lands." In *Gilgamesh* the more destructive side of his character is in evidence. He disputes angrily with Shamash in the divine council, brings about the death of Enkidu, and is responsible for the deluge. In the biblical text YHVH is equally interventionist, closely supervising the first couple and their children, micromanaging their affairs, making Noah's ark watertight, and coming down to see what was happening in Babel. Like Enlil, he has a special concern with agriculture and care for the soil in general. He plants his own garden and appoints a custodian in much the same way that Enlil has his own reserve in the Cedar Forest guarded by his appointee Humbaba.

As described in *Gilgamesh*, the behavior of the deities is on the whole less rational than that of the human characters. They quarrel when gathered in conclave, Ishtar is by turns petulant and abusive, and they all cower like dogs during the deluge and crowd like flies around the sacrifice (11.115, 161). While Genesis 2–3 is different in several respects, not least in there being only one deity among the dramatis personae, several commentators have noted an element of the irrational and arbitrary in the character of YHVH as rendered in this and other incidents in the so-called J source (e.g., Barr 1992: 11-14). The prohibition of eating the fruit from the tree that confers wisdom (Gen 2:16-17) remains without an explanation, the sentence of death is threatened for violating the prohibition but is not carried out, Cain's offering is rejected without explanation (4:3-5), YHVH decides to blot out human beings by a flood since all their thoughts and inclinations are evil (6:5-6), but after the decision is carried out decides not to do it again for the same reason expressed practically in the same words (8:21). In *Gilgamesh*, the deity responsible for the deluge is Enlil, who for some reason is angry with Utnapishtim, but then, after it is all over, relents and confers immunity from death on Utnapishtim and his wife (11.172-95).

Enlil's personal preserve or "paradise" is the Cedar Forest, located on a mountain and guarded by Humbaba. It is called "the dwelling place of the gods" (5.1.6) and in it there is one special tree, the great cedar, a thing of delight. While this does not look much like YHVH's Garden of Eden, we recall that in a parallel tradition the trees in Eden, the garden of God, are cedars and the garden or sacred enclosure is located on a mountain (Ezek 28:14; 31:8). The Garden of Jewels that Gilgamesh reaches after passing through the mountain (9.5.45-51) also brings to mind the precious stones in Ezekiel's Garden of God (Ezek 28:13; cf. Gen 2:11-12). The Garden of Eden story in Genesis 2–3 can be read as a narrative development of this "Garden of YHVH/Elohim" topos, which begins to appear in biblical texts with some frequency only in the Neo-Babylonian period (Isa 51:3; Ezek 28:13; 31:8-9; 36:35; Joel 2:3).

5

Can *Gilgamesh* help us to identify more precisely the principal theme of the Garden of Eden story? In trying to answer this question we must, in the first place, keep to the narrative logic of Genesis 2–3, staying within the story itself, interpreting it in its own terms, rather than starting our discussion from the standpoint of the Pauline-Augustinian doctrine of the fall and original sin. If we suppose that the story is about the lost opportunity for gaining immortality, even if immortality is understood as a permanent continuance of life without death rather than postmortem existence (as Barr 1992: 4), we must account for the fact that Adam and Eve had never been denied access to the Tree of Life, had never eaten its fruit, and yet were expelled to prevent them from doing so. We may have a clue in the incident in which Gilgamesh finds the magical plant and then loses it to a snake (11.266-89). The plant is called "the old man becomes a young man," and it serves therefore to rejuvenate the one who eats it, to reverse the process of aging. That is why Gilgamesh proposes to try it out on the senior citizens of Uruk and eventually, when old age sets in, on himself. Adam and Eve had not eaten the fruit of the Tree of Life because they had as yet no need to; but after their disobedience it would be too late.

Gilgamesh and the Genesis story therefore share the theme of the lost opportunity of immortality, in the sense of a permanent continuance of life without death. But to state it this way by no means exhausts the meaning of either of these seminal texts. Gilgamesh is aware of the current solutions to the problem of a life bounded by death. There is the heroic view

99

according to which death can to some degree be overcome by the great deed that will live in the memory of posterity. As he prepares for the encounter with Humbaba, Gilgamesh comforts himself with the thought that "if I fail, I will establish a name for myself," which, however, turns out to be cold comfort after the death of Enkidu. This, too, is a theme that runs through the biblical version of the primeval world history, especially in the final episode of the City and Tower of Babel. Death can also in some sense be transcended and the life cycle extended through children. It may be significant that the poem provides no hint that the hero has children. The address of Shiduri to Gilgamesh, perhaps the most quoted passage from the poem though present only in the Old Babylonian Version (10.3), is of interest in this regard. Rather than being a recommendation of the *carpe diem* variety, you only go round once so grab for all the gusto you can get, I take it to imply that she is urging the hero to take a wife, have children, and give up his futile quest for any other kind of self-perpetuation:

> Gilgamesh, whither runnest thou?
> The life that thou seekest thou wilt not find;
> [For] when the gods created mankind,
> They allotted death to mankind,
> [But] life they retained in their keeping.
> Thou, O Gilgamesh, let thy belly be full;
> Day and night be thou merry;
> Make every day [a day of] rejoicing.
> Day and night do thou dance and play.
> Let thy raiment be clean,
> Thy head be washed, [and] thyself be bathed in water.
> Cherish the little one holding thy hand,
> Let thy wife rejoice in thy bosom.

Gilgamesh's repudiation of Ishtar's offer of marriage may also be significant in this regard. If, as suggested earlier, this incident reflects the celebration of sacred marriage during the great *akitu* festival, in which the king and the goddess represented by her priestess played the leading roles (Bottéro 2001: 154-64), the hero's rejection of the offer would imply neglect of his civic and religious responsibilities, which also included begetting a son to succeed him. Gilgamesh appears to have been prevented from completing the ceremony by the irruption of Enkidu on to the scene (2.6); he was due to celebrate it after his return from the Cedar Forest, but by then he had been overtaken by events.

The turning point in the story is the death of Enkidu brought about by the inscrutable will of the gods. The event is described with great pathos. Gilgamesh cannot bring himself to accept that his friend is really dead; he is, as we say, in denial, until the seventh day, when a maggot falls from Enkidu's nose. It comes home to him, son of a goddess that he is, that this will also happen to him: "When I die, shall I not be like Enkidu?" (11.1.3). He therefore embarks on a journey to the ends of the earth, following the path of the sun, to consult with Utnapishtim, who alone of mortals has been exempted from death by direct grant of the gods, specifically by the god Enlil (11.189-97). At each stage of the journey he is told that the attempt is doomed to failure. The Scorpion Man tells him that no one but the sun god could pass through the dark tunnel of the mountain Mashu, yet Gilgamesh succeeds in doing so (11.3.6-14). Shiduri tells him that no one but the sun god had ever crossed the Waters of Death, yet Gilgamesh does so with the help of the Ferryman (10.2.21-27). And finally, when he reaches his destination, Utnapishtim attempts to convince him that there is no chance of success. Death is decreed for mortals, and he might as well get used to the idea. The failure of the final test and the loss of the prickly plant due to carelessness or inadvertence finally close off any further options.

Gilgamesh's failure to achieve the goal for which he set out might appear to justify Jacobsen's view that the poem is a tragedy without catharsis (Frankfort 1949: 227). But in fact the poem ends with the hero's return to the city, to the human center, and his acceptance of the task proper to his station of building the city. We are being told that the dangers and sufferings of the long journey away from and back to the center were not in vain since it is no small thing to pass from denial to acceptance. As the proem implies, the journey itself was the source of Gilgamesh's knowledge and wisdom. Perhaps we can leave room for something similar in Genesis 2–3. Whatever other meanings the story might render, perhaps we can say that Adam and Eve could not and should not stay as they were. They had to enter the world of work, sweat, and tears, of childbearing and the joys and frustrations of sexual relations (Gen 3:16-19), and they had to do so at the price of surrendering a life without risk and without end, the immortality of ego consciousness.

VII

Structure, Theme, and Motif in the Succession History (2 Samuel 11–20; 1 Kings 1–2) and the History of Human Origins (Genesis 1–11)

1

In this essay I invite the reader to read the dramatic account of Solomon's accession to the throne (2 Samuel 11–20 and 1 Kings 1–2) in juxtaposition with the narrative of human origins according to the Yahvist writer (conventionally J) in Genesis 1–11. My intention is to demonstrate that, in spite of the obvious difference between these two texts in genre and length, a consideration of structure, theme, and motif will reveal that they have much in common. Hopefully, the experiment of reading each in the light of the other may convey a deeper appreciation of both texts. It may also suggest that they originated in the same milieu, and thus contribute to identifying, at least in a general way, a very obscure chapter in Israelite literary history in the later biblical period. But first I should say something about the critical study of the two texts.

Beginning in the early nineteenth century, the weight of scholarly opinion favored the application to Samuel 1 and 2 (originally one book) of one or other version of the documentary hypothesis that dominated the study of the Pentateuch at that time (Eissfeldt 1965: 241-48, 268-81). Assigning much of the material in 1-2 Samuel to two or three narrative sources represented in the Pentateuch or Hexateuch could claim some justification, but adopting this documentarian approach inevitably obscured the distinctive character of blocks of narrative material in 1-2 Samuel, each with its own subject matter and themes. By the middle of the twentieth century, at any rate, this approach to the historical books as, in effect, an extension of the narrative strands in the Pentateuch or Hexateuch was no longer in favor. Its abandonment was in good part the result of Martin Noth's Deuteronom(ist)ic History theory, which cut off the Tetrateuch (Genesis to Numbers) from the historical books to which Deuteronomy could then be seen to serve as an introduction (Noth 1981).

Another factor was the influence of Leonhard Rost's *Die Überliefe-rung von der Thronnachfolge Davids (The Tradition of the Succession to the Throne of David)* (Rost 1982). In his study of 2 Samuel 9–20 and 1 Kings 1–2, Rost adopted a vertical rather than a horizontal approach to source division. By concentrating on narrative theme rather than the criteria employed by Pentateuchal critics, he identified the Succession History as one of several distinct but connected narrative blocks in 1-2 Samuel, following the Ark Narrative (1 Samuel 4–6 plus 2 Samuel 6), to which he also dedicated a detailed study.

Rost's main thesis has proved to be quite durable, though some scholars have raised doubts about the distinctive character and coherence of the Succession History or Court History. There is also considerable disagreement about its extent, where it begins, how extensively it has been edited, and, not least, when it was composed. First of all, no one doubts that the final chapters of Samuel, 2 Samuel 21–24, form a series of appendices and therefore are not continuous with the preceding narrative. On the assumption that the principal theme is the succession to David's throne, the narrative line clearly continues into 1 Kings 1–2, ending, in keeping with this central theme, with the statement that "the kingdom was established in the hand of Solomon" (1 Kgs 2:46b). Scholars also generally agree that some additions have been made to the narrative. David's deathbed admonition to Solomon shows unmistakable signs of the Deuteronomistic hand (2:1-4), and the record of David's death, the length of his reign, and Solomon's accession (2:10-12) looks like the standard annalistic conclusion to the account of a reign in the History (cf. 11:41-43: Solomon succeeded by Rehoboam). In this instance, however, the formulaic language does not serve to conclude the Succession narrative since Solomon's hold on the throne remained under threat until Adonijah was disposed of (in 1 Kings 1–2). Several commentators read the Nathan episode (2 Sam 12:1-15a), or at least the parable of the rich man and the poor man (12:7-15a), as a Deuteronomistic insertion, but this is not so self-evident, as we shall see.

If the Succession History has a definite excipit ("the kingdom was established in the hand of Solomon," 1 Kgs 2:46b), the same cannot be said for its incipit. Many commentators have followed Rost in including in this text the account of David's dealings with Mephibosheth, son of Jonathan and grandson of Saul, and the first campaign against the Ammonites and their allies (2 Samuel 9–10). But including David's actions designed to neutralize any possible remaining threat from the family of Saul obliged Rost to go back even further to include the king's rejection of Mikal, the wife given him by Saul (6:20-23), which then raised the question whether earlier incidents involving Mikal should not also be included (1 Sam 18:20-25; 19:11-17). Furthermore, the question with which the Mephibosheth incident opens — "Is there still anyone left of the house of Saul?" (2 Sam 9:1) — seems to offer a natural sequel to the grim account of the ritual murder of the seven descendants of Saul in one of the appendices referred to earlier (21:1-14). At this point it is becoming clear that including all of this material leads to the unraveling of the narrative as a distinct literary unity. The legitimation (mostly by morally dubious means) of David's own claim to the throne, his relations with Mikal, and the long account of his struggle to eliminate Saul and his family from contention are quite distinct thematically from the succession to David's throne. This issue arises only with David's liaison with Bathsheba and, eventually, the birth of Solomon (chaps. 11–12).

Solomon's allusion to his accession as the outcome of a promise made by YHVH (1 Kgs 2:24) persuaded Rost to include what he took to be the original nucleus of Nathan's dynastic oracle (2 Sam 7:11b, 16) as part of the Succession History. Since Rost attributed the Succession narrative to an author at the Judean court during the reign of Solomon, this was to be expected. But apart from the fact that Nathan's dynastic oracle does not require that Solomon succeed David, this is only one of several allusions in the Succession History to previous sayings and incidents recorded in the annals of the early monarchy. In recording the banishment of the priest Abiathar, for example, 1 Kgs 2:27 notes the fulfillment of the prophetic oracle in 1 Sam 2:27-36, implying no more than that the author of the Succession History was familiar with these parts of the history and felt free to refer to them.

In the early days of the investigation, a challenge to the essential unity of the Succession History came from Hugo Gressmann and Wilhelm Caspari, two pioneers in the study of biblical literary genres (Gressmann 1921: 163, 181; Caspari 1983: 153-83, 191-94). Their proposal was that the Court History was made up of a loosely connected catena of *Novellen* (e.g., the incident involving Amnon and Tamar in 2 Samuel 13–14) comparable to the Egyptian *Novelle* with its lively dialogue, love for significant and striking detail, and vivid characterization. Rost rejected their hypothesis since it seemed to him to undermine the unity of theme and authorship of the Succession History (Rost 1982: 67, 83-84), but the two views need not be irreconcilable. It may be possible, in other words, to read the separate incidents as relatively self-contained "novelistic" narratives without denying the essential stylistic, structural, thematic, and perhaps even authorial unity of the composition as a whole.

In the last resort, how one reads the story as a distinct composition will depend on what one identifies as the central, controlling theme. I take it that unity and cohesion are manifested in a plot that tells how Solomon, guided by a hidden providence, reached the throne against all the odds. I therefore read it as unfolding in four dramatic incidents in each of which basic themes, patterns, and motifs are replicated:

2 Samuel 11–12	David's adultery with Bathsheba, leading to the death of their child.
2 Samuel 13–14	Rape of Tamar by Amnon, leading to his murder by Absalom.
2 Samuel 15–20	Rebellion of Absalom, expressed in his occupation of David's harem and resulting in his death.
1 Kings 1–2	Rebellion of Adonijah, expressed in his attempt to possess David's concubine and leading to his death.

There are four sons in line for the succession ahead of Solomon, and the four incidents deal with their progressive elimination, leaving Solomon to ascend and maintain the throne without a rival. This outcome involves a double fratricide — Absalom kills Amnon in the second episode and Solomon kills Adonijah in the final one — and in each instance the course of events ending in death is set in motion by an act of a sexual nature. In addition, all four episodes are held together by motifs recurring throughout, motifs reminiscent of the so-called Yahvist (J) source in Genesis 1–11, as we shall see.

2

Comparison of the Succession History and the Yahvist account of human origins in Genesis 1–11 inevitably opens up the question of the milieu within which both works arose and their date of composition. Until fairly recently practically all scholars, including Rost, took it for granted that the Succession History was written by a contemporary or near-contemporary of Solomon, and a great deal of energy was expended in identifying the author, the principal candidates being the priest Abiathar active under David and Solomon and Ahimaaz, son of Solomon's priest Zadok. Such an early date had its attractions since it seemed to provide a historical source of incomparable value for a period notoriously lacking in documentation. Gerhard von Rad's description of the Succession History as "the oldest specimen of ancient Israelite historical writing" would have been widely accepted half a century ago, and some would still accept it (von Rad 1966: 166-204). In the present climate of opinion, however, these assessments will seem overly optimistic to many scholars. The ability to create lively and plausible scenarios is not confined to contemporaries or eyewitnesses — witness Job, Esther, Judith, Tobit, and the like. It is at least clear that the dialogue, through which to an extraordinary degree the plot and the motives of the actors are displayed, is fictional. The retrieval of a core of historical data from the story need not be ruled out, but it would have to be carefully assessed, and it would be prudent to bear in mind that there is no supporting evidence for any of the events recorded in this text. The core might include the circumstances of Solomon's birth, Absalom's elimination of Amnon as successor to the throne and his unsuccessful rebellion, and the accession of Solomon accompanied by further palace intrigue. This, then, could have been the basis on which the author, writing centuries later, constructed a dramatic and, on the whole, psychologically believable story.

The absence of the Succession History from Chronicles, in which David is presented as a figure of heroic and saintly proportions, is generally and understandably explained as a deliberate omission by the author, who generally follows his principal source, the Deuteronomistic History. In a brief study of what he calls "the Court History of David," however, John van Seters argued that the author of the History would have had the same reasons for not including this material as the Chronicler, since the presentation of David as a conniving and morally bankrupt figure in this work is clearly inconsistent with the ideal figure presented in the rest of the history. Van Seters therefore concluded that, rather than being a source for the Historian, the Court History is an antimonarchic and antimessianic addition to it from no earlier than the mid-sixth century B.C. (Van Seters 1983: 277-91).

Van Seters's thesis is ostensibly quite reasonable since the succession of murder, rape, adultery, incest, and treachery that the Succession History contains gives it the appearance of a *chronique scandaleuse* not calculated to edify or serve the purposes of a historian with a very explicit moral agenda. But it is important to note, on the other hand, that Solomon is declared to be the "beloved of YHVH" (2 Sam 12:25), and that the author describes both Solomon and David as accepted enthusiastically by the people (2 Sam 19:41-43; 1 Kgs 1:39-40). This looks more like pro-Solomonic propaganda than antimonarchic polemic. At a more basic level, the plot as set out above, which follows the pattern, familiar in biblical narrative, of the ascendancy of the youngest or the last in line, as in the election of Saul and David, conveys the message that the succession of Solomon was from the outset meant to happen. As for David, his sin was after all forgiven (2 Sam 12:13), and nothing related to the later vicissitudes of his life as described in this source is clearly at odds with the paradigmatic David of the rest of the History.

In agreement with Van Seters, I conclude nevertheless that the Succession History is a Second Temple composition and that it originated in a milieu quite different from that of the Deuteronomists. While by no means indifferent to religious issues, it focuses more directly on secular matters, and its often subtle insight into human motives and the interplay of social relationships is informed by a remarkable psychological realism. In contrast to the explicitly declarative and imposing god of the Deuteronomists, the deity of the Succession History acts from behind the scenes, and divine action works by indirection, more often than not through the often devious aims of the human agents. Only on very few occasions do we hear of divine interventions or divine judgments on what is transpiring (2 Sam 11:27b; 12:15b; 17:14).

The impression left with many readers that the Yahvist in Genesis 1–11 shares the same *Weltanschauung* as the author of the Succession History has inspired attempts to trace both works to a common source, in the first place — as noted earlier — by extending the Yahvist source (J) beyond the Pentateuch or Hexateuch into the Books of Samuel. Even those who rejected the existence of parallel strands (J and E) in the historical books recognized affinity with the spiritual and cultural world of the Yahvist in these books. The issue calls for a further brief comment at this point.

Throughout the modern period until recently there has been a critical consensus that the so-called Primeval History in Genesis 1–11 resulted from the combination of a Priestly source (P), beginning with creation, and a Yahvistic source (J for Jehovah, the older, incorrect reading of the Tetragrammaton YHVH) beginning with the Garden of Eden narrative. Until the last decades of the twentieth century, most critical scholars adhered to some form of the documentary hypothesis, which required dating J to the time of the early monarchy. The reasons for doing so are well known but may be recalled. They include its alleged "enthusiastic acceptance of agricultural life and of national power and cultus," its "delight in agriculture, cult, national power, the state, and kingship," and "the optimism of national and religious exultation" with which this source was thought to be suffused (Eissfeldt 1965: 200; Fohrer 1968: 157; Weiser 1961: 108). Others were impressed by its naive anthropomorphisms and antique flavor (Rowley 1950a: 25), and others again by its humanistic tone, reflecting what Gerhard von Rad was accustomed to refer to as the Solomonic enlightenment or its dimmer afterglow during the reign of his successor (von Rad 1966: 69).

In reading through this scholarly commentary, one is struck by the fact that von Rad rarely based his arguments for an early date for J on Genesis 1–11. This is understandable since, however well these generalizations may fit other parts of the Pentateuch or Hexateuch, they are not at all supported by a reading of Genesis 1–11, from which enthusiasm for agrarian life and religious and nationalistic optimism are conspicuously absent. We read instead of the curse on the soil, exile, and the vanity of human pretensions in general and their deployment in the political sphere in particular. One would think that this unenthusiastic diagnosis of the human situation and pessimistic assessment of moral capacity would correspond more closely to a time of failure and disorientation. The conviction of an ineradicable tendency to evil, expressed both before and after the deluge (6:5; 8:21: "the inclination of the human heart is evil from youth up"), is more reminiscent of some of the darker lucubrations of the later sages and prophets than of von Rad's "free-spirited Solomonic era." Job speaks of mortals being few of days and full of trouble (Job 14:1), and Jeremiah of the human heart perverse and devious beyond comprehension (Jer 17:9-10). One could almost take that as a comment on the story of crime and punishment in the Succession History.

It is not difficult to discern in Genesis 1–11 a foreshadowing of the history of Israel as one of repeated spiritual failure leading to disaster that is almost but not quite terminal, a disaster followed by a new beginning. In

Genesis 1–11 the great divide is the deluge, and in antiquity a deluge is a familiar figure for military defeat and political disaster, as in the lament over the destruction of the Sumerian city of Ur (Pritchard 1955: 458-59). Isaiah 54:9-11 can therefore compare the hoped-for restoration of "storm-tossed" Jerusalem to the renewal of the world after the deluge (Gen 9:8-17). Genesis 1–11 ends, as does the national history, with the forward movement stalled in Mesopotamia (Gen 11:1-9; 2 Kgs 25:27-30). The pattern is repeated on a smaller scale in the Garden of Eden story. Like Israel, the Man *hā'ādām* is placed in a favorable environment where permanence is contingent on obeying a commandment. Death is threatened for nonobservance, but what follows is not physical death but the social death of exile. Behind the seductive Snake and the Tree of Ambiguous Knowledge we discern cults carried out both before and after the fall of Jerusalem in gardens featuring sacred trees; and the role of the Woman in Eden recalls anxieties about women as the occasion for adopting such cults (Deut 7:3-4; Proverbs 1–9; Isa 57:3-13, etc.). These parallels suggest that reflection on historical experience viewed from the other side of disaster has generated a recapitulation and interpretation of the history transcribed into the categories of myth, following a familiar Near Eastern pattern in speaking of human origins most clearly articulated in the *Atraḥasis* myth.

That the biblical version of the history of early humanity originated in the postdestruction period is consistent with the absence of allusion to it in earlier texts. We begin to hear about the Garden of Eden and the deluge only from the time of the liquidation of the state and ensuing deportations (Isa 51:3; 54:9-10; Ezek 28:13; 31:9, 16; 36:35; Joel 2:3). The location of the Tower of Babel in Shinar (Gen 11:2) points in the same direction since this toponym appears predominantly, and perhaps exclusively, in the postexilic period (Isa 11:11; Dan 1:2; Zech 5:11). Genesis 11:1-9 could then be read as a critique of the Neo-Babylonian Empire, written at a time when Babylon had become a byword for godless political and imperial pretensions.

There is therefore some justification for alignment between the Succession History and J in Genesis 1–11. The paradigmatic character of the latter suggests if it does not absolutely require that it be dated later than the History, as several recent scholars have stated or implied (e.g., Schmid 1976), and its reactive relationship to P in the context of the *tôlĕdôt* scheme would also locate it later than that source, perhaps as presenting a more psychologically credible and less optimistic assessment of human nature (Blenkinsopp 2002: 49-62). In contrast to both the History and P, both the

Succession History and the J account of origins have a marked secular and lay character, and we can detect numerous indications in both of affinity with what is somewhat vaguely referred to as "late wisdom" (Whybray 1968). It is now time to test these conclusions by a closer reading of the four chapters into which I propose to divide the Succession History. The reader is invited to test the conclusions by a close reading of each of these sections in sequence.

3

The first of the four episodes (2 Samuel 11–12) is framed by the account of the second Ammonite campaign (11:1; 12:26-31). The siege of the Ammonite capital provides a chronological counterpoint to the events unfolding in Jerusalem. The chronicle of these more private and individualized events has been inserted into the military annals, but it was written expressly for insertion at this point since the siege provides the pretext for the elimination of the unsuspecting husband of Bathsheba and the complicity of the brutal army commander Joab.

A first echo of the Yahvist is heard with David walking about on the palace roof in the late afternoon or evening, reminiscent of YHVH walking about in the garden at the time of the evening breeze.[1] He sees a woman very beautiful in appearance *(ṭôbat mar'eh mĕ'od)* washing herself, finds out who she is, that is, the wife of a foreign mercenary, and summons her to the palace. After she returns to her house, her message to the palace that she is pregnant *(hārâ 'ānokî)* echoes Havva's cry at the birth of Cain, "I have gotten a man child with [the help of] YHVH" (Gen 4:1), a cry of triumph rather than a distress signal. The attempt to displace responsibility for the pregnancy onto Uriah begins with some small talk, after which the king grants him furlough, using crude sexual innuendo to urge him to sleep with his wife. (The sexual implication of "wash your feet" was noted by some medieval Jewish commentators who knew that "feet," *raglayim,* is a euphemism for the genitals). This invitation Uriah declines on account of a religious scruple, sexual abstention being de rigueur when on campaign (cf. 1 Sam 21:5-6). After David tries unsuccessfully to achieve his ob-

---

1. *vayĕhî lĕ'ēt hā'ereb . . . vayyithallēk 'al-gag bêt-hammelek* (2 Sam 11:2); cf. *YHVH 'ĕlohîm mithallēk baggān lĕrûaḥ hayyôm* (Gen 3:8).

ject by getting him drunk, the plot is finally consummated when Uriah returns to the front bearing his own death sentence, unsuspecting to the end (2 Sam 11:14-17). David reacts to the news of Uriah's death much as Joab had anticipated, mouthing the first of several traditional platitudes that occur throughout the Succession History — "Do not let this affair trouble you, for the sword devours now one, now the other" (11:25). The unsavory episode draws to a close with Bathsheba's ritual mourning, her transfer to the palace harem, and the birth of her child.

We may note in passing the stylistic device characteristic of both the Succession History and Genesis 1–11 of using direct speech in preference to indirect, reported speech to advance the action and reveal the intentions of the characters. This feature is in evidence in the dialogue between the Woman and the Snake (Gen 3:1-5), YHVH, the Man, and the Woman (3:9-19), YHVH and Cain (4:6-15), and the monologues in the Tower of Babel episode (11:1-9). In this first part of the first episode of the Succession History it is abundantly in evidence, as it is in the aftermath of the child's death in 2 Sam 12:17-23. Joab's oral instructions to his messenger provide a good example of the care taken by the author in constructing the dialogue: the anticipated reaction of David to the news of the military blunder the messenger is instructed to report is set in the a-b-a pattern ("Why did you approach the city? . . . Why did you approach the wall?"), and concludes with the announcement of Uriah's death (11:19-21).

Part or all of the account of Nathan's intervention (2 Sam 12:1-15) is often elided as an addition to the Succession History. This is understandable since 11:27b ("The thing which David had done was displeasing to YHVH") immediately preceding and 12:15b ("So YHVH struck the child that Uriah's wife had borne David, and it got sick") immediately following make a seamless connection, and the text between these two clauses comes away clean. Moreover, Nathan's indictment assumes the dynastic oracle of 2 Samuel 7 and at times has a Deuteronomic ring to it; compare, for example, the rhetorical question Nathan puts to David ("Why have you despised the word of YHVH?" 12:9) with the question Samuel puts to Saul in a similar situation ("Why did you not obey the voice of YHVH?" 1 Sam 15:19). There is also the question whether the parable makes a good fit with the situation it is intended to reflect. After all, the poor man's lamb is like a daughter to him, not like a wife, and the coercive actions in the parable and in real time are quite different.

While certainty in such matters is rarely attainable, it seems that the indictment has been touched up in the Deuteronomistic manner but that, if we can speak of additions, they were made with the idea of fitting the incident more completely into the narrative as a whole. This is the case with the oracular prediction that "the sword shall never pass from your household" (2 Sam 12:10), which serves as an ominous lead-in to the events that follow. The more specific prediction that David's "neighbor" will lie with David's women in the open air is fulfilled in Absalom's takeover of the royal harem (12:11; 16:22). It would also be too literalistic to rule out the parable as unsuited to the context. Like David's harem women (12:8), the lamb lay in its master's lap, and that it did so "like a daughter" *(kĕbat)* could have been suggested by Bathsheba's name *(bat-šebaʿ)*. We might note, finally, how the two segments of this first scene (11:2-27a; 11:27b-12:25) have been linked by means of the contrasting scenes of Bathsheba mourning the death of her husband, then being comforted with the birth of David's child (11:26-27a; 12:24-25).

4

In spite of the rapid pace at which the events described unfold, the second episode (2 Samuel 13–14) covers a period of at least seven years, two years elapsing between the rape and the murder of the rapist (13:23), the three years of Absalom's exile in Geshur (13:38), and the two years he was denied access to the court after his return (14:28). The episode is introduced with a vague temporal indication common in 2 Samuel (*vayĕhî ʾaḥărê-kēn,* "some time afterward"; cf. 2:1; 8:1; 10:1; 21:18). We are therefore not told how much time had elapsed since the birth of Solomon, but the connection with the previous episode is apparent. As Bathsheba went from mourning (perhaps disingenuous mourning) to consolation for the loss of her husband in the first episode (11:26-27; 12:24-25), so David for the loss of his son in the second (13:31, 39). In this second episode, the first of the two fratricides eliminates Amnon, Solomon's leading rival and the heir-apparent, and the way is prepared for the crisis of Absalom's rebellion in the following section. The unity of the narrative is therefore maintained with respect to structure, style, and theme in spite of the introduction of an entirely new set of dramatis personae.

The first of these is Tamar, an unmarried sister of Absalom and half-sister of Amnon about whom all we are told is that she was beautiful. We shall see that this motif of personal beauty, sometimes alluring and dangerous, runs throughout the entire story of David and his family. At the beginning we are told that David had beautiful eyes and was handsome in appearance (1 Sam 16:12; cf. 17:42). Absalom was also a handsome man (2 Sam 14:25), and *his* daughter, another Tamar, was a beautiful woman (14:27). Adonijah, the last of the sons to die a violent death, was also a fine-looking man (1 Kgs 1:6). It is tempting, and perhaps justified, to suspect a link with the old topos of *royal* beauty and wisdom, in its turn related to the beauty and wisdom of the First Man, the Man in Eden the Garden of God, full of wisdom, perfect in beauty (Ezek 28:12). Amnon, the crown prince, at any rate is not so described. In gratifying his lust at the expense of Tamar he replicates the pattern of his father's conduct, and in so doing he brings about his own death. The instantaneous change from love to hate after he had gratified his lust, and his treatment of the violated Tamar ("Get up and get out!" 2 Sam 13:16), make for one of the most chilling scenes in biblical narrative. His accomplice Jonadab, David's nephew (13:3, 32), is described as *'îš ḥākām mĕʾōd*, literally, "a very wise man," an embodiment of low cunning. Like the cunning Snake in the Garden of Eden story (Gen 3:1), he asks ostensibly innocent but in reality loaded questions. Two years later he is still at it, manipulating David for his own ends after the murder of Amnon at Baal-Hazor (2 Sam 13:32-36).

It does not require much skill at interlinear reading to detect in this section collusion between the cousins Jonadab and Absalom in the hatching of a plot to put the latter on the throne. Jonadab exploits Amnon's infatuation with Tamar to provide Absalom with a motive for murdering Amnon other than personal ambition, namely, avenging his sister's honor as Simeon and Levi avenged the honor of their sister Dinah (Gen 34:25-31). Absalom's attempt to persuade David to attend the sheep-shearing at Baal-Hazor with all his sons would seem to indicate his intention to make a clean sweep, and David's cautious rejoinder likewise indicates a degree of dubiety about Absalom's intentions (2 Sam 13:23-27). That Jonadab was able to reassure the king about what actually happened at Baal-Hazor before the messengers arrived strengthens the impression of collusion in this particularly sordid example of palace intrigue. We note, too, how he emphasizes that the deed was done to avenge Tamar and not out of political ambition (13:32-33).

The stratagem employed by the odious Joab, another cousin (2 Sam 17:25; cf. 2 Sam 13:3), to bring the banished Absalom back to the court suggests that he, too, was implicated in the plot to put Absalom on the throne. It involved the co-option of another wise agent, similar functionally to the wise Snake in the Genesis story, whose intervention would be successful in the short term but bring disaster later on. The dialogue between the "wise woman" and David is composed with consummate skill and involves the device of "the story within the story" or *récit à cadre,* a deliberate fictionalization of the situation between David and Absalom (14:4-11). Examples of this literary device are abundant from Apuleius's *Golden Ass* and *One Thousand and One Nights* to the play within the play in Shakespeare's *Hamlet* and Tolstoy's *Kreutzer Sonata.*

The theme, to which we will return later, replicates the primordial fratricide perpetrated by Cain in which the murderer is threatened with death on account of the blood vendetta but is granted protection by a higher power (Gen 4:1-16). The more somber and pessimistic tendency of the later sages, preeminently Qoheleth, but reflected also in the Yahvist's work, is heard as the wise woman reminds the king that "we must all die; we are like water spilled on the ground that cannot be gathered up" (2 Sam 14:14). Taken all in all, this chapter must be considered one of the masterpieces of Hebrew prose.

An interesting feature of the Succession History is the counterpoint between vivid episode — for example, Jonathan and Ahimaaz concealed in the well by a woman (2 Sam 17:17-22), or the bringing of the news of Absalom's death to David (18:19-32) — and long intervals of time empty of incident. There is an indeterminate amount of time between the first and the second segments (13:1), two years for the rape of Tamar to be avenged (13:23), Absalom's three-year exile in Geshur (13:38), his two years in his house in Jerusalem (14:28), and the four years during which the rebellion was brewing (15:7). In the third and longest segment of the work narrating the rebellion of Absalom and ending with his defeat and death and the restoration of David's rule (chaps. 15–20), we continue to hear echoes of the Yahvist writer in Genesis 1–11, including such familiar turns of phrase as "You are my bone and my flesh" (2 Sam 19:12-13; cf. Gen 2:23) and "knowing good and evil" (2 Sam 19:37; cf. Gen 3:5). There is the seduction motif, with Absalom stealing the hearts of the people (2 Sam 15:6). There is the wise or ostensibly wise agent, in this instance Hushai, following whose advice leads to disaster (17:5-14). Absalom's rebellion was set in motion after another sage, Ahithophel, advised him to occupy his father's harem (16:20-23). The finality and irreversibility of this act can be gauged by Solomon's reaction to Adonijah's request for Abishag (1 Kgs 2:19-25). Thus, all four chapters of the work begin with an act of a sexual nature that results in disaster and death. The sexual connotations of the Eden story are unmistakably conveyed in the reference to nakedness and shame, and perhaps also in the act of eating, a common euphemism for sexual activity (e.g., Prov 6:30; 30:20).

The presence in the final episode (1 Kings 1–2) of David, Bathsheba, Nathan, and Solomon links it with the first episode and rounds off the narrative. The recruiting of Abishag also highlights the effect of the passage of time on David since his summoning Bathsheba to the palace, accentuated by the notice that she was to lie in his lap (1 Kgs 1:2; cf. 2 Sam 12:3, 8). Themes by now familiar continue to resonate: Abishag is exceedingly beautiful (*yāpâ 'ad-mĕ'ōd*, 1 Kgs 1:4), and Adonijah is very handsome (*ṭôb-tō'ar mĕ'ōd*, 1:6). The widespread belief that the well-being of the people depended on the virility of the ruler explains why Adonijah's rebellion follows immediately on the notice that David did not know Abishag sexually (1:4-5); a fairly close parallel from the Ugaritic KRT cycle is the attempt of Yassib, son of king KRT, to replace his elderly and ill father on the throne (Coogan 1978: 52-74). After the rebellion was stifled before it got underway, Abishag would once again, and finally, be the occasion of Adonijah's undoing (2:13-25).

While the plan to insure the succession of Solomon was hatched by Nathan, the focus is on Bathsheba throughout. As elsewhere in the Succession History, character and intentions are revealed skillfully by means of dialogue. We hear her manipulating the old king in her own interests and those of her son (1 Kgs 1:15-21, 28-31). She reminds him of an oath he may or may not have made (1:17; cf. 1:30), and in her later dealings with Adonijah she accedes to his request for Abishag and passes it on to Solomon, knowing full well what the outcome would be (2:13-22). This is one of several indications that the Bathsheba of the Succession History is anything but a passive, good-natured, and rather stupid woman, as some commentators have suggested.

5

Our reading of the Succession History has revealed an impressive concentration of the same motifs that appear in the Yahvist's "primeval history" in Genesis 1–11, especially in the first episode featuring the Man, the Woman, and the Snake in the Garden of Eden. It may be helpful to summarize the main points. The traditional element of the beauty and wisdom of the primordial man is only implicit in Genesis 2–3 but explicit in the Ezekiel version of the myth (28:12, 17) in which the *Urmensch,* perfect in beauty and wisdom, is also a royal figure. It is not surprising that these qualities are incorporated into the profile of the ideal ruler; witness the theme of royal, Solomonic wisdom and the king as "the most beautiful of men" (Ps 45:3). We have seen how frequently the theme recurs in the Succession History. David's own beauty (1 Sam 16:12; 17:42) irradiates out among the members of his family, including by co-option Abishag, who is described as stunningly beautiful (1 Kgs 1:4). As for David, though he does not always act wisely, to say the least, his wisdom can still be compared to that of the angel of God (2 Sam 14:20).

Another motif inscribed or encoded in different ways in both texts is that of the *femme fatale,* the Woman Who Brings Death. The woman in question is generally a foreign woman. The struggle for the succession is set in motion by David's infatuation with Bathsheba (or Bathshua, 1 Chr 3:5), wife of a foreign mercenary, and it is not hypercritical to suggest that she is not assigned the role of the designated victim in the narrative. The motif reappears in the historian's judgment on her son who came to grief through his love for many foreign women (1 Kgs 11:1-3). It is pervasive throughout Genesis, a particularly relevant instance being the marriage of Judah to a Canaanite woman called Bathshua (Gen 38:2; 1 Chr 2:3; cf. 3:5) the death of whose first two sons is attributed to YHVH (Gen 38:7-10). This incident also features a Tamar, Judah's daughter-in-law, who remained unmarried and "dwelt in her father's house" (Gen 38:11) as the Tamar of the Succession History dwelt unmarried in her brother Absalom's house (2 Sam 13:20). Both Tamars are later vindicated at a sheep-shearing festival. The two texts are close enough to suggest a relation between them of some kind. The motif is expressed in the universalized language of myth in the first episode of the Yahvist history. The woman is the occasion of the sin of disobedience, though the seduction is displaced onto the Snake (Gen 3:13), and there results in due course the primordial fratricide.

The peril of ensnarement by the foreign woman is perhaps *the* prominent motif in Proverbs 1–9 (Blenkinsopp 1991: 457-73). It is emphasized that she seduces in the first place by means of language (5:3; 7:5) — she has a smooth tongue and smooth speech — and both Havva (Eve) and

Bathsheba are very dexterous with words. There is also the old motif, familiar from ancient Near Eastern iconography, of *die Frau am Fenster,* for the Greeks *Aphrodite parakyptysa,* the woman who allows herself to be seen (Prov 9:13, 18). Seduction is represented as offering forbidden fruit to eat. The verb for eating occurs fourteen times in Proverbs 1–9 and seventeen times in Genesis 3, and there is perhaps something of the same association in the scene of Amnon being fed from Tamar's hand (2 Sam 13:5). The link between Proverbs 1–9 and the Succession History will appear even more clearly when we compare Nathan's parable, in which David's adultery is represented as theft, with Prov 6:29-31:

> So is he who has relations with his neighbor's wife,
>   no one who touches her will go unpunished.
> Do not people despise a thief when he steals
>   to satisfy his appetite when he is hungry?
> If he is caught, he will pay sevenfold;
>   he will surrender all the goods of his house.

David insisted on sevenfold (following the ancient versions) restitution for the theft of the poor man's lamb, and he was, for a time, literally despoiled of the goods of his house.

There is a further link between the Eden narrative and this point in the Succession History: in both texts falling prey to seduction leads to a condemnation of death but one that is not carried out.

A consideration of the peculiar character of wisdom in the Succession History brings to the fore the motif of the wise agent following whose advice leads to disaster and death. Jonadab is (literally translated) "a very wise man" (2 Sam 13:3), but his advice to Amnon leads to the latter's death. Joab suborns the wise woman of Tekoa, but the stratagem that she skillfully implements leads to civil war and the death of Absalom. Ahithophel, filling the same role as the legendary Ahikar with the Assyrian army (Pritchard 1955: 427-30), advises Absalom to take possession of the harem, an irreversible act that seals Absalom's fate. In the Eden story, the Snake has this same attribute of dubious wisdom. He asks the same kind of leading questions as does Jonadab, and following his advice has the same disastrous consequences.

The fratricide motif, of frequent occurrence in ancient myth (e.g., Seth and Osiris, Romulus and Remus), reappears in the wise woman's fictionalized version of the relations between Amnon and Absalom. In this episode of the Succession History in particular we hear echoes of the language of the Yahvist writer in the story of Cain and Abel (Gen 4:1-16). The killing takes place in the open country (*baśśādeh*, 2 Sam 14:6; Gen 4:8); the fratricidal brother, in danger of imminent death, is protected by a royal (divine) decree; and the dead husband will be left without issue "on the face of the earth" (*ʿal-pĕnê hāʾădāmâ*, 2 Sam 14:7); compare Cain's banishment "from off the face of the earth" (*mēʿal pĕnê hāʾădāmâ*, Gen 4:14). Banishment and exile loom large in both Genesis 1–11 and the Succession Narrative, as they do in many biblical texts from the postdestruction period. Both David and Absalom are banished. In Genesis, the Man is driven out of the garden onto the arable land (*ʾădāmâ*, Gen 3:23), and Cain from the *ʾădāmâ* onto "the face of the earth" (4:14).

In the final resort, however, what J in Genesis 1–11 and the Succession History have most basically in common is a kind of theological anthropology that seeks to express through narrative the possibilities, constraints, ambiguities, and aporias of human existence. The aspect of human behavior most clearly in evidence in both works is the tendency to transgress limits, and the moral factor consists in the description of the consequences of doing so. This theme is often expressed in the aphoristic literature (e.g., Prov 11:2; 16:18; 18:12; 29:23), sometimes in a rudimentary parabolic form (e.g., 25:6-7). It is the theme that unites the succession of episodes in Genesis 1–11: the Man and the Woman in Eden, Cain in relation to his brother, Lamech intent on indiscriminate vendetta, promiscuous divine beings in relation to human women, the violence of the generation of the deluge, Nimrod the empire-builder, and the builders of the city and tower in the land of Shinar. In the Succession History the theme is abundantly in evidence. It is exemplified in most of the leading characters who are active or proactive as opposed to those who are acted upon, especially Uriah and Tamar. But it is especially in evidence in the three sons whose lack of restraint leads to their deaths. The author uses practically the same language in describing how both Absalom and Adonijah "exalted themselves" by putting together a force of chariots, horses (horsemen), and fifty outrunners (2 Sam 15:1; 1 Kgs 1:5); a good example of the author's ability to express basic human realities by means of concretely and precisely described situations.

It would be gratifying if we were able to round off our brief study by proposing a plausible setting for the composition of the two works. Unfortunately, our limited knowledge of the intellectual and literary history of the Second Temple period permits no more than a vague and ill-defined guess. If the J source in Genesis 1–11 was composed subsequent to and as a kind of supplement to P, and if its mirroring of the religious history of Israel presupposes the History, we would have to place it no earlier than the second half of the sixth century B.C. The affinity of both texts with the work of Second Temple sages (as expressed in Proverbs and Job), and their cultural ambient in general, suggest that they originated in the lay, intellectual milieu of Judah sometime in the second century of Persian rule. But whenever they were composed, they present us with a distinctive view of human reality *coram Deo* different in important respects from those of the Priests and the Deuteronomists.

VIII

The Judge of All the Earth
(Genesis 18:22-33)

The men left there and continued on to Sodom, leaving Abraham still standing in the presence of YHVH. Abraham drew near and said, "Are you going to sweep away the righteous with the reprobate? Suppose there are fifty righteous people in the city; will you sweep them away rather than pardon the place on account of the fifty righteous in it? Far be it from you to do such a thing, to kill the righteous together with the reprobate, so that the righteous are on a par with the reprobate! Far be it from you! Shall not the judge of all the earth give right judgment?" YHVH replied, "If I find in Sodom fifty righteous people in the city, I will spare the entire place on their account."

1

This is how the story begins; the rest is well known. The conversation between Abraham and YHVH about the fate of the city of Sodom (Gen 18:22-33) occurs in a remarkable incident in the sequence of stories about Abraham's trials and triumphs. The lead-up to the dialogue combines two themes: a visit of supernatural beings at Mamre near Hebron in which Abraham and Sarah, now aged, are assured that they will beat the odds and have a son; a meeting between Abraham and either two or three travelers whom Abraham hastens to entertain in good oriental fashion and set on their way to Sodom, where their overnight stay will be rudely disturbed.

Abraham's solicitude as host highlights by contrast the treatment by the inhabitants of Sodom of wayfarers unfortunate or imprudent enough to make a stopover in their city.

In spite of some minor inconsistencies of a kind not uncommon in biblical narrative, in particular whether Abraham entertained two or three passersby — which provided occasion for trinitarian speculation in the patristic period — this part of the story hangs together quite well. While most commentators in the modern period assigned it to the earliest narrative strand in the Pentateuch, credited to the so-called Yahvist writer (indicated by the siglum J), there was always a troubling suspicion that it did not fit the profile of this source, that it was anomalous, and therefore that it was probably a later insertion (e.g., Westermann 1985: 347-48, 352). One problem is that we are left wondering how Abraham knew of the decision to destroy the city, and though we were told in an earlier aside that its inhabitants were wicked (Gen 13:13), not enough was made of their moral turpitude to justify such a drastic punishment as total obliteration.

Now that the older consensus on the sources of the Pentateuch has crumbled, it is easier to question the once taken-for-granted date of J during the United Monarchy or shortly thereafter. One of the strongest argument for a later date arises out of the unique literary character of the passage. The dialogue is not of the usual kind that serves to display the character or intentions of the speaker. It is programmatic, in the sense of being set up deliberately to address problems of a theological or moral nature raised by the proposed annihilation of the city by divine decree. To that extent it is comparable to a certain type of postbiblical haggadic or narrative midrash on biblical texts. Rabbinic midrash was usually done on texts presenting theological or moral problems, texts that seemed to call for an explanation. But the explaining was usually done not by argument but by retelling the story in a different way or telling a new story to make the point of the original story in a different way. Hence midrash is one way of generating new narrative out of old, a characteristic abundantly illustrated in the present instance.

Midrash — the term means, literally, "inquiry" or "investigation" — is commonly understood to be a type of rabbinic commentary on biblical texts, either of a legal (halakic) or narrative (haggadic) kind. Some scholars want to define the term exclusively as a form of *rabbinic* biblical exposition, while others see an organic connection between postbiblical midrash and exegetical procedures within the biblical material itself (Seeligmann

1953: 150-81; Bloch 1954: 9-34; Sandmel 1961: 105-22; Vermes 1973: 8-9, 228). The point is made appositely in a remark by Weingreen: "There are literary elements in certain passages in the Hebrew Bible which are clearly not part of the original text and which, when isolated from the basic text, are identified as being of a rabbinic type of exposition" (Weingreen 1976: 55-75). If we are looking for parallels to this kind of dialogue between a *ṣaddîq* and God whose purpose is to thresh out a theological issue arising from a biblical text, we shall find them more readily in the great corpus of haggadic midrash than elsewhere in the Hebrew Bible. If therefore we hesitate to grant a monopoly of this genre to the rabbis, we might take the broad approach and accept, as a working hypothesis: first, that it is possible to read Gen 18:22-33 after the manner of midrash; second, that its purpose is to explain in narrative form some troubling features of the account of the annihilation of Sodom by divine decree in the following chapter; third, that, as such, it constitutes the first stage in a literary trajectory extending beyond the confines of the biblical texts in which new meanings are coaxed out of the text and new narrative generated out of old.

What, then, are the issues arising out of the account of the destruction of the city that seemed to the biblical midrashist to call for comment? The starting point is the divine decision to destroy the *entire* city. Though Sodom is to be annihilated on account of its moral depravity, it would be natural to assume the existence in it of some innocent people, at least innocent enough not to have merited total obliteration. If so, it would seem to be contrary to divine justice that they, too, should perish. If no distinction is made between the innocent and the guilty, the moral order is subverted and the ethical character of the God of traditional religion called into question. If that happens, the center no longer holds and everything falls apart. The idea behind this reasoning is that, in the matter of the administration of justice, we may hold God to standards at least as high as those accepted among the deity's devotees as expressed in laws and traditional societal norms. The point is made by Abraham in the most forceful way:

> "Are you going to sweep away the righteous with the reprobate? Far be it from you to do such a thing, to kill the righteous with the reprobate, so that the righteous are on a par with the reprobate. Far be it from you! Shall not the Judge of all the earth give right judgment?" (18:23, 25)

The fate of the innocent caught up in a guilty society is therefore the principal issue. But the question also arises whether the innocent, perhaps at a certain critical mass, can play a salvific role, even perhaps to the point of saving the corrupt society in which they live from the consequences of its depravity. The biblical midrashist answers this question in the affirmative, so much is clear, but the further question of the critical mass either remains unanswered or is answered implicitly as Abraham gets the number down from fifty to ten and stops there. Why he goes no further will call for consideration at a later point in the literary trajectory. These, then, are the issues that the dialogue in Gen 18:22-33 was written to answer, and they arise directly out of the destruction of a city. The city was Sodom, but it could have been Lisbon, or Dresden, or Hamburg, or Coventry.

It could also have been Jerusalem, and in fact one could make a strong case that our passage finds its place among other attempts to come to terms with the destruction of Jerusalem by the Babylonians in the autumn of 586 B.C. Much of the literature that has come down to us from the immediate postdestruction period was written to address these issues involving the ethical character of the deity, and whether it made any sense to continue thinking of the deity as the guarantor of justice and the protector of the innocent. Before taking soundings in this literature, we recall that conventional religious thinking in Israel and elsewhere in the ancient Mediterranean world and Near East, reflected in surviving legal and aphoristic formulations, simply took for granted collective and intergenerational moral accountability and liability. YHVH was not the only deity who visited the sins of the parents on the children to the third and fourth generation (Exod 34:7; Num 14:18). In Israel, however, the bonds between deity and people were particularly close and formulated in terms of reciprocal *moral* responsibility, at least in the classic Deuteronomistic formulation. The Israelite god YHVH freely obligated himself to protect and bestow blessing, but according to the standard view his commitment was contingent on the fulfillment of certain moral demands on the part of the people. That, in essence, was the conventional wisdom and theology, and the particularly close ties between the people and their God made for a more severe crisis of belief when the partnership did not seem to be working. Under normal conditions it sustained and reassured, but history teaches that normalcy is not guaranteed in the lives of societies and individuals.

Questions about the justice of God and the ethical character of the God of traditional religion therefore began to be raised in an acute form when the Babylonians destroyed Jerusalem and its temple. The crisis of faith found expression in the proverbial saying about the ancestors having eaten sour grapes and the effect of this diet on their descendants (Jer 31:29-30; Ezek 18:2). Ezekiel, in particular, comes to the defense of YHVH in his own scholastic way by arguing that each generation stands on its own with respect to the imputation and the consequences of guilt. The accusation that "the way of YHVH is not just" (Ezek 18:25, 29; 33:17, 20) is therefore unfounded. Ezekiel makes the point very clearly that the individual's fate is not decided by heredity. The same issue is addressed in the book of Job. In Ezek 14:12-23, Job is one of the three legendary just men, together with Noah and Daniel, who are living in a corrupt society overtaken by a succession of disasters and who, by virtue of their righteousness, will save themselves *and no one else, not even their own sons and daughters.* This is clearly a quite different solution from that of the author of Gen 18:22-33. We recall that the disasters that afflicted Job were part of a larger scenario of destruction in which *his* sons and daughters, and many in the land of Uz besides, lost their lives. And even though he lived to get another family and more property and livestock, those who had died at the beginning of the story stayed dead.

The close affinity between Job in the land of Uz and Abraham at Sodom supports the view that both these righteous ones are addressing the same issue and the same situation. Both hold that God cannot be asked to explain his decisions, yet both demand an explanation. Abraham asks, rhetorically, whether God will destroy the righteous with the reprobate, but Job goes further and affirms that he does so, and in doing so undermines the distinction between good and evil: "it is all one; he destroys the blameless and the wicked" (Job 9:22). Both also presume to speak though they are but dust and ashes (Gen 18:27; Job 30:19; 40:6). In general, both Abraham and Job struggle with the fate of the righteous in a world, or society, or city, in which injustice appears to triumph and yet over which the God of Israel claims jurisdiction as sovereign judge.

The fact that in the prophetic writings Sodom occurs as a code-name for corruption and annihilating judgment and, more specifically, as a symbolic designation for Jerusalem (Isa 1:9-10; 3:9; Jer 23:14; Ezek 16:44-63), strengthens the suspicion that, in spite of their very different literary forms, both Gen 18:22-33 and Job are attempting to come to terms with the fate of Jerusalem. This was the paradigm, the make-or-break test case of the reality, power, and ethical character of the God of traditional religion. The destruction of Jerusalem and its temple, together with the civil and religious infrastructure undergirding the life of Judean society, thrust upon the survivors questions about the reality, the ability, the will to intervene, and the benevolence of their God. But the most pressing question was whether God can be said to be just in anything like the ways in which justice is postulated of human beings and societies, whether human ideas about justice have any meaning when postulated of God. Abraham's questioning provided a point of departure for reflection but left many questions unanswered. Let us see how the midrash took up the challenge of this text.

2

One of the most striking features of the midrash on our passage is that it goes straight to the heart of the questions just posed by presenting God's judgment on Sodom in terms of a judicial process. As is often the case, the process is set in motion by a complaint, the demand for legal redress by a plaintiff. The "outcry" (the Heb ṣĕʿāqâ, Gen 18:21, is also a forensic term) is directed against the cities of Sodom and Gomorrah. The Jerusalem Targum explains that these cities oppressed the poor and decreed that anyone giving even a morsel of food to the needy would suffer death by burning. It adds that the complaint that came up to God derived from a young girl called Pelitit, meaning something like "Survivor," who makes a sudden and unexpected entrance into the story. So, in responding to the cry for redress, God as judge says: "I will now reveal myself and see whether they have acted entirely according to the outcry of the maiden Pelitit which has come up to me" (Ginsburger 1903: 29-30).

An explanation, ingenious and moving at the same time, is provided by Rabbi Levi, a third-generation Amora, reported in *Bereshit Rabbah Vayyera* 49:6, a major rabbinic commentary on Genesis. The story, repeated often with variations in later midrashim, is a good example of the midrashic genius for generating new narrative out of old:

> There were two girls who went down to draw water from the spring. One of them said to her companion, "Why do you look so sick?" and she answered, "Our food supply is exhausted, and we are already close to death." So what did she do? She filled her pitcher with flour and exchanged it for the other girl's, taking the one which was in the other girl's hand in place of her own. When they heard of it, the people of

the city seized her and condemned her to death by fire. The Holy One (Blessed be He) said, "The sentence passed on this girl does not permit me to remain silent." The proof of this is that the Scripture does not say, "according to their outcry" *(hakkěsaʿăqātām)* but "according to her outcry" *(hakkěsaʿăqātāh),* that is, that of the girl.

The girl therefore entered the story courtesy of the feminine suffix attached to the noun *sěʿāqâ,* "outcry," in Gen 18:21. Later identified with Lot's daughter (e.g., in *Pirke de Rabbi Eliezer*), she will win a place in Jewish folklore as the first martyr to charity. It is her cry for justice addressed to God that sets in motion the judicial inquiry that follows: "I will go down to see whether they have acted entirely according to the outcry which has come up to me; I mean to find out" (18:21).

Interestingly, the Targum tradition exploits the indeterminacy expressed in this verse to introduce the possibility of repentance or "turning" *(těšûvâ)* conceded to the corrupt citizens of Sodom, and therefore to absolve God of the charge of arbitrariness. Targum Neofiti, for example, paraphrases 18:21 as follows: "They are sinners; but if they pray for repentance and trust in their souls that their evil deeds may not be manifest before me, they will be before me as if I did not know them" (Diez Macho 1968: 101).

The people of Sodom would clearly have to undergo a radical change of heart in order to repent, since according to rabbinic teaching deeds of charity are the most powerful advocates or "paracletes" *(pěrāqlîṭîn,* a Greek loanword) before God (e.g., b. *Šabbat* 32a). The midrash on our passage therefore allows repentance, but emphasizes it rather less than we might expect. Rabbi Abba bar Kahana, a fourth-century Palestinian Amora, states that the Holy One left them an opening for repentance, understanding the indeterminacy or disjunction implied in Gen 18:21 as between utter guilt leading to destruction and a lesser degree of guilt meriting a less severe punishment. In the latter case, the Holy One would make known to them and manifest to others the right measure of justice in the world *(middat haddîn bāʿôlām),* presumably by inflicting an appropriate punishment short of total annihilation.

Bereshit Rabbah Vayyera 49:6 also quotes an opinion of a certain Rabbi Jeremiah ben Eleazar to the effect that over the span of a quarter of a century prior to the destruction God brought on the city earth tremors and assorted terrors to induce them to repent, but without success. Later commentators, for example, in *Midrash Haggadol Bereshit,* will interpret God's desire to know what is happening as a merciful knowledge (*yĕdî'at raḥămîn,* "a knowing of mercy") characteristic of God and God's righteous ones by which the true measure of justice is revealed. But in general not much is made of repentance, and the reason may be that it was not seen to make a good fit with the forensic model that predominates in the midrash.

After the complaint, the judicial inquiry follows: "I will go down and see whether they have acted entirely according to the outcry which has come to me." It is often noted that in the midrash this is one of ten "descents" *(yĕrîdôt)* of YHVH, the previous one being the investigation of the building of the tower and city of Babel in Genesis 11 (*Bereshit Rabbah Vayyera* 38:9; 49:6). Rabbi Abba bar Kahana takes the occasion of a syntactic feature of this verse (18:21) to insist on an interval between the investigation of the complaint and the execution of the verdict, offering the ingenious but implausible reading: "I will go down and see whether they have acted according to the outcry which has come to me — then destruction!" (*Bereshit Rabbah Vayyera* 49:6; *Pesikta Zutarta* 85).

Yet there must be an interval, since the rights of the defendant require the intervention of a defense attorney *(sĕnigôr,* borrowed from the Greek *synēgoros).* This is where Abraham comes in. As a good defense lawyer, Abraham seeks to find some merit in his client's case, or some mitigating circumstances that would at least result in a lighter verdict (*Tanḥuma Yelammedenu Vayyera* 9:13). Here, too, the midrash moves in a different direction from the Targum, which understands Abraham's intervention more as a form of intercessory prayer than a legal argument or plea bargaining — for did not Abraham stand before God as one stands and prays the *'amîdâ?*[1]

The forensic model is also used to elucidate the numerical sequence, perhaps the most remarkable feature of the passage. Rabbi Hiyya bar Abba, a fifth-generation Tanna, explains that Abraham was about to go directly from fifty to ten but was directed by the judge to do it in stages in order to insure a thorough defense of the accused. He uses the analogy of a water clock *(depsydra* or *klepsydra)* of a kind presumably used in tribunals at the time of writing: "This may be compared with a water clock filled with water. As long as there is water in it the defense attorney may continue speaking, but sometimes the judge wants him to speak at greater length so he gives the order, 'Add water to it'" (*Bereshit Rabbah Vayyera* 49:12).

---

1. The literal meaning of the word for the morning prayer is "standing." See Onkelos, Neofiti and Fragment Targum on Gen 18:22.

After counsel for the accused has finished speaking, the judge rises and leaves, signifying that the trial is at an end. So "YHVH went his way when he had finished speaking with Abraham" (18:33).

The articles of indictment assume different forms in different *midrashim*. For coercive homosexual activity we have to wait for Philo and other authors of the Greco-Roman period (*Abraham* 133-36; *Jub.* 16:5; Jude 7); there is no such article of indictment in the midrash. What is emphasized is oppression of the poor, failure to distribute wealth, and neglect of the basic norms of charity and hospitality. In this respect the authors of the midrash reproduce the radical teaching of the great prophets of the eighth century B.C., that a country or city that does not practice justice and righteousness does not deserve to survive. We find the same emphasis in the Targum, and Josephus moves in the same direction when he speaks of the city's pride, arrogance, and hatred of outsiders (*misoxenia*), all the result of excessive affluence (*Ant.* 1.194-95; cf. Wis 19:13-14). The authors of the midrash develop the theme in their own sometimes odd ways. According to one attestation, the people of Sodom even covered the trees to prevent the birds from eating the berries (*Pirke de Rabbi Eliezer* 182; *Tanḥuma Vayyera*, par. 8; *Zohar* 1:105b; *Midrash Haggadol Bereshit* 1:282-84, 309-10). Against accusations of this gravity, once verified by the judge, no defense could avail, and it simply remained for the angel-executioner to proceed with his task.

3

It is not astonishing that scholars have read both the biblical text and its midrashic transpositions and embellishments prejudicially as reflecting a huckstering or legalistic approach to God-human relations typical of that tradition. Otto Procksch (reported in Westermann 1979: 354), one of the older commentators, described Gen 18:22-33 as *echt jüdisch* ("authentically Jewish"), and the description was not meant to be complimentary. But quite apart from anti-Jewish prejudice, we would want to ask why anyone should object to regulating human conduct according to law. One would also think that the contemporary literary-critical partiality to multiple meanings would welcome the midrashic approach to texts, and we would want to ask whether this particular midrash does not in fact present an imaginative and illuminating reading of the biblical passage in terms of a familiar and important aspect of civilized social life. The point of the extended forensic metaphor is, I suggest, that if we are to take God into account at all, the affirmation of divine justice is in some way an essential prerequisite for sustaining faith, and that it is not unreasonable to assume that divine justice, even if it works in mysterious ways, will measure up to the best standards according to which human justice is administered. The midrash follows its own presuppositions, procedures, and narrative logic, which are not those of the post-Enlightenment study of the Bible. From the critical point of view its limitations will be obvious to us, but they were already obvious to several of the medieval Jewish commentators. In the present instance, however, it remains faithful to the basic sense of the biblical text, especially if, as I argued, the text is addressing the unparalleled disasters visited on Israel (Judah) toward the beginning of the sixth century B.C.

At one point, however, the judicial analogy limps, and it is interesting to see how the authors of the midrash deal with it. In civil and religious courts of law there is the possibility of appeal to a higher tribunal of justice, which is hardly an option where God is the judge. In interpreting 18:25 ("Shall not the Judge of all the earth do right?"), *Bereshit Rabbah* quotes Rabbi Judah in the name of Rabbi Shim'on (*Bereshit Rabbah Vayyera* 49:9; also *Midrash Haggadol Bereshit* 1:314):

> Human beings can appeal from the local commander to the governor, and from the governor to the commander-in-chief, but you, since there is no one who can appeal against you, will you not judge justly?

And again:

> When you proposed to judge your world you delivered it into the hands of two, namely, Remus and Romulus, so that if one of them wished to do something his counterpart could veto him; but you, since there is no one who can veto you, will you not judge justly?

The sages had evidently reflected closely on Abraham's rhetorical question. What led him to pose it? Is it not self-evident that God judges justly? They put themselves in the same situation as Job, who, in the extremity of suffering, pleads for an umpire, an independent witness, a vindicator over against the God whom he sees as the author of the disasters visited on him, his family, and his people (Job 9:33; 16:19; 19:25). But seemingly they were not prepared to go as far as Job, who refused to accept the traditional link between sin and suffering in terms of cause and effect, even though in so doing his own suffering remained tragically inexplicable. Much is at stake, for the demand for justice is an absolute prerequisite for faith. If one were to accept the Gnostic doctrine of the two powers, an immensely attractive option at all times, the problem would look very different. Rabbi Judah may have had it in mind in alluding to the founders of Rome, but he and his rabbinic colleagues felt that they had no option but to struggle with the issue within the bounds of traditional religious ideas.

Within these self-imposed limitations the authors of the midrash are not far behind Job in pushing their questioning to the extreme limits. Commenting on 18:25, *Bereshit Rabbah* makes a connection with Job 9:22 — "he [YHVH] destroys both the blameless and the wicked" — but adds that, unlike Abraham, Job was punished because he spoke with ill feeling (*Bereshit Rabbah Vayyera* 49:9). Later commentary is not so reticent. According to the midrash *Tanḥuma,* Abraham cleverly puts his own accusation against God into the mouths of those not yet born and therefore in the form of a counterfactual. If justice is not done here and now, and seen to be done, people will say: "This is his [God's] *métier,* destroying the generations in the measure of cruelty. He destroyed the generation of Enosh, the generation of the deluge, and that of the dispersion of the nations. He never leaves off his trade *('ênô mēnîaḥ 'ummānûtô).*"

It is typical of rabbinic theology in general that God answers the charge and takes responsibility for these acts of annihilating divine power. God even quotes Scripture in his own defense:

> So you have spoken. Come and observe: I will parade before you all the generations which I have destroyed, and I will demonstrate to you that I did not inflict on them greater punishment than they deserved. And if perchance you still think that I have not acted properly, you teach me how, and I will do it, as it is written: "Teach me what I do not see; if I have done iniquity I will do it no more" (Job 6:24).[2]

---

2. *Tanḥuma Vayyera* §10; also *'Aggadat Bereshit* 22:4 and following, repeated by Rashi, with echoes of Job, in his comment on *ḥālîlâ lĕkâ* ("far be it from you"): "It is a profanation for you, for they will say, 'This is his *métier;* he destroys all, the righteous with the wicked; thus you did to the generation of the deluge and the generation of the dispersion.'"

According to the midrash, then, God is not exempt from the responsibility of accounting for his actions. And since Scripture is one and indivisible, the imminent destruction of Sodom and Gomorrah can be set alongside other acts of destructive divine agency, and thus, if not explained, at least contextualized differently. The juxtaposition of the destruction of the cities with the deluge is further justified with reference to the exegetical rule of analogy *(gezera šava)*, since the word *rabbah,* "great," occurs in both texts (Gen 6:5; 18:20). But as often happens, appeal to one biblical text in support of another creates a new problem, namely, that after the deluge God had promised never to destroy his creation again. It is entirely typical of the remarkable theological audacity of the midrash to find Rabbi Acha of Lydda, a fourth-generation Amora, reminding God of his oath *(Bereshit Rabba Vayyera;* cf. *Midrash Haggadol* §18): "You swore that you would never again bring a deluge on the world. Are you now going back on your oath by saying, 'I will not bring a deluge of water but one of fire?' If that is so, you are not thereby released from your oath."

In other words, God cannot escape from honoring the oath by recourse to a legal quibble. In even stronger terms comes the reminder that God cannot apply strict justice *at all* if God wishes to preserve the created world:

If you desire the world, there can be no strict justice.
If you desire strict justice, there can be no world.
You cannot have it both ways.[3]

4

So far these questionings deal in a general way with divine responsibility for wholesale disaster and human suffering on a massive scale, but the more pointed issue of distributive justice, the suffering of the innocent individual caught up in the punishment inflicted on the unrighteous, is not far below the surface. Since the rabbis teach by preference in parables, *Bereshit Rabbah* illustrates the problem by quoting a parable attributed to Rabbi Jonathan of the early Amoraic period. Asked by a colleague for an

---

3. *Bereshit Rabbah Lek Leka* 39:6 and often in the later midrash. The last line reads, literally, "You would grasp the rope at both ends."

interpretation of Prov 13:23, "There is one swept away without justice," he told the following short story (*Bereshit Rabbah Vayyera* 49:8):

> It happened that a man was sent to collect taxes from the people of Tiberias and Sepphoris. While he was collecting in Tiberias he saw a man from Sepphoris, whereupon he at once apprehended him. "I am from Sepphoris," the man protested, but he replied, "I have warrant to collect in Sepphoris also." But before he finished collecting from the people of Tiberias there arrived an exemption from Sepphoris. There you have one who is swept away without justice.

— a sad case of being in the wrong place at the wrong time. The issue of distributive justice is raised in a different mode in a homiletic commentary on the phrase *ḥālilâ lĕkâ* ("Far be it from you!") in Gen 18:25. It makes its point by retelling the biblical account of the final phase of Sheba's rebellion against David (2 Sam 20:14-22) — a midrash within a midrash, therefore (*Tanḥuma Vayyera* §12; *'Aggadat Bereshit* on Gen 18:25):

> Abraham said, "Master of the universe, I see in the Holy Spirit that one woman will save an entire city and here I am, unable to save these five cities." And who is this woman? She is Serah, daughter of Asher; and it happened when Sheba ben Bikri rebelled against David and came to Abel, as it is written, "They came and besieged him in Abel, and all the people who were with Joab were battering the wall to throw it down" (2 Sam 20:15). When Serah noticed what was happening, she began to cry out, "Summon Joab." When he came, she said to him, "Are you Joab?" and he said, "I am." She said, "You are the wise one whom the Scripture praises: seated in your place you make me wise.[4] But (she continues) have you not read in Torah that 'When you draw near to a city to fight against it, you must offer terms of peace to it'? (Deut 20:10). And is it not incumbent on you to do so? . . . So why will you swallow up the heritage of YHVH?" . . . Joab answered, "Far be it from me that I should swallow up or destroy!" But you, who are merciful, is it your pleasure to destroy these people? Far be it from you to do such a thing!

4. This odd phrase is a punning translation of 2 Sam 23:8, where one of David's warriors has the strange name Yosheb Bashebet Tahchemoni. The Vulgate translates the last word *sapientissimus* ("Most wise").

So what did Joab say to her? "This is not the way it is; it is rather a question of one man from the hill country of Ephraim whose name is Sheba ben Bikri, a repulsive fellow, an idolater, a worthless chap." She replied, "I am one of those who are peaceful and faithful in Israel; it is I who have filled out the allotted number of Israel" — as it is written: the name of the daughter of Asher was Serah (Num 26:46). "Stay where you are, and I will bring about a peaceful settlement" — as it is written: "His head will be thrown to you over the wall" (2 Sam 20:21). She had such confidence as to promise Joab his head! Now look what she did: "The woman went in her wisdom to the people" (20:22). What does "in her wisdom" mean? It means that she said to them, "I know that Joab and all Israel are outside ready to kill us, our sons and our daughters." "Why?" they asked her, and she answered, "He wants to take a hundred people and then he will go away." They replied, "Let him take two hundred." Then she said, "He only wants fifty," so they replied, "Let him take a hundred." She continued, "He really wants only five," so they said, "Let him take ten." Finally, she said to them, "He wants only one, and his name is Sheba ben Bikri." When they heard this, they went at once and cut off his head, as it is written: "They cut off the head of Sheba ben Bikri" (20:22). See, then, how wise was this woman. In like manner, Abraham came in his wisdom before the Holy One. He went from fifty to forty, from forty to thirty, from thirty to twenty, and from twenty to ten. She acted in the same way: the woman went in her wisdom to the people. Solomon praised her when he said: "Wisdom is better than weapons of war" (Qoh 9:18). The wisdom of Serah outweighed the weapons in Joab's hand, for as soon as Joab had the head of Sheba ben Bikri, he left at once and did not harm the city.

Abraham said to the Holy One: "Master of the universe, if Joab was content to take the head of one man who was guilty, leaving intact the entire city, you who are merciful, will you destroy everyone? Far be it from you!"

Here we have a lively little sermon that, in the traditional manner of the homiletic midrashim, begins with a biblical passage quite different from the one under consideration and works its way back ingeniously, following its own narrative logic, to the text to be interpreted. The choice of the opening text (the *pĕtiḥâ*) is dictated by the phrase *ḥālilâ lî*, "Far be it from me!" spoken by Joab (2 Sam 20:20). Once this apparently rather arbitrary and inconsequential connection is established, other possibilities open up. Thus the phrase "in her wisdom" *(běhokmatāh)* in the Samuel text provides the pretext for explaining Abraham getting God down from fifty to ten. The manner is curious, but the point is transparently clear: if Joab refused to hold the entire city of Abel accountable and discriminated between the guilty and the innocent, how much more so must the Judge of All the Earth?

5

The debate on the related issue, whether the righteous can influence the fate of the unrighteous society in which they live, came to the fore as a result of the anticipation of disaster and the actual disaster of the destruction of Jerusalem and its temple, the loss of independence, and subsequent deportations. Jeremiah affirms hyperbolically that the presence of even one righteous person in Jerusalem would have saved the city (Jer 5:1), while, as we saw earlier, Ezekiel rules out this option: the *ṣaddîq* will save only himself, not even members of his immediate family (14:12-20). How, according to the author of Gen 18:22-33, is this mysterious transference to be understood? How is it supposed to work? It was accepted that the prayer of intercession, an activity associated with the prophetic rather than the priestly role, could affect the outcome, but it could do so only by bringing about a change of heart in those on whose behalf it was offered. The more paraphrastic Targums assume that divine judgment could be forestalled by the merit *(zěkût)* of the righteous, especially that of righteous ancestors, which had the power to confer validity on the intercessory prayer offered by them in union with the prayer of Abraham (e.g., *Targum Pseudo-Jonathan* on Gen 18:24, 29, 31-32). The assumption is plausible since the tradition recognizes Abraham as a prophet who intercedes (Gen 20:7), but the text remains silent on the why and the wherefore.

The "bargaining down" from fifty to ten also raises the issue, less amenable to rational explanation, of critical mass, and why Abraham, having gone so far, stopped at ten. Following a hint in the biblical text (19:4), Josephus affirms that ten would have sufficed, but that there was not even one (*Antiquities* 1.199). Some Jewish commentators tried to solve the problem by a head count of Lot's family, but the text clearly prescinds from these six individuals (Ginzberg 1961: 252). Then there is the theory that a *minyan* was required (Ginzberg 252-53), or that fifty signifies redemption based on the jubilee year, as suggested by Philo in his treatise *On the Migration of Abraham* (*Migration* 122–23). Other midrashists, followed by Rashi, divide the fifty among the five Cities of the Plain. This expedient narrowed the margin since forty-five would leave only one lacking in each city, forty would mean that four out of five cities would be saved, and so on.

At this point our text connects with the tradition, which will be familiar in one form to readers of André Schwarz-Bart's novel *Le Dernier des Justes (The Last of the Just)*, of a certain number of individuals whose righteousness, unknown to themselves, outweighs the mass of evil in the world and sustains the world in existence. For those of the sages who start out from our text, the designated number is fifty rather than ten. Rabbi Joshua ben Levi of the early third century represents Abraham as pleading with God to combine the good works of the righteous in Sodom so as to reach that number, leading to the tradition that "the world remains in existence through the righteousness of fifty" (*Bereshit Rabbah Vayyera* 49:9). Better known is the tradition of the thirty-six hidden righteous, the *lamed vavniks*, based on a cabbalistic reading of Isa 30:18: "Blessed are all those who wait for him" (Scholem 1971: 251-56).[5] An alternative opinion was that the world never lacks thirty individuals like Abraham, this time based on the numerical value of *yihyeh* ($y + h + y + h = 30$) in the clause "Abraham shall surely become *(hāyô yihyeh)* a great and mighty nation" (Gen 18:18) (*Bereshit Rabbah Vayyera* 49:3; *Pesikta de Rab Kahana* 1:191). There is also speculation that the number is to be divided between the past and the future: the tribal leaders together with Moses, Aaron, and Miriam in the past, the shepherds and princes of Zechariah 11 in the future. Or perhaps the number is to be divided between the land of Israel and the diaspora, or even between Jews and Gentiles. These are all variations on the biblical theme of the righteous remnant in its developed, more or less apocalyptic form, assuming a line drawn between the righteous and the reprobate, now an invisible line, but to be manifest in the last days.

5. The word *lô*, "for him," in the Isaianic text consists in the letters *lamed* and *vav*, whose combined value by gematria is $30 + 6 = 36$; hence the text can be read, "Blessed are all those who wait on the thirty-six." The origin of the belief is, however, to be sought elsewhere. Scholem suggests the "dean divinities" who preside over the zodiacal band covering 360 degrees divided into ten "houses."

6

Unlike Ezekiel, the author of Gen 18:22-33 believed that, by some mysterious dispensation, the righteous can counterbalance the enormous weight of evil in the world symbolized by the Cities of the Plain. Following its own logic, the midrash develops this basic insight while at the same time trying to clear up some of the problems that this text, more than most texts, leaves for its interpreters. That its answers were not in all respects philosophically satisfying will be apparent to the modern reader, as it was already apparent to medieval Jewish commentators (Rashbam, Ibn Ezra, Saadia Gaon). Midrash is no substitute for the historical-critical reading of biblical texts, but it would be a mistake and an impoverishment to regard it as an unscientific and superseded way of reading. The historical-critical method tends to concentrate on the prehistory of the text, while midrash projects the text along its own trajectory into the future. The example presented above will serve to show that, in its own unique fashion, it deals with serious issues in a serious way.

IX

Biographical Patterns in Biblical Narrative:
Folklore and Paradigm in the Jacob Story

1

Søren Kierkegaard is quoted as saying that the problem with human life is that it has to be lived forward but can only be understood backward. Some degree of self-understanding is nevertheless attainable as we blunder ahead in our lives, and patterns do emerge that can be discerned at least by others if not always by ourselves. But there is still a sense in which the significance of a life can be grasped only when viewed in its entirety, after it has come to an end.

If this is so, it is understandable that the history of autobiography follows a different trajectory from that of biography. The autobiographical genre is often traced back to Augustine's *Confessions,* but Augustine's great work can in no sense be regarded as an absolute beginning; it had many predecessors, and in fact it comes up for discussion only at page 637 of Georg Misch's classic history of the genre (Misch 1950: 625-37). It is possible to read the *Confessions* as the interiorization of the journey narrative exemplified by the *Satyricon* of Petronius (minus the pornography) and the more overtly autobiographical, but still fictional, adventures and misadventures of Lucius in the *Metamorphoses* of Apuleius (Scholes and Kellogg 1966: 73-81). But the first-person travel narrative, forerunner of the picaresque novel of Fielding and Smollett, goes back much further than the Roman period. Students of the ancient Near East will, for example, be familiar with the story of Sinuhe from the Egyptian Middle Kingdom and

Wen Amon's narrative of his journey from Egypt to Byblos over eight hundred years later (Pritchard 1955: 18-22, 25-29).

Inscriptions attributed to a ruler or other prominent individual and composed in the first person, many of which have survived from antiquity, record military campaigns, the construction of temples, and the like. Few if any of these have a distinctive literary character, and most of them are crudely propagandistic. Then there are memoirs written for a specific purpose, usually apologetic, like those of Ezra, Nehemiah, and their contemporary Ion of Chios. The apologetic memoir of this kind has the potential for developing into a kind of autobiography, something like the *Bios* of Josephus, perhaps the first clear instance of the genre (Momigliano 1971: 18, 35-36), but still lacking those qualities of interiority and self-questioning characteristic of Augustine's *Confessions*.

Insofar as we are able to reconstruct it, the early history of biography has a different profile. We may define biography in a very general way as an account of a person's life from birth to death. But records of human lives are of different kinds, of which the fully developed genre of biography is only one. If we may for the moment take the broad view, we could find the essentials of a life epitomized in a name and a couple of dates on a tombstone or, in a slightly less succinct form, in memorial brasses and epitaphs, such as the following brass from St. Mary's church in Wilton in the south of England:

Edmund the sonn of Edmund Philip alias
Sweeper of Burbridge farrer to the Earl
of Pembroke hoo died the 19 of January
and buried in this place. Anno 1677
Aetatis 70.

The tombstone notes name, parentage, place of residence, occupation, age, date of death, and place of burial. These are not unimportant data, but not much to go on if we are interested in the person of this Edmund and the meanings bestowed or imposed on the biblical span of his life. Another subject of a rudimentary biography is the Solomon Grundy of the old nursery rhyme:

Solomon Grundy, born on a Monday,
Christened on Tuesday, married on Wednesday,

138

Took ill on Thursday, worse on Friday,
Died on Saturday, buried on Sunday.
This is the end of Solomon Grundy.

In this case the meaning is not exhausted in the enumeration of natural events — birth, sickness, death — since there are also the Christian rites of passage accompanying birth, mating, and return to the earth. As in the creation account in Genesis the life is fitted into the liturgical week, and as in the Gospels an inordinate amount of space is taken up with how the life ended.

It was perhaps unnecessary to adduce these artless examples of rudimentary biographical schemata to make the point that the purpose of a biography is not simply that of providing biographical data, and few biographies apart from entries in *Who's Who* limit themselves in this way. We might therefore redefine biography as the attempt to grasp the meaning of a life by telling it in a certain way. This is certainly true of the early history — or prehistory — of the genre. Biographers of the Peripatetic School, principally Theophrastus of Lesbos and Aristoxenus of Tarentum, wrote the lives of exemplary individuals in such a way as to illustrate certain virtues, the subjects serving as paradigms of the ethical teaching of Aristotle and his school. Encomiastic biographies (*epainoi*), the earliest extant examples of which are lives of the Cypriot king Evagoras and the Spartan king Agesilaus by Isocrates and Xenophon respectively, are modeled on ancient celebrations of and lamentations for gods and divine men (Momigliano 1971: 74, 82). We note in passing that liturgical dirges and panegyrics have also served to add resonance to life stories. In the ancient sources (Plutarch, Appian) if not in Shakespeare, Anthony's funeral oration over Caesar's corpse bears unmistakable traces of ritual laments over the dead god of vegetation.

The memoirs and lives of Socrates, of which those by Xenophon and Plato are best known, fall far short of modern standards of objectivity, accuracy, and comprehensiveness. The reason is not so much that the writers in question were incapable of attaining these standards, but rather that this was not at all what they were about. In their view, as Momigliano has well put it (1971: 46), "He [Socrates] was not a dead man whose life could be recounted. He was the guide to territories as yet unexplored." The significance of this remark for appreciating the intent of the Gospel writers will be obvious. It is worth noting that Justin Martyr uses the term "memoirs" (*apomnēmoneumata, First Apology* 66:3) for the Gospels as Xenophon does for his account of the life of Socrates.

The few examples presented so far suggest that the history of the genre in modern times, beginning with Samuel Johnson's *Lives of the Poets,* is not the best place to start from in order to grasp in the broadest terms what is involved in telling life stories, and specifically biblical life stories. One problem with modern biography is that it has been drawn into the sphere of historiography and has tended to borrow from the latter its presuppositions and methods. The problem is adumbrated in Aristotle's *Poetics* (7-8, 23), where he argues that the literary representation of reality *(mimēsis)* cannot make a unity out of the succession of historical events or the events in the life of an individual. What is essential is the plot *(mythos)* understood as a complete action with a beginning, middle, and end. The agent must always be secondary to the action.

We can agree that the overall gestalt, the regularities and patterns of behavior that go to make up a life story, emerge from the decisions and deeds of the subject, that they are a precipitate of the different ways in which the subject marshals his or her resources in a particular life project. These are of course decisions and deeds selected by the observer and commentator as significant in keeping with presuppositions and prejudices that the biographer brings to the task; there is no such thing as an *innocent* interpretation of a life or of anything else.

But it is simply not the case that the process of making a whole of one's life involves only conscious activity. What is transacted at the conscious level must always be set in counterpoint to unconscious needs, desires, and fears revealed through dreams, sudden revelations of self-knowledge, the unanticipated tapping of unsuspected sources of energy and power, abrupt and, at the conscious level, inexplicable changes of direction. The most satisfying life stories do not hesitate to introduce a sense of fate, destiny, or providence that moves the subject in a direction quite different from that along which the subject is driven by conscious goals. The great Greek tragedians understood the point well, as the hymn to Zeus in Aeschylus's *Agamemnon* illustrates: "In our dreams, pain that cannot forget falls drop by drop upon the heart; and in our own despair, against our will, comes wisdom by the awful grace of God." Other analogues can be found in the way the spell functions in the folktale, oracles of deities in the Homeric poems, the ominous dreams of Gilgamesh and Enkidu in *Gilgamesh,* and the sense of a divinely willed destiny in the biblical story of

Joseph (see especially Gen 50:20: "You meant evil against me, but God meant it for good"). We even find it in the modern biography. "No one goes so far," said Cromwell to the French ambassador, "as he who knows not whither he goes." And even Hitler spoke of himself moving with the assurance of a sleepwalker.

2

In its earliest developments, then, biography attempted to bring out meanings by superimposing on the biographical data a pattern, paradigm, or grid of some kind. The question now arises whether the same strategy can be applied to biblical narratives with biographical content or, with apologies to Hans Frei, biography-like narratives (Frei 1974: 16). Literary critics have paid a great deal of attention to biblical narrative in general but have had little to say about biographical narrative in particular. They have discussed somewhat the "ideal biographies" exemplified by ancient Egyptian funerary inscriptions honoring viziers and other public figures. In these texts personal characteristics, the staple of modern biography, tend to recede before standard topoi dealing with title, family connections, call to public service, and vindication in the face of false charges. Some have claimed that this type of ideal biography provides the structural key for understanding the biblical presentation of the careers of Moses, Elijah, the Isaianic Servant, and other prominent biblical figures (Baltzer 1975).

The biographical or hagiographical *legendum* understood as an account of the activity, especially the miraculous activity, of a holy man or woman, is another kind of biography. A comparative study of (for example) the Elijah cycle, the life of the Pythagorean philosopher Apollonius of Tyana by Philostratus, rabbinic traditions about the Galilean rabbi Hanina ben Dosa, and the *Life of Anthony the Hermit* by Athanasius will, it is claimed, reveal common structural features (Jolles 1965: 23-61). There are, of course, different ways of defining and circumscribing narrative genres. In the New Testament context, both Bultmann and Dibelius distinguished the *legendum* from the miracle story, restricting the former to such episodes as the finding of the child Jesus in the temple and the temptation scene in the wilderness (Dibelius 1934: 104-9; Bultmann 1965: 209-74). Also generically distinct is aretalogy, the recital of the deeds of a god or goddess and therefore a kind of rudimentary divine biography or autobiography.

Since the boundaries between the divine and human were somewhat fluid in antiquity in general, accounts of the careers of a cult hero or *theios anēr* ("divine man") could be subsumed in the same category (Farnell 1921; Hadas and Smith 1965; Cox 1983).

Another narrative genre much discussed by biblical scholars is the folktale. Interest in the folktale dates to the early nineteenth century with the publication of the *Kinder- und Hausmärchen* of the brothers Grimm in 1812. Influenced by currents of Romanticism in Germany at that time, which also generated a revival of interest in the oral culture of the peasantry, early form critics Hermann Gunkel and Hugo Gressmann identified folktale motifs in several biblical narratives of a biographical kind, including the stories about the ancestors in Genesis (Gressmann 1910; Gunkel 1917, 1964). In some few instances the pattern is easily detected, as in the folktale motif of the "Grateful Dead" that underlies the narrative theme in the book of Tobit (Gerould 2000: 45-47, 155-56, 167-68). In more recent years, an often rather desultory search for folktale elements in biblical narrative has given way to a more systematic and theoretically sound analysis inspired by formalist and structuralist literary procedures. Since the method developed by the Russian Formalist Vladimir Propp has been one of the most influential of these in the biblical guild, it may be useful for those unfamiliar with his work to provide a brief summary of his analysis of traditional narrative (Propp 1968).

On the basis of a comparative study of a large number of folktales, Propp set out to distinguish between constants and variables by concentrating on internal organization. His method was to break down each sample into its smallest narrative units. The core constituent of the narrative was not a motif or theme but what he called a function, namely, the action of a character defined from the point of view of its contribution to the narrative as a whole. This study led him to the following conclusions. Functions serve as constant, stable elements independently of how or by whom they are performed; the number of functions in the folktale is limited; the sequence in which they appear is always identical; all folktales are of identical type with respect to structure. The analysis of his database along these lines — one hundred Russian folktales or fairy tales — resulted in a grid or template of thirty-one functions. Not all will be present in all examples of the type, but those that are present will always occur in the same order.

The narrative structure or pattern resulting from Propp's linear and syntagmatic analysis, a pattern that on his view fits all folktales, is the vehicle of the "message" of the folktale, which, in the broadest terms, moves from lack to liquidation of lack. The outline or grid is more or less as follows (Propp's functions are noted in parentheses). It begins with the acknowledgment of evil expressed typically as death (the death of parents) or absence (1). The victim falls under the power of an evil spell following the violation of an interdiction (2-3). This comes about through deception (4), generally involving self-deception or complicity with evil (5-7), leading to a lack (8a), often brought about by the casting of a spell or hex that blinds the victim to the true situation. For this situation of alienation, loss, or exile to be reversed, the evil must be acknowledged and some form of mediation sought (9). A journey away from the familiar (familial) world must be undertaken, either by the victim or by a donative hero on the victim's behalf (10-11). Tests, interrogations, and ordeals must be faced as the traveler meets hostile or only apparently hostile powers (12-13). Assistance will be necessary, usually in the form of a magical agent (14). The seeker eventually arrives at the scene of the desired person or object (15), but never without having to overcome the initial evil or villainy (16-18). Thus, the evil is removed (19) — one returns to life, one is set free, the evil spell is broken — and it is possible at last to return (20), though this, too, can be a hazardous undertaking (21-22). The narrative line can end here, but it will sometimes continue with the arrival of the victim-hero incognito (23), confrontation with false claims and the need to establish true identity (24-26), exposure of a false hero (27-28), and transformation, perhaps by putting on new clothes, punishment of the wicked, or marriage and ascent to the throne (29-31).

The point I am making here is not that Propp has uncovered the fundamental organization of all traditional narrative, though some have claimed that, but to present his analysis as one pattern on which the raw data of a human life as lived or narrated can be superimposed. Interestingly, Propp's decision to take structure as the primary vehicle of meaning in traditional narrative has some basic points in common with Aristotle's *Poetics.* Aristotle affirms the primacy of plot *(mythos)* over character *(ethos),* and he compares the plot to an organism in which the parts function by virtue of and for the benefit of the whole. A plot must have a beginning, a middle, and an end, and it must move through a *peripateia* (Propp calls it a "complication") to a final resolution. The protagonist must be like us *(homoios)* if the reader or hearer is to experience the purging of the emotions and recognize his or her own history as the narrative unfolds. The action, finally, is set off by a fatal or almost fatal error *(hamartia)*, corresponding to Propp's violation of interdiction and complicity with evil. Aristotle had tragedy in mind, but the comparison suggests that Propp's analysis has a more general applicability, can therefore stand us in good stead, and should be borne in mind in our attempt to decode biblical narrative with biographical features. With this we come finally to the life story of Jacob.

3

The story of Jacob is in the mainstream of biblical narrative, a mainstream fed by many tributaries, deepening and widening as it flows along. The heavy editing to which much of this narrative has been subjected, together with its *cumulative* character, in the sense that each segment has to fit into an existing context, creates serious problems for structural analysis of any kind. Taken in its entirety, the life story of Jacob from conception to death covers about half of the book of Genesis (25:19–50:14). But the situation is rather more complicated since Jacob's life history is intertwined with or superimposed on the story of Isaac, announced in the title ("This is the story of Isaac son of Abraham," 25:19), and taken up in the following chapter from which Jacob is completely absent (26:1-35). A good part of the narrative also deals with the birth of his children (29:31–30:24) and their adventures and misadventures, and here Jacob plays either a subsidiary role or no role at all (chaps. 34 and 37–50). This characteristic of the narrative, according to which the individual's life history is inseparable from that of the kinship group, justifies the designation "saga," understood as a family history traced over several generations, the *Gattung* associated with the ancestor narratives since Gunkel.

What material would an author setting out to write the story of Jacob, let us say sometime in the sixth or fifth century B.C., have had at his disposal?[1] He would very likely have been familiar with the biographical traditions about Jacob preserved in Hosea (12:4-5, 12), which include the

1. I leave out of account the contribution of the Priestly writer (P) consisting mostly of introductions and conclusions (25:19-20; 35:27-30; 37:1-2; 49:28-33), genealogical and archival material (35:22-26 and 36:1-43 in part; 41:46; 46:8-27), polemic against exogamous marriage (26:34-35; 27:46–28:9), and an alternative version of Jacob's vision at Bethel (35:9-15; 48:3-7).

extraordinary birth, the wrestling with a supernatural assailant, the vision at Bethel, and the flight to Mesopotamia where Jacob did service for one wife and guarded flocks for another. These traditions, reported at second hand, do not correspond precisely with the form in which they are presented in Genesis, where there is no allusion to Jacob weeping and the assailant is not identified as an angel (Hos 12:5). The hostility between Jacob and Esau as ethnic eponyms would also have been familiar to the author (cf. Amos 1:11; Obad 10; Mal 1:2-5), and the survival of Rachel's tomb tradition (1 Sam 10:2) provides one of several clues to the close ties to place, the *Ortsgebundenheit,* of biographical and hagiographical tradition in general.

Considerable skill must have been required to construct a psychologically believable life story of an individual called Jacob that at the same time serves as paradigmatic for the historical destiny of the people named for Jacob/Israel. Expressed somewhat differently, "the national archetypes have been made to assume the distinctive lineaments of individual human lives" (Alter 1981: 42). The paradigmatic intent is evident throughout the Jacob story. The birth narrative is structured so as to correspond to certain historical facts about Edom: that the Edomite kingdom came into existence before Israel attained statehood (Gen 36:31), and that it was destined to be conquered by Israel, as it appears to have been on several occasions. If, as some scholars have argued (Noth 1972: 87-101; Westermann 1985: 406), traditions were in circulation about distinct Cisjordanian and Transjordanian Jacobs, the composer of the text would have combined them, working up the former into the Jacob-Esau cycle and the latter into the Jacob-Laban cycle, and linking these two cycles in a master paradigm of exile and return. At any rate, it is interesting to note that the text that deals most fully with this theme, Isaiah 40–55, is also the text that refers to the contemporary Judean community most frequently as Jacob. We shall return to the paradigmatic character of the Jacob narrative later in the essay.

4

At this point we come back to what was said earlier about narratives, and narratives of human lives in particular, constructed on the basis of traditional, originally oral, folklore motifs ("functions" according to Propp), themes, and type scenes (Arend 1933; Alter 1981: 47-62). Our anonymous author, who certainly did not have detailed historical data about the characters in Genesis 25–35, or their doings, or transcripts of their conversations at hand, did what most ancient writers did when faced with the task of creating scenes from the past. He used folk motifs, archetypal plots, and their narrative developments and expansions as building blocks in constructing a work that was something less than history and something more than fiction. The technique is abundantly in evidence in the opening incident of Jacob's conception and birth (Gen 25:19-26; my translation):

This is the story of Isaac ben Abraham:
Abraham was Isaac's father; and at age forty Isaac took as his wife Rebekah, daughter of Bethuel the Aramean from Paddan-Aram. She was the sister of Laban the Aramean. Isaac entreated YHVH on behalf of his wife on account of her being infertile. YHVH granted his request, Rebekah his wife conceived, but the children were knocking each other around inside her. "If this is the way it is," she exclaimed, "why go on living?" So she went and inquired of YHVH. YHVH said to her:

"Two nations are in your womb,
When they leave your womb,
    two peoples will go their separate ways.
One people will be stronger than the other,
    the elder will serve the younger."

When her time came, twins were in her womb. The first came out all ruddy and as if covered with a hairy mantle; so they called him Esau. Then his brother came out, his hand gripping Esau's heel; so they called him Jacob. Isaac was sixty years old when he begot them.

Since in folk narrative conception and birth foreshadow the destiny of the protagonist, they are usually accompanied by remarkable events and circumstances and their portentous nature is evoked by the use of certain traditional literary conventions. Childlessness due to the infertility of the wife corresponds to Propp's initial situation, a lack that is liquidated by prayer for a son followed by an extraordinary conception and birth (Propp 119-20). The infertility of the wife, who nevertheless conceives with divine assistance, is a common biblical topos, beginning with the ancestresses all of whom were initially childless (Gen 11:30; 29:31; also Judg 13:2; 1 Sam 1:2; Luke 1:7). The birth oracle is another feature of annunciation scenes, usually following on a visit to a sanctuary and prayer either of the mother or of the husband on her behalf (Judg 13:2-7; Luke 1:8-20, 26-38).

One of the most stable elements of this type scene is the naming of the child to be born. The writer appears to be deriving the name Esau (*'ēśāv*) from *śē'ār*, "hair," but the latter connects rather with Seir, being both a personal name (Gen 36:20) and a toponym that came to be synonymous with Edom. In the same way *'admônî*, "ruddy," recalls Edom, "Redland," though Edom is also a personal name, identified with Esau (36:1). The names do not bode well for Esau. From the outset, personal characterization doubles as political satire, in a way comparable to the account of the conception and birth of Moab and Ben-Ammi (Ammon) from the incestuous union of Lot's daughters with their father (Gen 19:30-38). Esau/Edom is covered in hair like a fur coat and uncouthly reddened by the sun,[2] an Enkidu-like figure and, like him, a *lullu*, a primitive, the prototypical Wild Man. Jacob (*ya'ăqōb*) is explained with reference to *'āqēb*, "heel," on account of the circumstances, unique in the history of obstetrics if not of folklore, under which he saw the light of day. But the sobriquet is not meant to imply an innocent aberration, as with some of the Tricksters of folklore, much less a compliment, for the name would have suggested that the bearer is also *'āqob*, "fraudulent," "crooked" (cf. Jer 17:9). From this point on, the life story will tell by what trials and ordeals the bearer comes in due course to merit having a new name conferred on him, and what transformations must take place for the "Heel Grabber" to become the "God Wrestler" (25:26; 32:28).

Another familiar folktale motif is strife between brothers, often for obtaining the rights and privileges of primogeniture. Closely associated is the motif of parental preference for one son over the other. In this instance Isaac's preference for Esau was not just because Esau put food, good strong meat, in his mouth (if that is what *kî-ṣaid bĕpîv*, Gen 25:28, means) or, in an alternative translation, that Isaac had a taste for game that Esau satisfied. It had more to do with the father representing the social norms that sustained the patrilineal descent system, primogeniture in the first place, while by teaming up with Jacob the mother came to represent the subver-

---

2. In folklore right down to the present red is the color of misfortune and danger, and in some cultures redheads are associated with the occult. See the examples in Iona Opie and Moira Tatem, *A Dictionary of Superstitions* (Oxford and New York: Oxford University, 1989), pp. 325-26.

sion of social norms. This pattern of familial alliances reflects actual social configurations. Even in the cross-cousin type of marriage reproduced in these ancestral stories, the woman is imported into the household from outside and therefore to some extent remains an outsider and a potential threat to the traditional ethos of the household, especially because of her influence on the children during their formative years.

The pattern of sibling rivalry is often reproduced in biblical narrative. It will suffice to recall Cain the firstborn, who kills his brother but is rejected by God for no reason stated in the text (Gen 4:1-6). Then there is Ishmael, who is bested by Isaac (16:1-12), and Manasseh, who loses out to Ephraim (48:8-20). The same subversive principle is applied to Saul, David, and Solomon. The traditional folkloristic character of the Esau-Jacob rivalry, which begins with a struggle to be born first, comes more clearly into focus when we compare it with the account of the founding of Tyre reported by Philo of Byblos (fragments 2:7-8 in Eusebius, *Praeparatio Evangelica* 1.10.10). The quarreling brothers in this instance are Ousōos and Hypsouranios. Like Esau, the former is a great hunter; he was also the inventor of clothing made of skins, reminiscent of the fur coat (*'adderet śē'ār*) with which Esau appeared to be covered (25:25). Hypsouranios was the first builder of huts *(kalubai)* made of reeds, rushes, and papyri, which led some scholars to compare him with Jacob, who built booths for his cattle (33:17).

While a direct connection between the Phoenician and biblical traditions seems unlikely, that the Phoenician brothers are part of a foundation myth indicates more clearly the *political* reason why the biblical author incorporated this topos into his story. The account of the dual conception and birth suggests that, in the earliest stages of the history, Edom and Israel were branches of the same ethnos, joined by kinship and perhaps also by covenant (Heb. *'aḥîm* stands for "brothers" and "covenant partners"). The close relationship would also be compatible with what some ancient poems suggest about the Edomite region as the original residence of YHVH, the place from which he comes forth in splendor according to ancient Israelite poetry (Deut 33:2; Judg 5:4; Hab 3:3). Hence both Esau and Jacob were part of an ethnic origins myth, just as Ousōos and Hypsouranios were involved with the origins of Tyre and, for that matter, Romulus and Remus with the origins of Rome. And just as Hypsouranios alone is credited with founding Tyre and Romulus alone with founding Rome, so only Jacob was destined to found the dominant people Israel in spite of being the younger son.

Sibling rivalry and the struggle for precedence are intensified when brothers are twins. In many traditional societies the birth of twins is viewed as an ominous event and the children are killed. The struggle between Perez and Zerah, twin sons of Tamar, to descend the birth canal first (Gen 38:27-30) parallels the prenatal rivalry between Esau and Jacob. This is the only other biblical instance of twins struggling in the uterus, but the topos is a familar one in folklore and legend. In addition to Romulus and Remus already mentioned, there are the twins Osiris and Seth of Egyptian myth, Ormazd and Ahriman of Parsi legend, and Akrisios and Proitus, sons of a ruler of Argos, whose struggle for seniority began in the womb. This topos falls under Axel Olrik's "law of twins" *(Gesetz der Zwillinge)* rubric applicable to a wide range of folklore material (Dundes 1965: 135-36).

5

The extraordinary conception and birth, together with the oracular statement that interprets them, hinges the entire narrative on the relation between the brothers and determines the course of events from beginning to end. The story is structured around the journey away from the familiar (familial) world, the twenty-year absence, and the return attended as always with dangers and trials (Propp's functions 10-20). The *nostos* (homecoming) theme is a familiar feature of traditional literature and appears prominently in *Gilgamesh* and the *Odyssey* (bk. 23). Leaving home was necessitated by the hero's trickery after Esau sold his birthright *(běkōrâ)* under duress and then was tricked out of his father's deathbed blessing *(běrākâ)*. The narrative is kept moving in spite of apparent delays and detours. Genesis 26, dealing with Isaac's stay in Gerar, which some commentators take to be a rather unfortunate interpolation, serves to cover the period from the adolescence to the maturity of the brothers — from when they were mere youths *(ně'ārîm, 25:27)* to their maturity, the age of forty (26:34). Clearly, the author had nothing relevant to the Jacob story to narrate for this period.

The hiatus also provided the opportunity to link up with the more inclusive story of the ancestors of which it is a part by introducing once again the Abrahamic promise of land and posterity (Gen 26:2-5, 24) and replicating the theme of the endangered ancestress (26:6-11). At the purely literary level, it serves as a dramatic postponement, a rallentando, slowing down the pace before reaching the decisive point of Jacob's flight from home; this is a common technique of traditional storytelling.

Unlike Esau's sale of his birthright (25:29-34), the theft of the paternal blessing by the mother-son team of Rebekah and Jacob (27:1-45) is told at considerable length and with much detail. The author/editor also records the emotions of the actors — the cool, calculated approach of Rebekah and the conniving attitude of Jacob contrasted with the violent trembling of the old man and the great and bitter cry and the tears of Esau on discovering the deceit (vv. 33-34). Several commentators have argued that both the sale of the birthright (25:29-34) and the vicissitudes of Isaac in Gerar (26:1-33) have been interpolated since 25:28 ("Isaac loved Esau . . . but Rebekah loved Jacob") looks like the perfect introduction to the theft of the blessing (Gunkel 1997: 291; Westermann 1985: 414). But as the narrative now reads, the loss of birthright and paternal blessing *(běkōrâ/běrākâ)* belong together, and in fact Esau complains that he has been "jacobed" twice (*vayyaʿqěbēnî zeh paʿămayim*, 27:36).

The story of the deception is told straight through with no authorial intervention or tongue-clicking and no unnecessary sidetracking. What the reader needs to know, that Isaac is on his deathbed[3] and blind, is told at the outset. The situation is briefly described (27:1-4), the plot is hatched (vv. 5-17) and successfully implemented (vv. 18-40), and its outcome, Jacob's flight to Haran, leads on into the central *peripateia* of the Jacob story (vv. 41-45).

Folklore motifs and stereotypical roles as formative elements in the narrative are apparent here as they are throughout. One of the most familiar of these roles is that of the Trickster, celebrated in African, Native American, and other oral cultures and exploited in literary contexts (e.g., once again, Odysseus). Deathbed blessings and last words in the form of portentous prophecies also correspond to familiar folk narrative scenarios (e.g., Patroclus and Hector in the *Iliad*), and are especially portentous if the speaker is blind (e.g., Tiresias). In the present narrative, however, one suspects not only that the juxtaposition of these traditional motifs will be disturbing to most readers but also that the writer is conscious of moral

---

3. This information is demanded by the motif of the deathbed blessing and clearly assumed by the other characters (e.g., 27:41, where Esau anticipates an end to the statutory mourning in the near future). They were wrong, however, since Isaac will live twenty years longer and die at the age of 180 years (35:27-29).

ambiguity. Rebekah does not hesitate to spy and eavesdrop to attain her end, and she takes on the risk of the dread curse of a dying man without a moment's hesitation (27:5-7, 13, 42). The irony of describing Jacob as *tām* (25:27), usually translated "morally upright," "perfect" (cf. Job 1:1), was noted earlier, and irony may also be intended in his own ambiguous self-description as "a smooth man" (27:11). Like his mother, he has no objection to involving the deity in his lies (vv. 19-20), and whatever comedy might be extracted from the scene finally disappears with the kiss that persuades the old man to give him his blessing (vv. 26-27).

As suggested earlier, Jacob's departure for Mesopotamia, his twenty-year period of indentured service, and his eventual return from exile constitute both the core of the narrative as life story (Propp's functions 10-20) and the master paradigm. The dream-vision at Bethel at the point of departure (28:10-22) and the encounter with angels, including an angelic assailant, at the point of return (32:2-3, 23-33), function to bring out the depth-dimension of the story and serve as counterpoint to the devices and stratagems doggedly pursued by the human actors. A similar function is played by dreams in the Joseph story. In addition, both stories convey the impression of a hidden providence at work, often drawing the action in directions contrary to those in which the actors are driven by their own devices and desires.

Apart from a command to return (31:3), repeated in a dream-vision of YHVH in the guise of the deity El Bethel (31:10-13), the twenty-year interval is a time of the silence of God. True to the pattern of the folktale, the fratricidal hatred between the brothers can only be overcome, in Proppian terms the lack can only be liquidated, by tests, interrogations, ordeals, and sufferings. Laban is the agent responsible for all of this, a kind of anti-donor, forcing Jacob into two periods of indentured service and achieving the well-nigh impossible feat of tricking him into marrying the wrong woman. Jacob's first choice as wife is initially infertile, as was her mother-in-law (29:31), and only after all but one of his children are born in exile — in a cloud of etymological puns — is he free to return.

We can do little more than enumerate the folklore motifs and type scenes that have gone into the making of this central part of the Jacob narrative. It begins with an encounter at a well between the hero and his destined bride (29:1-19), a type scene replicated in the life stories of Isaac (Gen 24:10-51) and Moses (Exod 2:16-22). A common feature of this scene at the well (N715.1 in Stith Thompson's Folklore Index) is a feat of strength or daring performed by the hero to impress the woman who is to be his wife (Gen 29:8-10; Exod 2:17). A great deal of Trickster activity characterizes the relations between uncle and nephew. Jacob the Trickster is out-tricked by Laban, in most spectacular fashion in the Substituted Bride type scene (Thompson 1977: 117-20). The careful reader will note the irony in Laban's retort to the expostulations of Jacob the Supplanter that it is not the custom to give the younger in marriage before the firstborn (*habbĕkîrâ*, 29:26). These setbacks notwithstanding, Jacob comes out on top in the curious incident of prenatal conditioning of the sheep and goats (30:31-43) and in abandoning Laban by guile (31:20). In this final deception he is assisted by some subsidiary trickery on the part of Rachel in her theft of Laban's household gods (31:19, 33-35), perhaps with the idea of promoting fertility or assisting in childbirth.

We come now to the incident of the perilous fording of the wadi Jabbok (32:23-33; Eng. trans. 32:22-32), the subject of a vast amount of commentary to which we cannot aspire to do justice in this essay. The incident is fully integrated into the Jacob story. Though the verbs are different, the wrestling with the supernatural assailant echoes the wrestling *in utero* at the beginning, and he who was rightly called "Heel Grabber" or, less literally, "Supplanter," is now renamed "God Wrestler." The stolen blessing in the early stages also parallels the blessing that the mysterious assailant is compelled to bestow before departing. Attention is therefore still on the brothers, since the struggle with the "man" (32:24) or the "angel" (Hos 12:4) is clearly a preparation for or anticipation of the encounter with Esau. The connection is also made more allusively: Jacob calls the place Peniel or Penuel ("Face of God") since "I have seen God face to face and have survived" (32:30); and then, after surviving his encounter with Esau, he tells him that "seeing your face is like seeing the face of God" (*pĕnê 'ĕlohîm*, 33:10). A further point: one of the many wordplays in the episode — more easily grasped when spoken than when written — is the contrast between the wrestling with the assailant (verbal stem *'bq*) and the embrace of the two brothers (verbal stem *ḥbq*, 33:4). The exploitation of familiar folk motifs has therefore been well integrated into the narrative as both life history and paradigm.

The crossing of dangerous waters, like the waters of death in *Gilgamesh* and the *acqua perigliosa* in Dante's *Inferno* (1.22-24), is rich in symbolic resonances that are left for the reader to discover and savor. The cluster of motifs that have gone into the underlying folktale are familiar: a malevolent demon or deity (sometimes a monster or animal) guarding a river crossing or a spooky wilderness location (cf. Exod 4:24-26); night as the time of danger; nocturnal spirits, ghosts, or demons that, like the vampire and the ghost of Hamlet's father, must leave before daybreak; the numen who refuses to reveal his name since to know the name is to have the power to summon up or expel (cf. Judg 13:17-18; Mark 5:9).

Whether these and no doubt other familiar motifs in this incident occur in a haphazard way or cohere into some kind of pattern may be tested by matching them with the Proppian grid mentioned earlier. In his celebrated interpretation of the passage, Roland Barthes claimed to find a high level of overlap with the functions toward the middle of Propp's sequence, that is, 15 to 19 (Barthes 1974: 38). Jacob has been forced to leave home and go into exile, corresponding to Transference of the Hero (15); he experiences combat with his opponent (16); he comes out of the combat marked for life — his hip has been dislocated and, like Oedipus, he is lame (17), corresponding to Propp's "branding of the hero" function. He is victorious since he is able to coerce his assailant into giving a blessing, corresponding to Victory of the Hero (18); the lack (i.e., absence) is finally liquidated with his return to Bethel and, eventually, to the father (Gen 35:1-15, 27-29). Whether either this incident or the Jacob narrative as a whole makes a perfect fit with Propp's structuralist and actantial analysis may be doubted, but it is close enough to illustrate the biblical author's creative use of traditional narrative patterns in constructing a credible human life story.

The encounter with Esau (33:1-17), who in the meantime has evolved from a hunter to a pastoralist, leads to a reconciliation of sorts, though the brothers never bring up the past. Jacob's crafty arrangement of his troupe with the women and children in front, his cautious approach to his brother, the offering of a gift as implicitly making up for the stolen blessing (33:11: "my gift," literally, "my blessing," *birkātî*), and his tactful insistence on their going their separate ways show that the transformation signified by the name change has left his native cunning unimpaired. On the other hand, his acknowledgment that it was God who had graciously given him a large family (33:5) contrasts with his disingenuous claim at the beginning that God had granted him success in hunting the game offered to his father (27:20), thus reinforcing the impression that he is a changed man. With the disappearance of Esau from the scene (33:17) the Story of Jacob, in reality the Story of the Two Brothers, comes to an end. From the point of view of plot and structure, the misadventures at Shechem that occasioned the return to Bethel, and the return to the father who could then die old, full of days, and presumably reconciled to his wayward son, are appendices.

6

I recall, once again and finally, how this story of personal transformation in an individual human life doubles as a paradigm of the historical destiny of the two peoples. We may suppose that this is how the author, writing, let us say, in the late sixth or early fifth century B.C., intended it to be read. Exile in Mesopotamia as a time of indentured service (e.g., Isa 40:1-2), the need for moral transformation, and the return to the land are clearly inscribed in the story. Hostility between the Judeans and the Edomites, personified as Jacob and Esau, is abundantly attested for the period before and after the Babylonian conquest, calling eventually for terms on which the two peoples could coexist, as Israelites had coexisted with other peoples in the land from the outset, Deuteronomic prohibitions notwithstanding. Interestingly, the book of Job, which can also be read paradigmatically as a communal response to disaster, is set in the land of Uz, namely, Edom (cf. Lam 4:21).

Correspondences exist even in such subsidiary features as the four groups into which the sons, eponyms of the tribes, are divided, the unique situation of Benjamin as the one born in Palestine, and the prominence of the Bethel sanctuary visited by Jacob/Israel before and after departure from the land (Gen 28:10-22; 35:1-15). The Jacob story, then, combines a personal life history, generated from traditional, archetypal themes, with a kind of political allegory in which a certain understanding of the past is inscribed, resulting in what is in effect a new narrative genre.

· X ·

What Happened at Sinai?
Structure and Meaning in the
Sinai-Horeb Narrative (Exodus 19–34)

1

One of the most anomalous features of the Pentateuch read as a literary work is its narrative tempo. The Israelite camp in the wilderness of Sinai en route from Egypt to Canaan occupies from start to finish about a third of the total length of the Pentateuch (Exod 19:1–Num 10:28; 1,987 verses out of 5,848), yet it lasts less than one year out of the 2,706 from creation to the death of Moses. This narrative anomaly indicates the transcendent value assigned to law in the life of Israel, but it leaves open the question when this became part of the record. Several features have led some scholars to suspect that the entire Sinai/Horeb story has been inserted into an existing narrative account of origins. The account of Moses' meeting with his Midianite father-in-law and the institution of judges and elders immediately preceding the arrival at Sinai (Exodus 18) is taken up and completed immediately after the departure (Num 10:29-34; 11:16-17, 24-30). Stories about the provision of food (manna and quails) and water also occur before and after the Sinai/Horeb narrative (Exod 16:1-36; Num 11:4-15, 31-35; 20:2-13). It was the presence of these duplicate versions that first suggested the possibility that the entire narrative of what transpired at Sinai had been inserted into an account, in some important respects parallel, of what happened at another "mountain of God" in the wilderness at which the encounter between Moses and his father-in-law took place.

The hypothesis that an early tradition of law giving located at the Kadesh oasis was supplanted by an account of the giving of the law at Sinai, both traditions featuring Moses as principal actor, goes back like so much else to Julius Wellhausen and was developed further by Eduard Meyer (Wellhausen 1957: 342-43; Meyer 1906: 51-71; on which see Nicholson 1973: 4-6). The Wellhausen-Meyer hypothesis held that the Sinai narrative submerged an earlier tradition of law giving and judicial activity located at the Kadesh oasis in the wilderness of Sinai that, according to Wellhausen, was the true location of the Mosaic history. Max Weber also located the origin of Israel's religion and law at Kadesh. He stated this clearly in his remarkable monograph on ancient Judaism: "From the beginning his [YHVH's] seat was on the mountains. However, the oldest tradition considered the oasis Kadesh, in the Sinai desert, his true sanctuary. This was where the tomb of the prophetess Miriam was located and where presumably decisive acts of Israel's self-constitution took place. The place of his organized worship most important for the origin of the Levites was at the "waters of strife" of Kadesh (Deut 33:8), that is, at the spring of the oasis where his priests gave judicial oracles" (Weber 1952: 122).

According to the hypothesis, the *disiecta membra* of this Kadesh tradition can be pieced together from accounts of episodes reported as taking place during the Israelite journey through the wilderness. The Marah (Bitter Water) incident where the Israelites received a statute and ordinance belongs here (Exod 15:22-26), and the similar incident at Massah and Meribah (Exod 17:1-7;[1] cf. Num 20:1-13) is explicitly located at Kadesh (Num 20:1, 22). The place where the miraculous provision of water took place is also known as Rephidim, site of the campaign of extermination against the Amalekites (Exod 17:8-16), and this incident is followed immediately by the meeting between Moses and his father-in-law, the Midianite priest Jethro, elsewhere known as Hobab and Reuel (18:1-27). Thus, the entire section Exodus 17–18 reproduces narrative traditions originally associated with Kadesh.

Allowing for the great disparity in length, the parallels between the Sinai story and this older Kadesh tradition are impressive. Legal enactments and judicial activity take place at both Sinai/Horeb (Exodus 19–34) and Kadesh. YHVH made a statute and ordinance for Israel at the Bitter Waters (15:25); Moses taught the people, issued statutes and instructions

---

1. The phrase *bĕḥōrēb*, "at Horeb," in Exod 17:6, which provoked Paul's odd midrash of the rock that followed the Israelites across the desert (1 Cor 10:4), is an addition with the purpose of linking the Kadesh and Sinai/Horeb traditions; see Noth 1962: 140.

(tôrâ), and set up a judicial system on the alternative "mountain of God" (18:13-27), another version of which is located immediately after the Sinai/ Horeb pericope (Num 11:10-17, 24-30). Both Sinai (Exod 24:1-2, 9-11) and Kadesh (18:12) feature sacrifice and a ritual meal in which Moses, Aaron, and the elders participate; both take place on or near a mountain, and the issue of guidance through the wilderness is raised in both versions (Num 10:31; cf. Exod 23:20).

The hypothesis is also consistent with those descriptions of the wilderness journey from which the Sinaitic covenant and law are conspicuously absent. The itinerary in Numbers 33 is generally assigned to the Priestly source (P), but it is reasonable to suppose that it contains older local tradition. The wilderness of Sinai is the eleventh of the forty-one stages of this itinerary, but nothing is recorded as having happened there. They arrive and then they depart (Num 33:15-16). The omission could be deliberate, but why mention the death of Aaron at the thirty-third station (vv. 37-39) and say nothing about Sinai? The same conclusion follows from those passages in which the journey through the wilderness is mentioned only en passant. In negotiating with the king of Edom for safe passage through his territory, Moses informed him that his people had arrived in Kadesh from Egypt and were now preparing for the last leg of their journey. The impression is given that Kadesh was the goal of the journey from the beginning, and that it also served as the staging post for the occupation of Canaan (20:14-17). Or again, Jephthah gave the Ammonite king a similar account of Israel's itinerary that omits any mention of Sinai and also implies that Kadesh was the destination of the trek from the beginning (Judg 11:14-18).

We can add an argument *e silentio*. Wherever the place name Sinai occurs in early, preexilic texts, it is never connected with Moses and the giving of the law. YHVH comes from Sinai and the mountains in Seir (Edom) or Paran or, alternatively, from Sinai in the wilderness. As was pointed out earlier, this is where YHVH was originally at home. With one possible exception (Mic 6:4), Moses is mentioned only in late prophetic texts (Isa 63:11-12; Jer 15:1; Mal 4:4), and he is mentioned as a guide and intercessor but not as a lawgiver.

The hypothesis of a massive insertion, described by Wellhausen as "a most melancholy, most incomprehensible revision" (Wellhausen 1957: 342), certainly involves a radical reshaping of the traditional material that came eventually to form the Torah canon, but it does not necessarily imply that the Sinai story is completely disconnected from other traditions recorded in the Pentateuch. In his well-known essay "The Form-Critical Problem of the Hexateuch," Gerhard von Rad used the hypothesis as the starting point for his theory of the origin and growth of the Hexateuch. Von Rad argued that the occupation of the land promised to the ancestors had to be part of the base narrative, which therefore must have included the book of Joshua, thereby constituting a Hexateuch. Von Rad maintained that this "baroque elaboration of simple dogmas" grew from traditions originating in the ceremonial of the Israelite tribal amphictyony in the earliest period of the history. The tradition of the exodus from Egypt and conquest of the land originated in historical recital during the celebration of Shavuot (the Feast of Weeks) at Gilgal, while the law tradition developed from the covenant-renewal festival of Sukkot (the Feast of Tabernacles) at Shechem. These originally quite distinct traditions were first combined during the time of the early monarchy by the Yahvist, for whose work von Rad had the highest regard. At this point the traditions were transformed from cultic recital to literature (von Rad 1966: 1-78).

Von Rad's thesis has been subjected to frequent criticism, and few scholars if any endorse it today (Nicholson 1973 passim; 1998: 63-92). It concerns us in the present essay only insofar as it emphasizes the original, relative distinctiveness and isolation of the Sinai narrative. According to von Rad, the amalgamation of the two traditions involved disrupting the existing Kadesh tradition, but the gain outweighed the loss since the combination resulted in a comprehensive statement of the basic message of the Bible as a whole, which for von Rad, as a good Lutheran, could be summarized as Law and Gospel (von Rad 1966: 54).

One reason for the abandonment of von Rad's hypothesis is the early date he assigned to his Yahvist writer, whom he regarded as the one responsible for the insertion of Sinai into the mainline historical account of origins. Those many scholars who now date the J material in the Pentateuch several centuries later and bring it into closer association with the standard History would hold an alternative view. The idea would be that in the period of reconstruction after the disasters of the early sixth century B.C., it was felt necessary to create a more complete, coherent, and paradigmatic foundational narrative that would place the emergent Second Temple community on a firm basis of law. If in the process of elaborating this narrative existing traditions about origins were pushed into the background, this must have seemed a small price to pay.

The presence of sources in the Sinai-Horeb pericope is admitted by all critical commentators, though as always with much disagreement on matters of detail. The position I adopt in this paper can be stated briefly as follows. The core Sinai/Horeb narrative (Exodus 19–34) basically results from the combination of a Deuteronomistic (D) and a Priestly (P) narrative. Both these narratives have their own consistency and integrity, and both belong to larger narrative complexes. Here as elsewhere P provides the solemn proemium and exordium to the narrative (Exod 19:1; Num 10:11-36). This is a common feature of this narrative strand, and it does not imply that P stands for an editor rather than an author. It seems rather that the final editing involved the incorporation and combination of material from distinct narrative works. It does not seem likely that P as *Endredaktor* would have retained the account of the calf cult in which Aaron, eponymous ancestor of the Jerusalem priesthood, plays a disreputable role. I believe that we can identify with a reasonable degree of assurance the respective contributions of D and P in the Sinai/Horeb story. This compositional dualism does not, however, exclude the incorporation of older traditions, written or oral, traditions that could have originated in Shechem or Kadesh, nor does it rule out the expansion of the basic narrative with later additions, for example, the passing of the divine glory before Moses (33:17-23) and the latter's facial transfiguration (34:29-35), both of a marked midrashic character (Blenkinsopp 1977: 54-69, 80-85; 1992: 183-97).

2

We begin with the Priestly writer since his voice is the first we hear as the Sinai story begins. In what follows I am assuming that the siglum P stands for a multigenerational source comprising a great amount of cultic and ritual prescription worked into a history beginning with creation. The conclusion of this history is not so self-evident; some scholars confine it to the Pentateuch, where it terminates with the death of Moses, while for others it includes the occupation and settlement of Canaan, ending with the setting up of the wilderness sanctuary in the promised land (Joshua 18–19). It is relatively easy to disengage the main lines of the P version of what happened at Sinai. The Israelites arrived in the Sinai wilderness on the first day of the third month, counting from the exodus from Egypt (Exod 19:1-2a), and departed processionally on the twentieth day of the second month in the following year (Num 10:11). This last date was chosen to accommodate those who had incurred ritual uncleanness and were therefore obliged to celebrate the delayed Passover as prescribed in Num 9:9-14. For P, Passover marks the establishment of the Israelite wilderness commonwealth *('ădat yiśrā'ēl):* "This month shall be the first month of the year for you" (Exod 12:1), foreshadowing the celebration of the first Passover following the dedication of the rebuilt temple in the sixth year of the reign of Darius I (Ezra 6:19-22). By providing a solemn introduction and conclusion to the narrative, a P writer wished to identify it as recording a distinct and important phase in the overall P history.

According to P, then, the Israelites arrived in the Sinai wilderness, whereupon Moses went up the mountain and was granted a vision (Exod 24:15b-18a). In the vision he received detailed specifications for the construction of a mobile sanctuary with its equipment, and equally detailed instructions for the cult to be carried out in it and for the appointment of liturgical personnel (25:1–31:17). Like the Sumerian king Gudea of Lagash, Moses was also given a model or blueprint *(tabnît)* of the sanctuary to be built (25:9, 40), reminiscent of the pattern or model *(toknît)* of Ezekiel's visionary temple (Ezek 43:10). The construction of the sanctuary and its apparatus was to conclude with the celebration of sabbath, officially instituted at this point (Exod 31:12-17; 35:1-3) though anticipated at an earlier stage of the journey through the wilderness (16:4-30). The detailed account of the implementation of the visionary instructions (chaps. 35–40) was probably the work of a clerical editor anxious to make the point that the instructions retained their validity even after Aaron had compromised himself in the Golden Calf incident.

The numerous cultic and ritual enactments in Leviticus and the first part of Numbers (to Num 10:28) are all recorded as being issued or implemented at Sinai. For the purposes of this essay these do not call for comment, but it is interesting to note how they fit into the well-organized structure of the P history. The nodal points of this history are: the creation of the world as the space in which the worship of God is to take place (Gen 1:1–2:4a); the erection and dedication of the wilderness sanctuary (Exod 40:1-33); and the setting up of this sanctuary at Shiloh, an action that put the seal on the settlement in Canaan and marked the foundation of a theocratic commonwealth as recorded in Joshua 18–19 (Blenkinsopp 1976: 275-92). This structure with its fundamental concern for worship is reinforced at different points. The vision on the mountain takes place on the seventh day (Exod 24:16), the creation of the wilderness sanctuary is followed by a day of rest as was the original creation (31:12-17; 35:1-3), and worship can finally be initiated after the ceremony of the ordination of priests, which also lasts seven days (Lev 8:33; 9:1). The wilderness sanctuary is set up on the first day of the first month, that is, New Year's Day (Exod 40:1, 17), corresponding to the first New Year's Day of creation and the day on which, according to P, the purified earth emerged from the water of the deluge, that is, the first day of the new creation (Gen 8:13).

The most notable feature of P's Sinai account is not, however, what it says but what it omits. *It has nothing to say about the making of a covenant.* The instructions delivered to Moses in the vision conclude with an injunction to observe sabbath that is described as a perpetual covenant (*běrît ʿôlām*, Exod 31:16). This marks the official institution of sabbath, the last of the three rites (circumcision, Passover, sabbath) that do not require the mediation of priests and are therefore, according to P, instituted before the ordination of priests and the setting up of the sacrificial cult. But the institution of sabbath is clearly not the P equivalent of the covenant making recorded at an earlier point of the narrative (Exodus 24). Like the rainbow and the circumcised foreskin (Gen 9:12-17; 17:11), sabbath is a *sign* (*ʾ ôt*, 31:17) pointing to creation and the sanctification of the people. The historical context appears to be that of the early Second Temple period, when sabbath observance could stand by metonymy for covenant observance. We hear an Isaianic author at that time assuring foreigners and eunuchs that "all who observe the sabbath and do not profane it, who hold fast to my covenant," are members in good standing in the community (Isa 56:1-7).

The standard explanation of this remarkable omission in the P Sinai story relies on the hypothesis that P never existed as a self-standing narrative, but only as a redactional strand to be read in conjunction with a narrative already in place (Cross 1973: 293-325). But even if this were so, we would still have to explain why at all important junctures of the history except this one P has either an independent account (the Abrahamic covenant, Gen 17:1-14; the call of Moses, Exod 6:2–7:7) or a significant contribution to a conflated version (the deluge, Gen 6:5–9:19; the Egyptian plagues, Exod 7:8–11:10). The highly distinctive structural features of the P history referred to earlier would also indicate an independent narrative, though not necessarily a history written by one author at one point in time.

A clue to the narrative logic of P in this section of the history can be found at the important point of the revelation of the divine name, which in P takes place not in the wilderness, as in the alternative account, but in

Egypt. The location may provide a clue to the social and political situation in which the P narrative originated. Ezekiel's chariot-throne vision in the Babylonian diaspora meant that YHVH could now appear and be present to his people in a land under the jurisdiction of other deities or, in biblical terms, in a land polluted with idolatry. Hence the experience of life in the diaspora could explain why in P the revelation could take place in Egypt rather than in the wilderness. In this version, YHVH identifies himself with the God who appeared to Abraham, Isaac, and Jacob and made a covenant with them (Exod 6:2-9). No further covenant was needed since YHVH heard the groans of his oppressed people and *remembered* the ancestral covenant. The subsequent course of events, culminating for P in the inauguration of worship and sacrifice, flowed from that moment when YHVH's memory was reactivated by human suffering.

We can therefore conclude that the absence of a P version of covenant making at Sinai, whether distinct or conflated, is a deliberate omission and corresponds to an important feature of the theology of P. According to this narrative source, the first covenant was with humanity in the restored but damaged world following the deluge (Gen 9:8-17), and the first and only covenant with Israel was made with the ancestors (Gen 17:1-21). Both are described as perpetual *(běrît ʿôlām)*, a term that designates a covenant not requiring periodic renewal and revalidation, as was the case with covenants and treaties in the political sphere. The Priestly writer has therefore substituted for serial or sequential covenant making of the kind attested in Deuteronomy and the associated History a once-for-all double dispensation: first, with the damaged postdiluvian world; then with Israel at the beginning of its history. Continuity over time between these past moments and the ever-changing present is established by God remembering; God's memory guarantees historical continuity, and the divine memory is activated by crisis and suffering (Exod 2:24; 6:5; Lev 26:42, 45).

The P covenant is also distinctive in that, unlike the standard D understanding of covenant, adhesion to certain commitments on the part of God (YHVH) as originator of the covenant is not contingent on the observance of stipulations imposed on and accepted by the human partner. P has therefore moved away from the idea of a contractual basis for the religious life in the direction of antecedent divine dispositions or dispensations. In linguistic terms, this major shift in religious thinking is expressed in the move from covenant to testament (as in "the new testament"), in Greek from *synthēkē* to *diathēkē*.

3

Aside from P, there has never been a consensus on the identification of sources in the Sinai story. The initial address in which Israel is described as "a priestly kingdom, a holy nation," has, for example, been assigned at different times and by different scholars to every Pentateuchal source including P. The situation is worse in the account of the sealing of the covenant in Exodus 24 in which, as Lothar Perlitt put it, sources might as well be assigned "durch Losorakel," which we might translate "by drawing straws" (Perlitt 1969: 181). One way of getting past the roadblock would be to start out with the Horeb event as presented in Deuteronomy. In this version the sequence of episodes is not always transparently clear. The topographical point of reference is Beth-peor just east of the Jordan valley, which dictates the perspective of the narrator (Deut 3:29; 4:44-46), and the historical lead-in covers the period from the departure from Horeb to Beth-peor, with Kadesh as an intermediate stage (1:1–3:29). But an account of what happened at Horeb comes up only in the homiletic parts of the book. We are told that YHVH himself spoke the Ten Commandments out of the fire to the people gathered about the mountain, after which "he added no more," which I take to mean that the promulgation of the individual stipulations of law as contained in the "book of the covenant" in Exodus 21–23 was left to Moses for later promulgation (Deut 4:10-13; 5:5b-22). YHVH then wrote the Decalogue on stone tablets (5:22b). Terrified by direct contact with the deity, the people requested that Moses act as a go-between, the request was granted, and Moses was charged to promulgate detailed stipulations of law at a later time (4:14; 5:31). Moses went up the mountain to receive the tablets (9:9-11), and the people led by Aaron took advantage of his absence to engage in an orgiastic bull cult (9:12-14; cf. 4:15-20). On discovering what had happened, Moses smashed the tablets, fasted, interceded for Aaron and the people, and was told by God to make new tablets and a box in which to put them (9:15–10:5).

The close correspondence of this sequence of events with the sequence in Exodus 19–34 (after subtracting the P version) has suggested the hypothesis that the non-P version in Exodus was either assembled and edited or perhaps even composed by one or more D authors as an expanded version of the reminiscence of Moses. Not all agree with this, of course, but several scholars have accepted the hypothesis in recent years, with differing degrees of emphasis and enthusiasm and many variations and modifications in detail, though it is by no means a new idea (see especially Perlitt 1969; Kutsch 1973). The hypothesis is supported by the frequency of D vocabulary and themes in the Exodus version. Then, on this hypothesis, at some stage and under circumstances unknown to us, this D-type version was amalgamated with and framed by the P version. If so much is accepted, Exodus 19–34 could be read as a conflation of D and P versions, and as offering two different, in some respects fundamentally different, options for the religious life of the emergent Judean community in the postdisaster period. But before examining these options we must take a closer look at what, in its final form, we may, without denying the incorporation of older traditions, call the D (Deuteronomistic) version.

The D version begins with the first of several ascents of the mountain by Moses (Exodus 19:3a). These ascents represent symbolically the role of Moses as mediator and his elevated status vis-à-vis the people. The mountain is the space intermediate between God and the people, the place of mediation, and the place where God's voice can be heard. The initial discourse is of special importance as recapitulating the event in advance (19:3b-6):

> "Thus you shall say to the household of Jacob, and proclaim to the Israelites:
>
> *You have observed what I did to the Egyptians, and how I bore you up on eagles' wings and brought you to myself. And now, if you will indeed obey my voice and observe my covenant, you shall be my own special possession from among all the peoples, for all the earth is mine. You shall be for me a kingdom of priests and a holy nation.*
>
> These are the words that you shall speak to the Israelites."

The themes in this brief discourse and the language in which they are expressed are transparently Deuteronomistic: appeal to collective experience (cf. Deut 1:19; 4:3; 11:7; 29:1); Israel as a "special possession" (*sĕgullâ*, Deut 7:6; 14:2; 26:18); the fact that this privileged position and ensuing benefits are contingent on obedience and covenant observance (Deut 7:9, 12; 29:8); Israel borne aloft on eagles' wings as a sign of divine providence in passage through the wilderness (only here and in Deut 32:11). The much-discussed phrase "a kingdom of priests and a holy nation" *(mamleket kōhănîm vĕgôy qādôš)* is not found in Deuteronomy or anywhere else in the Hebrew Bible, but in the context of international relations Israel can be called a *gôy* (Deut 4:7-8, 34; 9:14; 26:5) and can be addressed as a holy people (*'am qādôš*, Deut 7:6; 14:2, 21; 26:19; 28:9). The phrase "a kingdom of priests" (or "a priestly kingdom") occurs only here but fits the D view of Israel's relationship with other nations and ethnic groups, a matter of particular urgency in the early postexilic period (Blum 1989: 288-90; Perlitt 1969: 174-75).

The postscript to the inaugural divine discourse on the mountain recalls the opening words, and therefore the title, of the book of Deuteronomy: "These are the words *('ēlleh haddĕbārîm)* that you shall speak to the Israelites" (Exod 19:6b; cf. Deut 1:1). Moses then summoned the elders and set before them all the words that YHVH had commanded him, to which the people gave their unanimous assent: "All that YHVH has spoken we will do." Clearly, the "words" *(dĕbārîm)* are now commandments, stipulations of law, as in the sealing of the covenant in Exod 24:3 where the same formula of assent occurs, and yet at this point no law has been promulgated. The solution seems to be that this introductory interchange involving YHVH, Moses, and the people is intended as a recapitulation or proleptic summary of the Horeb event from a D author. A D origin is also suggested by the role of the elders in connection with the law (cf. Deut 5:23; 27:1; 29:9; 31:9, 28) and the insistence on an attitude of obedience and trust with regard to Moses as the mouthpiece of YHVH (Exod 19:9a). In the D understanding of covenant, the explicit acceptance of the stipulations by the people, here expressed in the formulaic expression "we will do" (19:8a) — a performative utterance like the "I do" of the marriage ceremony — is an essential precondition for YHVH to honor his covenant commitments.

In the parallel version in Deuteronomy there is no ritual preparation of the people for encounter with God as in Exod 19:10-15, and the theophany itself (Exod 19:16-25 plus 20:18-21) is only sketchily referred to (Deut 5:4-5, 22, 25-26). This would be consistent with the adaptation by the D writer in Exodus of an old theophanic tradition associated with Sinai as YHVH's place of origin, of the kind reproduced, for example, in the Song of Deborah and Psalm 68, where YHVH is hailed as "He of Sinai" (Judg 5:5; Ps 68:9). But the basic sequence of events in Exodus runs parallel in its broad lines with the version in Deut 5:2-33: promulgation of the Decalogue by God directly to the people, expostulation of the people and request for mediation, and communication of the law book to Moses alone with a view to later promulgation. This way of structuring the narrative encodes the idea of the transcendent authority of the law in general and the special

status and function of the Decalogue over against the individual stipulations of the law in particular.

The communication of these stipulations to Moses follows at once
(Exod 20:22–23:19), no doubt with a view to promulgation at a later time.
The initial statement — "You have seen that I have spoken to you from
heaven" (20:22) — contains the typically D appeal to experience combined
with a way of expressing the ultimacy of divine communications, whether
prophetic or legal, which is equally characteristic of the D school (cf. Deut
4:36; 26:15; 1 Kgs 8:22-53). Following the insertion of the law book there occurs a passage dealing with the theme of divine guidance and the measures
to be taken, or to be avoided, following on occupation of the land. This
passage is as Deuteronomic as anything in the book of Deuteronomy
(23:20-33). The key to understanding the role of the angel-messenger
(mal'āk) sent by God to guide the Israelites and communicate God's commands is the theory of prophecy expounded in Deut 18:15-20. Like the
angel-messenger, the prophet (nābî') is presented as continuing the work
and mission of Moses after Sinai, communicating divine commands, a
function that called for absolute obedience. A fairly close parallel can be
found in Judg 2:1-5, in which an angel-messenger delivers what is essentially a prophetic address to the Israelites after the conquest of Canaan. It is
therefore not surprising that eventually mal'āk came to function as one of
several synonyms for nābî' (e.g., Hag 1:13; Mal 3:1, 23).

Scholars generally concede that the collection of case laws and apodictic statements in Exod 20:23–23:19 (the so-called "covenant code") has
been spliced into the Sinai-Horeb narrative, but at what time and under
what circumstances we do not know. The insertion has occasioned some
dubiety as to the referent for the "words and ordinances" and "the book of
the covenant" in the account of covenant making (24:3, 7). If we put the
law book in parentheses, we can trace the outline of the D version, beginning with the inaugural address and followed by the promulgation of the
Decalogue and Moses' ascent of the mountain to take delivery of the stone
tablets on which God had himself inscribed the Decalogue. The absence of
Moses provided the occasion for setting up a bull cult, the annulment of
the covenant was signified by the smashed tablets, and the inauguration of
a new dispensation was signified by new tablets.

The account of the concluding ceremonies (Exod 24:1-18) has proved
to be mined terrain for proponents of all variations of the documentary
hypothesis (Nicholson 1986 passim). Broad agreement exists that several

scenarios have been conflated, differing as to location, participants, and ceremonial. The first (vv. 1-2, 9-11) features Moses, Aaron, his two sons and seventy elders and consists in a vision and a meal on the mountain. It has nothing in common with Deuteronomy, which evinces little interest in and no sympathy for Aaron and his followers. It is, however, reminiscent of the meal "before God" in which Moses, Aaron, and the elders participated on another mountain near Kadesh (Exod 18:12). Somewhat incongruously, an account of a covenant-sealing ceremony at the foot of the mountain has been sandwiched into this first version (24:3-8). The inserted account has several archaic features pointing to a covenant-making ceremony at Shechem with which the D school was certainly familiar (Deut 11:26-32; 27:1-26; cf. Josh 8:30-35). Since it appears to refer to the so-called "covenant code," it was probably added after the insertion of the law collection.

A similar "sandwich" technique accounts for the arrangement of the second half of the chapter in which the P version of the vision granted to Moses (24:15b-18a) is spliced into the continuation of the mainline D narrative of the event (vv. 12-15a plus v. 18b), which is taken up again in the Golden Calf episode and its sequel (31:18–34:35, with additions). I read this as a considerably expanded version of the account in Deuteronomy 9–10, where the episode is presented as one of several "rebellions" in the wilderness.

A rich variety of traditions about covenant making seems to have been known at the time when the narrative attained its final form. Rather than decide on one version to the exclusion of the others, as a modern editor might well have done, those responsible for the final form wisely chose to transmit a rich mix of traditions, disregarding the contradictions resulting from their juxtaposition.

Common to both the Exodus and Deuteronomy versions is the existence of a law written on stone tablets (Exod 24:12; Deut 9:9, 11). This means that Israel's relationship with God rests on a contractual basis the terms of which are available in writing. The basic moral obligation into which Israel has contracted by accepting the terms of the agreement ("All that YHVH has spoken we will do") is encapsulated in the Decalogue. The ultimacy of the authority of this document is expressed by the fact that YHVH is both its author and engraver (Exod 31:18; 32:16; 34:1; Deut 4:13; 9:10). The choice of writing surface (stone) likewise indicates permanence and permanent relevance, in contrast with the papyrus book or scroll on which the individual stipulations of law would have been written (Exod 24:7).

The D school clearly assigned great importance to the distinction between the Decalogue, containing the basic moral norms defining the kind of community Israel was meant to be, and the individual stipulations of law, which could be updated, expanded, or even abrogated in keeping with changing situations and circumstances. The distinction will help to explain why the Decalogue is repeated in connection with the laws in both Exodus (Exod 20:1-17) and Deuteronomy (Deut 5:6-21). The tablets on which the Decalogue is inscribed are also preserved with greater care than the compilations of casuistic and apodictic laws. They are placed in an ark or chest specially made for them and deposited in the inner sanctum of the temple (Deut 10:5; 1 Kgs 8:9), while the "book of the law" is placed at the side of the chest (Deut 31:26). This contrasts with the P source, which describes the contents of the ark *('ārôn)* simply as "the testimony" *(hā'ēdût,* Exod 25:16, 21, etc.) without further explanation.[2] The focus of divine presence is above the ark cover *(kappōret)* between the cherubim, and it is from that location that divine communications were thought to proceed (Exod 25:22; Num 7:89).

4

A feature of much Pentateuchal narrative that can easily be overlooked is its paradigmatic function. Genesis 1–11 covers the early history of humanity but it also corresponds to the history of Israel viewed from the religious perspective as a failed history leading to disaster (the deluge) and a new beginning, or, alternatively, as a series of events leading to dispersion in Mesopotamia where the "primeval history" ends (Gen 11:1-9). The Garden of Eden story likewise can be read as a prefiguring of Israel placed in a congenial environment, that is, the land of Canaan, gifted with the Torah, failing to observe it, and in consequence being exiled from the land. The paradigmatic function of Jacob's exile in Mesopotamia and eventual return, upon which he assumes the name Israel, is also unmistakable.

One of the clearest and most explicit of these paradigmatic stories is

2. The translation of *'ēdût* is uncertain. In the P source, the *'ēdût* is a written document placed in a chest (Exod 25:16, 21; 40:20) located in the wilderness sanctuary (Exod 25:22; 26:33-34, etc.) the custody of which is entrusted to Levites (Num 1:50, 53; cf. Josh 4:16). The term is characteristic of but not exclusive to P since it occurs in parallelism with *tôrâ* in psalms (19:8; 78:5; Neh 9:34) and in other non-P contexts (Exod 31:18; 32:15; 34:29). P apparently prefers *'ēdût* to *bĕrît,* more characteristic of D.

the account of what happened at Horeb while Moses spent forty days and nights on the mountains and received the two tablets of the law. The account begins with Moses being commanded to ascend the mountain to receive the tablets of stone inscribed by YHVH himself. Before leaving with his acolyte Joshua, Moses subdelegates judicial authority to Aaron (not represented as a priest) and Hur for the period of his absence (Exod 24:12-15a, 18b).

After a long intermission filled with the P account of Moses' reception of the detailed prescriptions for initiating the cult (24:15b-18a plus 25:1–31:17), we reconnect with the D narrative in Exod 31:18: "When he [YHVH] had finished speaking with Moses on Mount Sinai, he gave him the two tablets of the 'testimony,' stone tablets written with the finger of God." The expression "stone tablets inscribed by God" is Deuteronomic, but "Mount Sinai" is not, nor is the reference to "tablets of testimony (*'ēdût*)." Since, moreover, God's speaking to Moses can refer only to the preceding cultic instructions, the verse probably represents an editor's way of linking the two quite different accounts of the Sinai/Horeb event.

The D version resumes with the account of the manufacture during Moses' absence of a cult object, the notorious "golden calf," in the presence of which the people, led by Aaron, sacrifice, eat, drink, and participate in an orgiastic ritual.[3] Comparison with the account of Jeroboam's cult establishment at Bethel and Dan (1 Kgs 12:26-32) provides the clearest example of what I have called a paradigm narrative in the Pentateuch. The cult object is similarly described: it is a calf made in a mold (*'ēgel massēkâ*, Exod 32:4, 8; cf. 2 Kgs 17:16; Neh 9:18), gold-plated (Exod 32:2-3, 31; cf. 1 Kgs 12:28, 32; 2 Kgs 10:29), representative of the bull cult prevalent throughout the Northern Kingdom (Hos 8:5-6; 13:3). The acclamation of the newly installed deity is identical — "These are your gods, O Israel, who brought you up from the land of Egypt!" (Exod 32:4; 1 Kgs 12:28). Both Aaron and Jeroboam institute a new and (from the Jerusalemite perspective) heterodox festival, since Jeroboam moved the celebration of Sukkoth from the seventh to the eighth month (1 Kgs 12:32). Both offer sacrifices on the altar they have erected, and the Bethel altar is served by non-Levitical priests

---

3. What the people did when, after eating and drinking, they "rose up to play" (*lĕṣaḥēq*, 32:6) is further specified in the dancing witnessed by Moses (v. 19); but the verb elsewhere has a distinctly sexual connotation (Gen 21:9; 26:8; 39:14 and probably Judg 16:25). After Gideon made a cult object in Ophrah, all the people "prostituted themselves" in its presence (Judg 8:22-27).

(1 Kgs 12:32). Since Levites volunteer to punish the worshipers of the golden calf, and do so with a will (Exod 32:25-29), it would follow that Aaron represents the illegitimate priesthood of Bethel, at least from the author's point of view. This will seem strange in view of the prominence of the Aaronite priesthood in the P source, Chronicles, and postbiblical texts, but the only mention of Aaron in Deuteronomy, apart from the notice of his death (Deut 10:6), is not favorable (9:20), priests are "sons of Levi" or "Levitical priests," never "sons of Aaron," in Deuteronomy, and the same book records the appointment of Levites to the priestly office in the wilderness (10:8-9), parallel in some respects to the Levitical "ordination" in Exod 32:29.

Comparison between the two texts justifies the conclusion that the Golden Calf episode, whatever its connection with the parallel version in Deut 9:8-21, is a fictionalization of the historical incident of Jeroboam's cult establishment as described in 1 Kgs 12:26-33. As such, it serves as the hinge or pivot on which the entire Sinai/Horeb narrative turns. In its simplest terms, the Sinai/Horeb narrative resolves itself into an account of the making, breaking, and remaking of the covenant; or, more concretely, since the motif of the stone tablets serves as a principal instrument of cohesion and unity in the narrative, the making, breaking, and remaking of the tablets. This simple structure corresponds in broad outline to the history of Israel viewed from the other side of disaster. Moses' smashing the tablets on returning to the camp (Exod 32:19) therefore encodes a theological evaluation of the kingdom founded by Jeroboam and an explanation of its eventual fate (cf. the Historian's comments in 2 Kgs 17:16 and 18:12). But since Judah also "walked in the customs that Israel had introduced" (2 Kgs 17:19), the debacle at Sinai/Horeb, in its final form a postdestruction literary composition, as we have seen, could serve as a paradigm of Judah's spiritual failure and its inevitable consequences as well.

5

If the Sinai-Horeb event inscribes a religious interpretation of Israel's history as a history of failure written from the other side of disaster, the question arises whether it contains any prescriptions for a new beginning or, in other words, whether the experience of religious failure and collective moral incapacity had generated any new thinking. Contemporary or near-contemporary biblical texts leave us in no doubt that the disaster of 586 B.C. resulted in widespread disorientation and questioning of traditional beliefs, a situation whose reflection can be discerned in the Sinai/Horeb narrative in its final configuration. The survivors mourning the absence of their God and his guidance after the apostasy (Exod 33:3-5) could evoke the situation following on the fall of Jerusalem and the deportations interpreted as the result of religious failure. Something similar could be suggested about the issue of guidance, whether by means of the angel-messenger *(mal'āk)*, perhaps with reference to prophetic guidance (33:2), or the face of God *(pānîm)*, perhaps hinting at liturgical experience (33:14-16), or the glory of God *(kābôd)* reflected in Moses' face, perhaps indicating the transcendent value of law as the ultimate source of authority (34:29-35).

Reading the D version of Exodus 19–34 paradigmatically as proposed does not, at first sight, suggest that disaster gave rise to new thinking in the religious sphere. The reissue of the same moral code — new tablets, old law (34:1-4) — suggests rather one more religious reform comparable to the many attempted with limited success during the monarchy. But if we take account of those parts of the Deuteronomistic corpus that reflect the disaster, we will see that the situation is more nuanced, and that the experience of disaster has made a difference. In the first place, the idea of moral obligation understood as adhesion to divinely revealed and imposed norms is expressed in the broader and more affective terms of seeking God with total dedication ("with all your heart and soul"):

> From there [i.e., the place of exile] you will *seek* YHVH your God, and you will find him if you *search* after him with all your heart and soul. (Deut 4:29)

> When you *search* for me, you will find me; if you *seek* me with all your heart, I will let you find me . . . and I will restore your fortunes and gather you from all the nations. (Jer 29:13-14)

Seeking God is also associated with the idea of repentance or, more biblically, returning (Deut 4:30; 30:2, 10), an anticipation of Buber's "true turning" *(tĕšûbâ)*, implying a change of direction, a reorientation of one's life.

While, therefore, it does not seem that the Deuteronomists had learned any radically new lessons from the experience of failure and collapse, we detect the beginnings of a process in which law observance, a straightforward rules morality, is being recontextualized, broadened in scope, and interiorized. Pointing in the same direction is the contrast between the law engraved on stone tablets and the law written on the heart, the clearest expression of which is the "new covenant" passage in Jer 31:31-34. The origin of this passage has long been a matter of dispute. It is, on the one hand, consonant with the strong sense of moral incapacity in sayings generally attributed to Jeremiah — about the inability of the leopard to change its spots (13:23) and the desperate sickness of the human heart (17:9-10) — but the new covenant passage also has close affinities with Deuteronomy. Deuteronomy speaks of the law in the heart, the internalized law (6:6; 11:18; 30:14), but it also assigns great importance to instruction that, according to Jer 31:34, will not be needed in the future. ("No longer shall each one teach neighbor or brother, for they shall all know me, from the least of them to the greatest.") While, therefore, the Jeremian text expresses a sense that individual and collective moral incapacity calls for a new initiative on the part of God, it provides no clue as to what form this might take or how the newly established relationship might be socially embodied.

The idea that a radical inner change, a kind of spiritual heart transplant, is needed to assure conformity with a divinely revealed law is not confined to the Jeremian text, which, in fact, may have drawn on those texts in Ezekiel that speak of a renewal of heart and spirit enabling conformity with revealed law (Ezek 11:20; 36:26-27). Ezekiel was a priest, and the book named for him expresses much the same worldview as the Priestly history in the Hexateuch. For Ezekiel as for P, and unlike Deuteronomy, the covenant is perpetual (*bĕrît 'ôlām*, 16:60; 37:26), it is activated by God remembering (16:60), and it is put into effect by the place, instruments, and acts of common worship (37:26-28).

With this we return to the P version of Sinai, the most remarkable feature of which we have seen to be the absence of any explicit mention of covenant making. This does not of course mean that these priest-authors were indifferent to divinely revealed law, but it does imply that their idea of the God-people relationship was significantly different from that of the Deuteronomists. The difference can be deduced from the language used. According to P, a covenant is not "cut" (verbal stem *krt*), as in cutting a deal between two partners, but "granted" (verb *ntn*) or "established" *(hqym)*. It is, as noted earlier, perpetual, once for all, and therefore unrenewable. We saw earlier that in the P version the document corresponding to "the tablets of the *běrît*," or some variation of that expression in D, is simply called *hā'ēdût*, "the testimony," which can be taken to signify a pledge of fidelity on the part of God. The main point is that the primeval covenants with the damaged postdiluvian world and with Israel's ancestors remain in force regardless of human behavior. In other words, no obligations are laid on the human partner contingent on the observance of which the preservation of the relationship rests and depends. The so-called Noachic laws are not covenant stipulations since they were issued prior to the announcement of the covenant (Gen 9:1-17). In the P version of the covenant with Abraham circumcision is, like the bow in the clouds, the *sign* of the covenant (17:11; cf. 9:12-13, 17). It is a necessary condition for membership in the community but not a stipulation of covenant law analogous to the Ten Commandments.

In his *Theology of the Old Testament,* Walther Eichrodt made the point that since the only Priestly covenant with Israel is antecedent to the revelation of the ceremonial law and the institution of worship, the implementation of the latter, described in great detail in Exodus 35–40 and on into Leviticus and Numbers, was not thought of as a human performance by which the covenant became effective but rather Israel's way of appropriating the covenant offered to them in the person of Abraham (Eichrodt 1961: 1:56-57). On this view, the finality of the covenant is not to provide a theological basis for moral obligation but to create a community united in worship. This takes place in an orderly fashion beginning in the pre-Sinaitic period with the three institutions not requiring the participation of the priesthood: circumcision (Gen 17:9-14), Passover (Exod 12:1-28), and sabbath (Exod 31:12-17; 35:1-3). The climax is the establishment of the sacrificial cult divinely revealed to Moses and the setting up of the sanctuary in the promised land.

The blending of the D and P accounts of what happened at Sinai/Horeb represents, therefore, a combination of different religious options facing the emergent Jewish communities of the postdisaster period. The P account of the Sinai event did not contain the Golden Calf episode featuring a compromised Aaron, and therefore did not reproduce the making-breaking-remaking pattern of the Deuteronomists. (Its place was taken by the sin of Aaron's two oldest sons, their punishment, and a ritual of atonement, Lev 10:1-7; 16:1.) The removal of the contractual element from the God-people relationship is consistent with the heightened sense of divine freedom, transcendence, and distance in P. The God of the Priestly writers is not a God who micromanages human affairs. Contrary to the prejudicial views about P at one time practically universal, this source leaves more room for human freedom of action and for the hallowing of time and space.

We do not know how and under what circumstances these distinctive religious perspectives were combined in one canonical text. If the proponents of imperial authorization during the Persian period are right, external pressure would have played a part (Watts 2001). In any event, the combination of these two mainline narratives mirrors the religious tensions and sometimes conflicting tendencies within Second Temple Judaism. Their juxtaposition in the Sinai/Horeb story and throughout the Pentateuch, together with the older traditions they incorporate, corresponds to a certain dialectic characteristic of ancient Jewish editing, and therefore ancient Jewish thinking, that continued on into the rabbinic period and perhaps beyond.

XI

Deuteronomy and the Politics
of Postmortem Existence

1

Deuteronomy, "the second law,"[1] was in every respect crucial for the emergence of Judaism as a religion based on law and one in which the written word was destined to play an important role. To risk an anachronism, we can describe it as the first *canonical* biblical text, one that in principle excludes the possibility of subsequent alteration: "Do not add to the word I command you and do not subtract from it" (Deut 4:2). It also represents the first attempt to impose an orthodoxy and orthopraxy by systematically prescribing certain forms of religious life and proscribing others. It marks the transition from the old to the new. As Wellhausen succinctly observed, "The connecting link between old and new, between Israel and Judaism, is everywhere Deuteronomy" (Wellhausen 1957: 362).

In both the laws (chaps. 12–26) and the homiletic discourses (chaps. 1–11, 27–34) in which it is embedded, Deuteronomy insists on the worship of one deity. The emergence of monotheism in Israel is a complex issue only one aspect of which, the *political* aspect, will concern us in what follows. It is a truism that in antiquity religion cannot be separated from politics. Whatever else it is, Deuteronomy is a political document, whether we read it as a

1. The title of the book is generally said to derive from the LXX translator's misunderstanding of Deut 17:18, which stipulates that the ruler must be guided by "a copy of this law" (*mišnēh hattôrâ hazzo't*). But the LXX has *deuteronomion*, not *deuteron nomon*, which suggests that the title "Deuteronomy" was already in existence, based on the correct perception that the book does in fact contain a second law.

blueprint for a reformed kingdom when Judah still existed as a kingdom, or as the sketch of an ideal future kingdom put together after the fall of Jerusalem, or both successively. Whatever the motives of those who drafted the law, the demand to centralize the sacrificial cult with which the Deuteronomic law opens served a political purpose, and the insistence on the worship of one god, the national and dynastic deity, was also a matter of *raison d'état.* The significant midpoint of the legal compilation contains clear directives for state officials, including what is in effect a constitutional monarchy (Deut 16:18–18:22). That these state officials include religious functionaries (priests and prophets) corroborates the point about religion and politics and provides another incentive to pursue its implications further.

In the present essay I want to do so by looking at one somewhat neglected aspect of the issue, the Deuteronomic legislation directed against the cult of the dead, which in effect means the cult of ancestors. This aspect is also open to a *political* explanation, in the sense that in a society like ancient Israel, organized according to kinship relations, the passage to statehood necessitates transferring allegiance from the kinship network to the state. I believe that this can be maintained whether one thinks of the Deuteronomic law as a law intended for implementation in the Judean state or as an aspiration for the future, a kind of utopian manifesto. Since mortuary cults were, and still are in some societies, an essential, integrative element of social systems based on lineage, it was inevitable that they would be opposed by a centralized state and its own official cult laying claim to the exclusive allegiance of those living within the national borders. One can therefore view laws concerning death rites and forbidding commerce with the dead in Deuteronomy as part of a broader strategy of undermining the lineage system to which the individual household belonged. This, anyway, is the argument I will present in this essay.

The presentation of the argument does not involve displaying new data. The aim is to highlight one neglected aspect of Deuteronomic political and social ideology by viewing certain laws, especially those dealing with mortuary practices, from a different perspective. This strategy may provoke reflection on the social as well as the psychological and religious aspects of beliefs about death and postmortem existence in Israel during the biblical period and even in the contemporary world. It may also help to nuance the common assumption that belief in postmortem existence was absent during the biblical period. We shall see, finally, that it has implications for the emergence of monotheism in ancient Israel.

Since we now have several in-depth studies of death cults and ancestor cults in Iron Age Israel (Spronk 1986; Lewis 1989; Schmidt 1994; Jeffers
1996; van der Toorn 1996), it will not be necessary to spend time arguing
that these practices were actually going on in Israel at that time. Some
scholars have nevertheless from time to time rejected the idea that ancestor cults in particular were practiced in Israel (Kaufmann 1960: 311-16; de
Vaux 1961: 56-61), so we may as well at least clarify how the terms are to be
understood. We must distinguish, in the first place, between ceremonial
acts carried out in connection with the disposal of the dead or destined to
perpetuate their memory, for which the term "funerary rites" seems to be
most appropriate, and acts inspired by the belief that the dead, and specifically dead kin, live on in some way and are in a position to influence the
living for good or ill — for example, by healing, by providing information
not otherwise obtainable especially about the future, or by haunting and
inflicting physical or psychic harm (Humphreys 1983: 151-64). These we
will call "mortuary cults." If this much is accepted, the further question
arises whether in Israel of the biblical period the dead were merely hon-
ored, placated, or consulted according to the circumstances, or whether
cult in the narrower sense, defined as a complex of religious acts directed
to divine beings, or beings thought to be in some way within the sphere of
the divine, was offered to them.[2]

In Ugarit of the Late Bronze Age the status of the recently dead was
distinguished from that of the long dead, one of the terms for whom was
rp'm (rāpa'imu?), corresponding to the biblical Rephaim. These were considered to be in some way within the realm of the divine, and in both
Ugarit and Israel the dead, or some of the dead, could be referred to as
'lhym, "divine beings" (Num 25:2; 1 Sam 28:13; Isa 8:19; cf. Ps 106:28). This is
not so surprising in view of the fact that in antiquity the boundary between the divine and human was for the most part fluid and permeable,
and some texts give the impression that the dead formed a kind of buffer
zone between the worlds of the human and the divine. In brief, I assume in
what follows that in ancient Israel it was believed that the dead, including
and especially dead ancestors, lived on in some capacity, that under certain
circumstances the living could communicate with them, that such interac-

---

2. This is to admit that there can be different grades or levels of cult depending on the
object. In Roman Catholicism, for example, a traditional distinction is made between
latreia, cult offered to God, and *douleia*, the cult of the saints.

tion was an important integrative element of the social, religious, and emotional bond of kinship, and that it took the form of cult acts offered to dead kin or on their behalf.

It would be appropriate to refer, in parenthesis, to the best-known biblical example of interaction between the living and the dead, namely, the conjuring up of Samuel from the underworld by the "mistress of the spirits" at Endor (1 Samuel 28). From this incident we learn that the dead Samuel could still communicate in Hebrew and had knowledge at least of the immediate future. But passing over to the other side does not seem to have done much for his general disposition or significantly modified his ethical ideas, for example, on how to deal with enemies like the Amalekites (Blenkinsopp 2002: 49-62).

The recent surge of interest in death cults among scholars in biblical and related fields represents an at least small-scale revival of the enthusiasm for this theme during the early days of *Religionsgeschichte* in the later nineteenth century, a theme associated with the names of such *viri illustres* as Numa Fustel de Coulanges, Sir Edward Burnett Tyler, Sir James Frazer, and William Robertson Smith. Interest in postmortem existence reached an all-time high in the late Victorian period, which was also the heyday of spiritualism (Conan Doyle, Henry Sidgwick, William James) and of the ghost story (Sheridan Le Fanu, Montague Rhodes James). The subsequent falloff in interest was due in part to exaggerated claims made for ancestor cults by some of these scholars. In his *La Cité Antique* (1864), for example, Fustel de Coulanges traced the origin of religion and culture in general, and private property in particular, to the cult of the dead. Herbert Spencer made similar claims for ancestor worship as providing the original impulse for the development of religion. Nobody makes these claims today, but a more open and sympathetic reading of the biblical texts bearing on religious practices, together with the volume of relevant archaeological data now available (Bloch-Smith 1992), has prompted a new look at the subject.

2

Max Weber noted many years ago that the consolidation of a civil and religious bureaucracy, together with the concentration of power and wealth in urban centers, inevitably works against a kinship system and tends to undermine its ethos (Weber 1952: 61-70; 1978: 1:370-84). This is a matter not just of conflicting ideologies but of economic urgency. The state needs land as a source of revenue and to reward or placate retainers, and the need will often be satisfied at the expense of the patrimonial domain, the plots of land on which the economy of the household and the clan rests and on which the survival of a subsistence peasant farming economy depends. Taxation placed a severe burden on such an economy, leading often to insolvency, indentured service, loss of land, and the breakup of households.

The creation of a centralized judicial system answerable to the monarchy would also have impinged on traditional ways of settling disputes and would have restricted local jurisdictions and the more or less informal ways in which they operated. To judge from protests directed against the state and its functionaries by the eighth-century-B.C. prophets, this process of state encroachment was well underway by that time. Several of the stipulations in the Deuteronomic legal compilation (Deuteronomy 12–26) can be interpreted along these lines. The establishment of a state-appointed local and central judiciary (16:18-20; 17:8-13) imposed serious limitations on the exercise of authority by the paterfamilias and the local elder *(zāqēn)*. Disputed cases involving homicide, torts, and legal rights in general had to be brought before the civil and religious authorities in session "in the place YHVH your God will choose," and their decisions were binding under pain of death (17:8-13). The "officers" *(šōṭĕrîm)*, often mentioned together with magistrates *(šōpĕṭîm)*, had a broad supervisory function, and in addition served as military commissars to keep the peasants conscripted to fight the king's wars in line. State-appointed magistrates supervised village elders in the investigation of a homicide the perpetrator of which remained undetected (21:1-9), and cases involving false witnessing were reserved to the central judiciary (19:15-21).

The authority formerly wielded through the traditional mechanisms of the kinship network was restricted in other ways. Full discretion in disposing of the estate was no longer left to the head of household (Deut 21:15-17). The practice of blood vengeance, a traditional aspect of tribal justice, was phased out in favor of a state-mandated law of sanctuary (19:1-13). The prohibition of returning runaway slaves to their masters (23:15-16) represented a remarkable departure from legal practice in the Near East (e.g., the Code of Hammurapi §§15-20). It may seem enlightened, but it would have tended to erode the property and labor base of the more prosperous households. The requirement that a member of a household practicing non-Yahvistic cults, which would include cults of dead ancestors in the first place, be summarily dispatched by his immediate kin can be read as a blatant attempt to sabotage the solidarity of the basic kinship unit from within (13:7-12). Even the statement rejecting the traditional idea of intergenerational accountability ("visiting the sins of the fathers on the children") can be seen as removing a prop supporting a traditional way of life (24:16).

Certainly these developments were not uniformly bad. Replacing the blood feud and the indiscriminate killing to which it must often have led with legal procedures and a cooling off period that sanctuary at least theoretically provided was hardly a bad thing. Placing limits on the absolute authority of the male head of household was also a step toward reducing seriously abusive treatment of dependents. But the protests of those dissidents we call the classical prophets, beginning with Amos, Micah, Isaiah, and Hosea, directed against state-sponsored violence, bribery, and the manipulation of the judicial system (e.g., Isa. 1:23; Amos 2:7; Mic 3:9-12) suggest that the drive towards statehood left many casualties in its wake.

We noted earlier that a state bureaucracy, especially in its formative period or when its existence is threatened, will attempt to strengthen the individual spousal bond while working to undermine the larger-scale configurations of the kinship network. The representatives of the state will therefore tend to act on the tacit assumption that the strength of the bond between spouses is in inverse proportion to the strength of attachments to their respective families of origin (Goode 1959: 38-47). This consideration may help to explain the severity of penalties, including the death penalty, for adultery (Deut 22:22) and other sexual offenses (Deut 22:23-29); it may also explain the law governing palingamy (second marriage), designed either to discourage divorce or protect the second marriage, more likely the latter (Deut 24:1-4). The liberal policy of a year's exemption from the military draft for newly wedded husbands could also be seen in this light.

3

A survey of the Deuteronomic laws from this perspective will help to contextualize regulations aimed more specifically at ancestor cult, which, perhaps not by accident, have been placed at the beginning, at the end, and at the center of the compilation. The first stipulation in the law code is that sacrifice must be carried out exclusively at the one central sanctuary, "the place that YHVH your God will choose . . . to place his name there" (Deut 12:5). The point is made redundantly (12:5-7, 11-12, 14, 17-18, 26-27): the Israelite and members of his household must sacrifice, partake of the sacrificial meal, and eat tithed food only at the central sanctuary, a requirement that necessarily involved the desacralizing of butchering at the regional level (12:15-16, 20-25). At the conclusion of the compilation, the offering of first fruits at the central sanctuary (26:1-15) forms an *inclusio* with this demand for centralization at the beginning, similar in this respect to the religious laws with which the so-called Covenant Code begins and ends (Exod 20:23-26; 23:12-19).

Looking more closely at this concluding paragraph, we see that the handing over of the tithe for Levites, aliens, and other indigent categories, the tithe of the third year, is accompanied by a solemn six-member declaration that forms a kind of negative confession (26:12-15). The donor affirms that the legal requirement has been fulfilled and that no part of the offering has been consumed during a period of mourning or a memorial service for the dead. Memorial services for the dead are well attested for Iron Age Israel outside of Deuteronomy. According to Hosea (9:4) "mourners' bread" defiles, and Ps 106:28 speaks of sacrifices offered to the dead by the apostates at Peor. Jeremiah (16:5-9) is forbidden to go to "the house of mourning" *(bêt marzēaḥ)* in which the relatives and associates of the deceased assuage their sorrow by self-laceration, shaving the head, feasting, and drinking deep, in some (but only some) respects similar to the traditional Irish wake.

These final prescriptions of the Deuteronomic law are balanced by the requirement of cult centralization at the beginning. Thus the entire legal compilation is bracketed with a positive command at the beginning addressed to households to partake of sacrificial meals only at the central sanctuary, and a prohibition of food offered to the dead as part of a mortuary ritual at the end. This seems to me to provide a significant clue to the agenda of those who drafted the Deuteronomic laws.

The requirement, coming at the conclusion of the festival calendar, that adult males present themselves at the central sanctuary, is part of the same agenda (Deut 16:16). A similar prescription occurs in the so-called Covenant Code, but without the codicil that this must be done at the central sanctuary (Exod 23:17; 34:23). Being present at the *central* sanctuary is therefore a specifically Deuteronomic requirement. The intent would be to redirect attention away from the annual clan sacrificial get-together, the *zebaḥ hayyāmîm*, attendance at which was mandatory for adult members of the kinship group (1 Sam 1:21; 2:19; 20:5-6, 28-29). Such occasions are well attested, their purpose being to legitimate and sustain a social order based on patrilineal descent, to provide a highly visible verification of membership in the phratry, to confirm the hierarchy of social status within it, and to nourish the emotional life of the group.

The relevant biblical texts make no mention of the participation in these annual clan gatherings of dead members of the kinship group, those recently or not so recently "gathered to their people," or of cult offered to them, or of their being given food and drink. This is not in itself surprising in view of the Historian's rejection of the cult of the dead in any shape or form. However, solidarity between the living and the dead is a normal feature of societies organized by patrilineal descent. The social life of the group and its persistence through time were bound up with ownership of a parcel of land that also served as a burial plot. Both Jacob and Joseph extract an oath from their nearest kin to bury them in the plot bought by Abraham at Mamre (Gen 50:4-14, 24-25). Naboth's perhaps ill-advised and in the event fatal refusal to trade in his ancestral plot was motivated by the same atavistic compulsion (1 Kgs 21:3). The wise woman of Tekoa feared that she and her son would be cut off from the "heritage of God," an expression that probably amounts to the same thing. The old Bethel prophet predicted that his prophetic colleague from Judah would not be interred in the burial plot of his ancestors, a grim fate indeed for a prophet (1 Kgs 13:22). There was therefore in the society for which Deuteronomy was legislating, and which it was attempting to bring within the orbit of the developing state system or within its own vision of the ideal state, a close connection between ownership of land, burial practices, and the perpetuation of the kinship network. These interconnections are detectable in the narrative cycles about the early ancestors, beginning with Abraham's purchase of a burial plot near Hebron in which he himself, his wife, and their descendants were buried.

Before taking a closer look at explicit references to funerary rites and communication with the dead in Deuteronomy, we should comment on the central cult place as the location of the name of YHVH. It is noteworthy that Deuteronomy speaks about the divine name being *placed* in the central sanctuary, or *dwelling* in it (12:5, 11, 21; 14:23-24; 16:2, 6, 11; 26:2), but never of the name being remembered or invoked there (*zkr* Hiphil), as in the altar law of the Covenant Code: ". . . in every place where I cause my name to be remembered/invoked *('azkîr)"* (Exod 20:24). To invoke the name of a god, a spirit, or the dead was to evoke or conjure up a presence. Invocation of the name of deceased forebears was thought of as a reality-conferring act, a warding off of the eventual fate of oblivion. It was an important aspect of mortuary cults throughout the Near East, whether in the Mesopotamian *kispu* festival (Bayliss 1973: 115-25; Alster 1990), in Ugarit (Pope 1981: 159-79; Lewis 1989: 5-98), and in Syria (Huehnergard 1985: 430). In Israel, too, the dead were remembered and no doubt invoked in commemorative celebrations and by means of mortuary steles. Absalom lamented not having a surviving son to keep his name in remembrance and therefore erected for himself a stele *(maṣṣēbâ)* in the King's Valley (2 Sam 18:18). The avoidance in Deuteronomy of this formulation, remembering or invoking *(hazkîr)* the name of YHVH, may therefore be dictated by the need to dissociate the cult of YHVH as cleanly as possible from one of the most important religious practices of the household and the clan.

4

The prohibition of self-laceration and tonsure[3] as mourning rites occurs early in the Deuteronomic legal compilation (14:1-2), and similar prohibitions are found in Lev 19:28 and 21:5, both belonging to the so-called Holiness Code. The prohibition in Lev 19:28 occurs in the context of necromantic practices, as is explicitly true of Deut 14:1 *(lāmēt,* "for the dead"). Lev 21:5 is limited to the priesthood, and possibly the prohibition originally applied exclusively to priests. Since the dietary restrictions following immediately after the proscription of mortuary practices in Deut 14:1-2 (i.e., Deut 14:3-21) represent an expanded form of the list in Lev 11:2-23, the most probable explanation of the connection is that Deut 14:1-2 drew on the stipulations in Leviticus and therefore belongs to a late edition of the laws. At any rate, the practices in question, together with similar mortuary customs such as tearing one's clothes (e.g., Jer 41:5), wearing sackcloth (e.g., Jer 48:37), and sharing a meal with the dead (Jer 16:6-8; Tob 4:17), are mentioned in the prophetic writings as a normal part of the ritu-

---

3. Unlike the monastic practice, this entailed shaving and rounding off the hair at the front of the head — in the biblical idiom, "between the eyes."

alized reaction to death in Israel and Judah, as they were just about everywhere else in antiquity.

The two apodictic commands couched in the plural in Deut 14:1-2 (against self-laceration and shaving the forelock) are introduced by a declaration whose purpose is to motivate the reader to observe them: "You are the sons *(bānîm)* of YHVH your God." To my knowledge, von Rad is the only commentator who has noticed that this expression occurs nowhere else in Deuteronomy or for that matter in the Hebrew Bible (von Rad 1966: 101). In Deuteronomy one or more variations on the expression "You are the *people ('am)* of YHVH" is normal, but not "the sons of YHVH." I suggest that the choice of this formulation at this point is deliberate, and that its purpose is to set up a contrast between acts performed on behalf of deceased kin, those to whom filial *pietas* is due on the part of the son, and cult appropriate for those who are sons of YHVH.

To summarize: the Deuteronomic legislation on funerary practices and cults of the dead was part of a general strategy of shifting the emotional focus of the religious life of the people, and therefore ultimately their allegiance, away from the lineage system with its immemorial practices and beliefs toward the state and its institutions. The idea was to undermine certain deeply ingrained and widely accepted beliefs by striking at the social practices — rituals of reenactment, commemorative ceremonies, or funerary practices — that embodied and sustained the beliefs. Commemorating and communing with the dead was a powerful means of preserving that continuity with the past without which a society cannot easily preserve its identity. That it was the norm rather than the exception we gather from the rhetorical question addressed to Isaiah: "Should not a people consult their ancestral shades, the dead, on behalf of the living?" (Isa 8:19). The promise to the ancestors, prominent in Deuteronomy, could be read as an alternative "orthodox" linkage with the past. The same could be said for the insistence that the God of Israel is a God of the living, not the dead, that he is "the living God" (*'ĕlohîm ḥayyim,* Deut 5:26; 1 Sam 17:26, 36; Jer 10:10; 23:36).[4]

---

4. In a dispute with Sadducean opponents, Jesus cited Exod 3:6 ("I am the God of your father, the God of Abraham, the God of Isaac, and the God of Jacob") to prove that God was a God of the living, not the dead. The same scriptural argument occurs in Philo's treatise on Abraham (*Abraham* 50–55).

The Deuteronomic prohibitions are not limited to funerary customs. Deut 18:9-14 lists eight religiously abhorrent practices (*tôʿēbôt*, "abominations") represented as foreign and contrasted with prophecy understood to be the form of mediation proper and unique to Israel. We know of course, and presumably the author also knew, that prophecy was not unique to Israel and that the rival practices were not exclusively foreign, but the contrast is deliberate and calculated. It implies that the practices listed are presented under the rubric of mediation between this world and the other world — the world inhabited by gods, spirits, and the dead — as is apparent also in the use of verbs of asking, inquiring, and listening throughout this section (18:9-22). The point can be verified by a brief look at how the eight practices function. In doing so we should keep in mind that English equivalents of the terminology used in this list will generally be no more than approximations and that there will probably be overlap in the semantic range of these designations.

1. The list begins with "passing one's son or daughter through the fire," that is, the cremation of live infants (18:10a). This prohibition seems at first sight to be in a category of its own, but we notice that more often than not where the practice is condemned it is linked with necromantic rites of one kind or another (Lev 20:1-6; 2 Kgs 17:17; 21:6). This crematory practice was also associated with Molech (Lev 20:3; Jer 32:35), a chthonic deity whose domain was the underworld. The Sorceress (alias Jerusalem) denounced in vitriolic language in Isa 57:3-13 is accused of sacrificing children (v. 5) but also consorting with the dead (vv. 6, 13), offering cult to Molech, and sending her envoys down to him in Sheol (v. 9). Far from being foreign, the ritual burning of infants was part of the national Yahvistic cult (e.g., Isa 30:33; Ezek 20:25-26) and was practiced in, or at least in connection with, the Jerusalem temple (Lev 20:3; Ezek 23:39). It was no doubt on account of its associations with the underworld that the Deuteronomic author lists it with forms of mediation between the living and the dead (Heider 1985; 1992 *Anchor Bible Dictionary* 4:895-98).

2. *qōsēm qĕsāmîm*, usually translated "augur," "practitioner of augury." Neighboring lands, including Philistia, Ammon, and wherever Balaam came from had their augurs, but so did Israel and Judah. The practice could involve mediumistic contact with the dead, and though dead ancestors are not explicitly mentioned, it is to their own departed kin that the

common people would have turned in the first place. The elite had other options. According to Ezek 21:26, one of the forms of divination or augury practiced by Nebuchadrezzar, definitely a member of the elite, was by *tĕrāpîm*. The meaning of this term has been much debated. While it could have meant different things at different times and in different places, scholars generally agree that it can refer to a physical representation of an ancestor, one that could be used for oracular purposes or as a means of receiving a communication from the world of the dead that the *tĕrāpîm* inhabit, a kind of ventriloquistic medium (van der Toorn 1990: 203-22). To take once again a more familiar example: Saul consulted a professional medium to conjure up Samuel's ghost (1 Sam 28:3-25). The woman is called a "mistress of the spirits" *(baʿălat ʾôb)*, not a female augur *(qōsemet)*, but Saul asks her to do an augury *(qsm)* for him by means of a ghost, which she does.

3. *mĕʿônēn*, usually translated "soothsayer" or "sorcerer." This, too, was a specialization that, according to the biblical texts, was found in Israel as well as in other lands (e.g., Lev 19:26; Judg 9:37; 2 Kgs 21:6; Isa 2:6). The word has been variously explained as referring originally either to rain making, or to the evil eye, or to the humming or chanting of spells. But if *mĕʿônēn*, a participial form in the Poʿel conjugation, derives from a verbal stem ʿ*nn* meaning "appear," "cause to appear," the preferred option in the dictionaries, a connection with conjuring up and communicating with the dead would be indicated. A special case, referred to earlier, is the denunciation of the ʿ*ônĕnâ* ("sorceress") and her offspring in Isa 57:3-13, reminiscent of the "outsider woman" *(ʾiššâ zārâ/nokriyyâ)* in Proverbs 1–9. The enumeration of the activities attributed to this personified female, including necromancy and sexually explicit rites, would be more appropriately encapsulated in the designation "sorceress" than "soothsayer," and that is in fact the term usually applied to her in the translations and commentaries.

4. *mĕnaḥēš*. The only specific contextual clue to the meaning of this term is the allusion to Joseph's cup, which he used to obtain information by magic (Gen 44:5). The precise technique is not apparent; it perhaps involved inspecting the lees or residue of the wine, the ancient Egyptian equivalent of reading tea leaves. Whatever it was, it was only one of numerous ways of looking for signs in the immediate environment. We are told that Balaam, of uncertain repute in biblical texts and postbiblical tradition, was convinced that Israel was blessed and therefore no longer went

looking for chance omens (Num 24:1). On a mission to the Israelite court at the time of the Omri dynasty, a group of Syrian emissaries were on the alert for omens that their plea for mercy to the king would be heard (1 Kgs 20:33). Though not very informative, these instances suggest that the *mĕnaḥēš* was a specialist in divination and the interpretation of omens. The practice was, in any case, condemned, and therefore presumably in vogue, in Israel as it was elsewhere (e.g., Lev 19:26; 2 Kgs 17:17; 21:6). This is one specialization that does not seem to have any mortuary connotations, though the database is too exiguous to justify excluding consultation with the dead. In view of the chthonic aspects of snakes and snake cults, it is tempting to make a connection between the *mĕnaḥēš*, a participle in the Piel conjugation of the verb *nḥš*, and *nāḥāš*, "snake." Perhaps, then, the Woman in the Garden of Eden wishes us to understand that the Snake was deceiving her by magical means (Gen 3:13).

5. *mĕkaššēp*, "sorcerer," "magician." The related verb *kšp* denotes a strong kind of magical practice, capable of inflicting physical and psychic harm. In a Ugaritic incantation text describing an exorcism, an abjuration is directed in the course of an exorcism against the *kšpm* who have afflicted a possessed youth (Avishur 1981: 13-25). Like most practitioners of these specialized occupations, the practitioner of *kĕšāpîm* can be male or female, but the biblical associations are generally with a female individual (Jezebel, 2 Kgs 9:22) or a city represented as female (Nineveh, Nah 3:4; Babylon, Isa 47:9, 12; Dan 2:2). The death penalty in the Covenant Code applies only to the sorceress *(mĕkaššēpâ,* Exod 22:17; cf. Akk. *kaššaptu),* and sorcery is frequently linked with sexual deviance on the part of the female (2 Kgs 9:22; Isa 47:8-9; Mal 3:5). All of this could of course simply reflect the prejudicial view of women of frequent occurrence in biblical texts. None of these texts makes an explicit association with mortuary cults, but the diatribe against the *'ônĕnâ* (the sorceress) in Isa 57:3-13 does make the connection, as we have seen, and there can have been little if any practical difference between the *'ônĕnâ* and the *mĕkaššēpâ*.

6. *ḥōbēr ḥeber*, "caster of a spell" (NRSV, NEB, JPS) or "snake charmer" (Ps 58:6; Sir 12:13). The verb *(ḥbr)* has the meaning of binding, in this instance by magical means, by putting a hex on an individual. It occurs only with reference to Babylonian practice (Isa 47:9, 12), which is probably also reflected in Ezekiel's detailed but obscure denunciation of the practices of Judean female magicians (Ezek 13:17-23); it was one of several indications that in the last years of the Kingdom of Judah prophecy

was losing out to magical and necromantic practices of different sorts. But there is no obvious connection with necromancy in any of this.

7. *šōʾēl ʾôb vĕyiddĕʿōnî,* "one who consults the spirits of the dead." The formulation makes it clear that the *šōʾēl* is the human medium and, wherever the terms occur, the *ʾôb* and *yiddĕʿōnî* are the spirits of the dead, not the human agents, a point sometimes obscured in modern translations. The so-called Holiness Code prohibits "turning to," that is, having recourse to, an *ʾôb* or *yiddĕʿōnî* (Lev 19:31; 20:6), or "whoring after" them (20:6), language pointing once again to the sex-death connection. The penalty of death is threatened against anyone, male or female, who has a spirit of the dead in them or, in other words, is regarded as being in touch with or possessed by a ghost (Lev 20:27). In the story of the encounter between Saul and the ghost of Samuel (1 Sam 28:3-25), the comment that Saul had "put aside" or "cut off" the *ʾôbôt* and *yiddĕʿōnîm* (vv. 3, 9) does not oblige us to identify those expelled as witches and warlocks. The Historian would have thought of it as a campaign of spirit-cleansing that would also of course have affected their controls. The female medium is, moreover, described as a *baʿălat ʾôb,* one who commands the spirits, a female shaman.

At a later point of the history, the notice that Manasseh made *ʾôbôt* and *yiddĕʿōnîm* (2 Kgs 21:6 = 2 Chr 33:6) has led to a similar misunderstanding. These would be objects, probably statues, representing the spirits of the dead, similar to the *tĕrāpîm* and assorted cult objects Josiah removed (2 Kgs 23:24), as also of the Roman *lares et penates.* Saul's spirit-cleansing operation as described by the Historian would therefore have consisted in objects representing and symbolizing the dead, dead ancestors in the first place, and in putting the mediums who manipulated them out of business.

The attempt to establish more precisely the meaning of *ʾôb* and *yiddĕʿōnî* has focused on etymologies, not always a reliable guide to meaning. The former has been interpreted in the light of the hapax legomenon *ʾôbôt* in Job 32:19 referring to wineskins, with the idea that a wineskin or bottle was used by the medium *qua* ventriloquist (the LXX translates *ʾôb* with *engastrimythos,* meaning literally "one who speaks in the stomach," i.e., a ventriloquist). On the basis of Semitic and non-Semitic cognates, others have connected the term with a ritual pit from which the dead were thought to speak, a hypothesis that goes back to van Hoonaker toward the end of the nineteenth century (van Hoonaker 1897/98: 157-60). The word has also been derived from *ʾāb,* "father," with reference to ancestors (Lust

1974: 133-42; Spronk 1986: 252). The theory that seems to be currently in favor, however, derives the word from the Arabic cognate *'āba*, "to return," thus giving *'ôb* the meaning of a revenant, a ghost. But none of these derivations is secure.

There has been much less debate about the *yiddĕʿōnî* since scholars have generally agreed that the word derives from the common verb *ydʿ*, "to know." The *yiddĕʿōnîm* are therefore "the Knowing Ones," those from whom information otherwise unavailable, especially concerning the future, could be solicited. In Isa 8:19 they are identified as *'ĕlōhîm*, "gods," referring to chthonic deities who were consulted especially in critical situations, and in Isa 19:3 they are listed with the *'iṭṭîm*, the ghosts (cf. Akk. *eṭemmu*) that the Egyptians will consult in vain.

The fact that "The Knowing Ones" are always paired with "Those Who Return" suggests that these designations functioned as a kind of hendiadys, signifying the spirits or shades of the dead who could be induced to return, or who returned spontaneously, and could communicate with the living and impart information not otherwise obtainable.

8. *dōrēš 'el-hammētîm*, "necromancer." This last designation does not occur elsewhere, though Isa 8:19 speaks of consulting (verbal stem *drš*) the dead on behalf of the living. It does not represent a specialization distinct from the ones preceding it, and it may have been intended to serve as a summary.

6

To summarize: The Deuteronomic law code may be read as a political document one of whose aims was to impose the official state cult of YHVH to the exclusion of competitors. The artifactual and inscriptional information accumulated over the last century or so, combined with a close and critical reading of the biblical texts, presents us with a picture of a highly diversified religious life among the populations of Syria and Palestine inclusive of the Hebrew-speaking kingdoms. In these kingdoms there were, in addition to YHVH, gods imported from other lands (e.g., the Phoenician cities), indigenous gods and goddesses, and a cult of ancestors that the representatives of the official cult have done their best to cover up.

For those who drafted the Deuteronomic legislation it was essential to combat allegiance to the kinship network, and one of the ways to accomplish this was by legislating against the veneration of ancestors that formed the religious and emotional core of household and clan. The importance of these measures can be gauged by their situation at the beginning, at the end, and in the middle of the legal compilation (Deut 12:5-7; 14:1-2; 18:9-14; 26:14). The so-called Deuteronomistic History also denounces practices promoting the veneration of and communication with the dead, including and especially ancestors. We note that the frequent reforms carried out by rulers deal exclusively with the removal of cultic abuses, never with the social abuses denounced in several of the prophetic books. By the same token, the Historian explains national disaster in terms not of social injustice but of heterodox religious practices, among which mortuary cults had a prominent place.

This is not to imply that the imposition of the exclusive cult of YHVH as the state religion was dictated by *purely* political considerations, much less a cynical concern for *raison d'état,* or that it constituted a Deuteronomic innovation. Devotion to YHVH alone had roots in older tradition; it seems to have been the driving force for some of the "primitives" associated with Elijah, Elisha, Jonadab, and no doubt others involved in the struggle against the devotees of the Phoenician Baal and Asherah in the ninth century. But it was the Deuteronomic centralization policy that marked the decisive first step in the direction of a monotheistic faith and its corresponding expressions in worship, and the argument presented here is that this was one aspect of political centralization. In other words, an important impulse toward the concentration of religious allegiance and religious practice in one supreme being and in one location was the aspiration toward a unified and centralized political system. The delegitimation and (at least in theory) decommissioning of local centers of worship with their cults also implied the concentration of the many local manifestations of YHVH — comparable to the many local manifestations of Baal — into one central hypostasis: "Hear, O Israel, YHVH our God is one YHVH" (Deut 6:4).

The Deuteronomic campaign against traditional family and clan religious thinking and practice should lead us to move beyond the conventional wisdom that excludes belief in meaningful postmortem existence from discussions of "the religion of Israel." While we have to wait for the book of Daniel (12:2-3) in the second century B.C. for the first unambiguous statement of belief in the resurrection of the dead, or of some of the dead, we can pick up intimations of an ongoing life with God arising out of the experience of worship (e.g., Ps 73:21-26) or the peremptory demand for justice (e.g., Job), or even as a result of external influences, as has been suggested from time to time. This subject is in need of still further reflection and study.

XII

"We Pay No Heed to Heavenly Voices":
The "End of Prophecy" and the Formation of the Canon

On that day Rabbi Eliezer brought forward all the arguments in the world, but they were not accepted. He said to them: "If the Halakhah [the proper decision] agrees with me, let this carob tree prove it." Thereupon the carob tree was uprooted a hundred cubits from its place; some say, four hundred cubits. They replied: "No proof may be brought from a carob tree." Then he said: "If the Halakhah agrees with me, let this stream of water prove it." Thereupon the stream of water flowed backward. They replied: "No proof may be brought from a stream of water." Then he said: "If the Halakhah agrees with me, let the walls of the schoolhouse prove it." Thereupon the walls of the schoolhouse began to totter. But Rabbi Joshua rebuked them and said: "When scholars are engaged in halakhic dispute, what concern is it of yours?" Thus the walls did not topple, in honor of Rabbi Joshua, but neither did they return to their upright position, in honor of Rabbi Eliezer; still today they stand inclined. Then he said: "If the Halakhah agrees with me, let it be proved from heaven." Thereupon a heavenly voice was heard saying: "Why do you dispute with Rabbi Eliezer? The Halakhah always agrees with him." But Rabbi Joshua arose and said (Deut 30:12): "It is not in heaven" (Deut 30:11-14). What did he mean by that? Rabbi Jeremiah replied: "The Torah has already been given at Mount Sinai [and is thus no longer in heaven]. We pay no heed to any heavenly voice, because already at Mount Sinai You wrote in the Torah (Exod 23:2): 'One must incline after the majority.'"

> *Rabbi Nathan met the prophet Elijah and asked him: "What did the Holy One, blessed be He, do in that hour?" He replied: "God smiled and said: My children have defeated me, My children have defeated me."*
>
> b. Baba Meṣi'a 59a-b

1

The debate between these combative rabbis was about a relatively insignificant matter, whether an oven with an unusual construction was subject to the laws of clean and unclean, but it raises some not insignificant issues about the source of religious authority. History instructs us that once firmly established, organized religions seek to preserve and perpetuate themselves by appealing to a sacred, normative past and excluding the possibility of the new. Truth has been given once and for all and need only to be transmitted. God has said all that he will ever say, and therefore prophetic revelations uttered in the name of the deity are no longer either necessary or desirable. In a sense, God is not permitted to intervene once the law has been laid down. In a textual religion like Judaism the transmitted truth, the *depositum fidei,* is contained in writings. These writings are not subject to alteration, but the catch is that they do require interpretation, and it is therefore on the field of the interpretation of sacred texts, especially legal texts, that the battle for and against religious innovation has always been fought in Judaism, Christianity, and Islam.

But first some facts about "canon." The idea of a scriptural canon arose in a Christian not a Jewish milieu, and the word itself, as referring to a catalogue of biblical books, shows up no earlier than the fourth century, in *The Decrees of the Council of Nicaea* and the *Festal Letter* of Athanasius, the former around A.D. 350, the latter seventeen years later. Lists of biblical books were in circulation in Christian circles earlier, but no comparable compilation is attested in Jewish sources prior to a well-known passage in the Babylonian Talmud listing titles of books and their authors (*b. Baba Batra* 14b-15a).

Many of the traditional ideas about the formation of the canon, including the role of the "men of the Great Assembly" and the "Council of Jamnia/Yavneh," are now known to be anachronistic even if they contain some grains of historical truth. Nevertheless, some texts were regarded as

193

authoritative during the Second Temple period and were deposited for safe-keeping in the temple archives. The much later report that Nehemiah established a library containing historical, prophetic, and liturgical material is unverifiable but not implausible (2 Macc 2:13). The law book of Moses was to be deposited in the sanctuary beside the ark of the covenant (Deut 31:26), and the priest Hilkiah is reported to have found such a book in the temple during the reign of Josiah (2 Kgs 22:8). If this information is not historical, it may still reflect practice obtaining at the time of writing.

Canonicity therefore has a long prehistory, but much ambiguity and uncertainty remains. Textual fixity is rightly considered an important criterion, but as late as the production of the nonbiblical Qumran scrolls it appears that there were segments of Judaism that thought of themselves as operating within what can be called anachronistically a canonical process rather than working with a fixed canon already in place. No doubt both the Qumran community and early Christian groups considered themselves to be in possession of revelations of overwhelming importance that were new even if presented as derived from existing authoritative texts.

At any rate, the process eventuating in the biblical canons now in use (Jewish, Protestant, Catholic, Eastern Orthodox, etc.) was long and complex and can be reconstructed only very tentatively. In this essay we will be concerned with only one aspect of this historical trajectory, namely, the neutralization and redefinition of prophecy as an essential corollary of canonicity.

The familiar passage about the canon in Josephus's treatise against Apion (*Against Apion* 1.37-41) will serve as a convenient point of departure. In Henry St. John Thackeray's translation it runs as follows:

> It therefore naturally, or rather necessarily, follows (seeing that with us it is not open to everybody to write the records, and that there is no discrepancy in what is written, seeing that, on the contrary, the prophets alone had this privilege, obtaining their knowledge of the most remote and ancient history through the inspiration which they owed to God, and committed to writing a clear account of the events of their own time just as they occurred) — it follows, I say, that we do not possess myriads of inconsistent books, conflicting with each other. Our books, those that are justly accredited, are but two and twenty, and contain the record of all time.

> Of these, five are the books of Moses, comprising the laws and the

traditional history from the birth of man down to the death of the lawgiver. This period falls only a little short of three thousand years. From
the death of Moses until Artaxerxes, who succeeded Xerxes as king of
Persia, the prophets subsequent to Moses wrote the history of the
events of their own times in thirteen books. The remaining four books
contain hymns to God and precepts for the conduct of human life.

From Artaxerxes to our own time the complete history has been
written, but has not been deemed worthy of equal credit with the earlier
records, because of the failure of the exact succession of the prophets.

In this passage Josephus, in his orotund and self-important way, gives us
something of a list, though no book is named. There are twenty-two
books; no more, no less. The first five were written by Moses and cover the
period from creation to the author's death. (Later Jewish tradition will
avoid the inconvenience of Moses writing a circumstantial account of his
own death and burial by assigning the last verses of Deuteronomy to
Joshua.) The next thirteen take the story from Moses' death to Artaxerxes,
presumably Artaxerxes I nicknamed Long Arm (465-424 B.C.), and are of
prophetic authorship. The final four contain liturgical and didactic-
moralistic material. According to the opening statement, all twenty-two
books were written by prophets. In fact, what makes the difference between the myriads of inconsistent books of the Greeks and the strictly limited number of duly accredited *(dikaiōs pepisteumena)* compositions of the
Jews is the requirement among the latter that only prophets may compile
official records since they alone enjoy the privilege of divine inspiration
(epipnoia).

Another peculiar feature of Josephus's list is that the corpus consists
essentially in a historical record. The last four (Psalms, Proverbs, Ecclesiastes, and Canticles) comprise something of an appendix, but the remaining
Hagiographa (Ruth, Chronicles, Ezra-Nehemiah, Esther, Job, and Daniel)
are subsumed under the rubric of history. Furthermore, the composition
of inspired and therefore accredited writings is limited chronologically,
coming to an end in the fifth century B.C. To a fixed number of "canonical"
books, therefore, there corresponds a "canonical" epoch, one that ends
with the failure of the prophetic succession *(diadochē)*.

Clearly, to begin with, this presentation of the literary patrimony of
the Jews is polemical and tendentious. One of Josephus's principal aims in
writing the treatise was to refute Apion and others who had criticized his

historical writing and questioned his arguments for the great antiquity of the Jewish people. This led him to contrast the records of his own people with those of the Greeks, which he described as self-contradictory, often mendacious, and vitiated by their failure to keep public records (*dēmosia grammata*). But it is obvious that his contrast between the myriad of Greek books produced without quality control and the strictly limited number of Jewish compositions is not only unfair but absurd, for he is contrasting the entire corpus of Greek literature with a small selection from the literary output of the Jews. It would have made better sense to compare the Homeric poems as in some sense canonical with the Jewish texts he catalogues — both incidentally with twenty-two components — but this would not have served his purpose.

The cutting off of the prophetic succession in the reign of Artaxerxes I can be explained with reference to Josephus's chronology of the biblical period in his *Antiquities of the Jews* in which he paraphrases the biblical books in what he took to be the correct chronological sequence. For Josephus, Artaxerxes is the Ahasuerus (Asueros) of Esth 1:1 and passim. The story recorded in this biblical book, which Josephus retells at inordinate length as a piece of history writing contemporaneous with the events recorded in it (*Antiquities* 11.184-296), concludes the biblical part of his narrative. This suggests that the idea of the end of prophecy derives from the prior acceptance of certain books as scriptural or canonical. Later Jewish tradition will justify the canonicity of Esther either by elevating the heroine to prophetic status (*Seder 'Olam Rabbah* 21) or by identifying Mordecai with the prophet Malachi and making him the author of the book (*b. Megilla* 15a). Neither of these options occurred to Josephus, though they would have been consonant with his approach in *Against Apion*.

In keeping with his understanding of the Jewish literary patrimony, Josephus from this point on refrains from using the term *prophētēs* of any individual who otherwise might have seemed to merit it, though he does not hesitate to brand contemporary failed messiahs as false prophets, *pseudoprophētai*. In speaking of his own prophetic gifts, opportunely discovered or activated as he awaited capture and possible execution in the cave at Jotapata in the Galilee, he is careful to note that they derive from his priestly descent and status, his exegetical skill, and his expertise in dream interpretation (*Jewish War* 3.351-54). While therefore remaining faithful to his views on the prophetic succession, he manages to insinuate his own qualifications as continuator of that tradition. Nevertheless, he refrains from speaking of himself directly as a prophet.

2

The idea of prophecy in the past tense is attested on numerous occasions in Tannaitic and Amoraic rabbinic texts. Rabbi Abba states that "after the last prophets Haggai, Zechariah, and Malachi had died, the Holy Spirit departed from Israel but they still availed themselves of the *bat qôl*" (*b. Yoma* 9b; *b. Soṭah* 48b; *t. Soṭah* 13.2-4). In this context the Holy Spirit (*rûaḥ haqqōdeš*) is identified with the "spirit of prophecy" *(rûaḥ hannĕbû'â)*, and the *bat qôl* (heavenly voice; literally, echo) is the standard surrogate for prophetic mediation now no longer available (Foerster 1961/62: 37-49; Schäfer 1970: 304-14; 1972: 23-26). The cessation of prophecy with the death of the last prophet, Malachi, makes a reasonably good fit with the reign of Artaxerxes as a terminus ad quem, especially in view of the drastic foreshortening of the two centuries of Persian rule in later Jewish historiography (*Seder 'Olam Rabbah* §30). It was evidently established at any early date that Haggai, Zechariah, and Malachi came at the end of the prophetic series (*sôp hannĕbî'îm;* see *b. Baba Batra* 14b).

An alternative opinion placed the terminus at the destruction of the First Temple when, as Abdimi of Haifa noted, prophecy was taken from the prophets and given to the sages (*b. Baba Batra* 12a). This view is consistent with the topos of the five things present in the First and absent from the Second Temple. There are different versions of the list, but they all include the Holy Spirit (*b. Yoma* 21b; *b. Soṭah* 48a). It resulted that in the post-prophetic dispensation not even the holiest and most learned rabbis such as Hillel or Akiva could claim inspiration by the Holy Spirit, and not even the most charismatic such as Hanina ben Dosa could claim to be a prophet.[1] Inspiration and guidance for living were not to be sought in miracles, oracular utterances, and divine voices, but were entrusted exclusively

---

1. John R. Levison (1997: 46-47) understands *t. Soṭah* 13:2-4 to imply that Hillel and Samuel the Small did exceptionally receive the Holy Spirit on account of their righteousness, but the point is that they were worthy to receive the Holy Spirit and would have done so had the situation permitted it, but it did not since the Holy Spirit had departed from Israel with the death of the last prophets. On Hanina and his refusal of the title "prophet," quoting Amos 7:14, see Vermes 1972: 28-50; 1973: 51-64.

to the sages and their teaching — a point made famously in the dispute between Rabbi Eliezer and Rabbi Joshua about the oven of Akhan quoted at
the head of this essay.

The thesis about the end of prophecy would also have served to
counter the Christian claim to have inherited the prophetic mantle from
Judaism, a claim implicit in several New Testament texts (e.g., Acts 2:1-21)
and advanced by Justin in the second century (*Dialogue with Trypho* §52).
We do not know who the third-century Amora Rabbi Yohanan had in
mind with his dictum that, since the destruction of the temple, prophecy
had been taken from the prophets and given to fools and children (*b. Baba
Batra* 12a). But he could have been thinking of Christians, and the saying is
in fact curiously reminiscent of the so-called Johannine logion (Matt 11:25)
in which revelation is vouchsafed not to the wise but to babes and suck-
lings. Scholars have occasionally argued that the thesis aimed to counter
the claims of the first Christians that the Holy Spirit, and therefore the
spirit of prophecy, had passed to them (e.g., Urbach 1945/46: 1-11).

It may be possible to trace this idea of prophecy in the past tense
back much earlier than Josephus and the rabbis. We should first exclude
from consideration complaints about the absence of prophetic guidance of
the kind we would expect to hear in times of disorientation and crisis (e.g.,
Lam 2:9; Ps 74:9; The Prayer of Azariah 1:15). The author of 1 Maccabees
has it that at the rededication of the temple in 164 B.C. the priests disman-
tled the desecrated altar and stored the stones until there should come a
prophet to tell them what to do with them (1 Macc 4:46). This could also
refer to a *temporary* absence of prophetic guidance, in the same way that
Ezra 2:63 implies the temporary absence of priestly guidance. But the situation is different some years later when, during the campaigns of the Syrian general Bacchides, we are told that there was such distress in Israel as
had not been since the time prophets ceased to appear among them
(1 Macc 9:27). This is a programmatic statement about a situation of depri-
vation beginning at a definite time in the past, and therefore implying a
qualitative difference between the prophetic past and the nonprophetic
present.

We need hardly labor the point that this redefinition of prophecy as
essentially a past phenomenon is an ideological construct designed to sustain the worldview and hegemonic position of a particular class. It does
not describe the actual state of affairs and therefore does not decide the
question whether prophecy actually continued in existence, to what extent,

and under what forms. In any group in which claims for legitimacy and authority must be made in religious terms, control of the "redemptive media," and therefore of the means of mediating religious guidance toward salvation, translates very readily into social and political control. It is characteristic of biblical prophecy to claim the right to speak and be heard outside officially sanctioned channels. Hence the relegation of prophecy of this kind to the past would, if successful, remove a powerful irritant for those whose authority rested on a traditional basis, especially the basis of a written law, the right to interpret which they reserve to themselves.

As a matter of historical fact as opposed to theory, prophetic activity did in fact continue after the time when, according to the thesis, it should have passed from the scene. Some of the older biblical commentators spoke of prophecy drying up after the Babylonian exile, but they omitted to explain why it dried up then rather at some other time. In Judaism charismatic and prophetic phenomena continued throughout the rabbinic period down into the Middle Ages and beyond in counterpoint to the repeated assertion of the demise of prophecy. Philip Alexander has provided examples of the solicitation and reception of direct divine communication, ecstatic phenomena including glossolalia and visions throughout this long period. He also notes how the Oral Law involved a doctrine of ongoing revelation disguised as traditional Sinaitic teaching (Alexander 1995: 414-33). The "end of prophecy" thesis cannot therefore be explained as an account of what actually happened to prophecy, but it is itself a historical datum calling for an explanation in the context of wide-ranging political and social changes in the late biblical period. To grasp these changes and their effects may bring us closer to understanding how the idea of canonical texts emerged within the biblical period itself.

3

We begin with Deuteronomy, which even on a fairly superficial reading betrays the intention of being what we might call anachronistically a canonical document. It contains a strict injunction against adding to it or subtracting from it (4:2; 12:32), the ruler must have a copy near him (17:18-20), and it is to be deposited in the temple and read from in public session on certain stated occasions (31:10-13, 26), a practice that we are told was followed (2 Kgs 23:1-3; Neh 7:73-9:5; 13:1-3). The book, inclusive of the law, is therefore presented as an official, public document. Deuteronomy is also the first biblical text to speak of "the Torah" or "the book of the Torah" as a single, complex entity. Prior to Deuteronomy, a *tôrâ* was an individual stipulation of law, or a decision handed down by one authorized to do so, or a piece of advice or instruction; after Deuteronomy, the individual stipulations are referred to as "words of the Torah" *(dibrê hattôrâ),* never as *tôrôt* (plural). Deuteronomy, finally, is presented in the form of a last will and testament left to his people by Moses on the last day of his life. The contents of the law show that it was intended to provide a comprehensive and binding blueprint for the commonwealth to be established (or re-established) after settlement (or resettlement) in Canaan (Judah). It therefore defines, inter alia, the scope and function of essential public offices, including the monarchy, the judiciary, the priesthood, and the prophets, and legislates on such important matters of concern as qualifications for membership and suffrage in the community.

What, then, does Deuteronomy have to say about prophecy? By speaking of it in the section dealing with the organs of statecraft (16:18–18:22), the authors betray their concern to confine it within the institutional grid of their ideal commonwealth (18:15-22). In contrast to the foreign "abominations" listed in 18:9-14 — all of which were, however, practiced in Israel — prophecy is presented as a uniquely Israelite phenomenon. Prophecy is also a charismatic phenomenon, by virtue of being "raised up" by God. But the prophetic office is now concerned primarily with the law, revealing divine commands rather than mysteries about the future, and therefore prolonging the activity and ministry of Moses as lawgiver. So redefined, prophecy had its origin at Sinai/Horeb in response to the appeal for mediation. Where Deuteronomy speaks of other aspects of prophecy, especially predicting the future, the tone is unmistakably deterrent. Unauthorized prophets and, a fortiori, those who speak in the name of deities other than YHVH, are subject to the death penalty (18:20; cf. 13:1-5). Prophets of this kind are bracketed with dreamers (13:1), and those whose predictions turn out to be mistaken automatically lose their prophetic credentials (18:21-22).

Whatever conclusion is reached on the origins of Deuteronomism and the authorship of Deuteronomy, a subject of interminable debate, the book presupposes the existence of scribes skilled in the drafting and interpreting of legal material. Their role can be considered a response to historical exigencies arising in the course of the history of the kingdoms and the postdisaster Judean community. The fall of the Kingdom of Samaria in the late eighth century B.C. would have intensified the need among the survivors to preserve the common patrimony, including the legal patrimony, and to do so in writing. Proverbs 25–29 is attributed to "the men of Hezekiah," the first Judean ruler without a counterpart in the Kingdom of Samaria, and a rabbinic tradition (*b. Baba Batra* 15a) expands the scope of their activity to take in the compiling and editing of Isaiah's sayings, and even the composition of Canticles and Ecclesiastes (Qoheleth). At about the same time, incidentally, the Homeric poems were being put together, and a movement to preserve the national heritage is attested for Mesopotamia and Egypt.

Some scholars have suggested that an early draft of Deuteronomy may have been part of this scribal activity under Hezekiah. While this possibility cannot be excluded, the connections with Josiah (640-609 B.C.) and the religious reforms carried out during his reign have for a long time (since the early years of the nineteenth century) been much more in evidence, though this would not prove that the book was composed at that time. The roughly quarter of a century between the death of Josiah and the fall of Jerusalem witnessed a crisis of confidence in prophecy and was therefore a time of uncertainty and danger for prophets of either the supportive or the critical kind represented, respectively, by Hananiah and Jeremiah (Jeremiah 28). One aspect of this crisis can be traced to hostility between law scribes and prophets critical of the political establishment. If the point of view of the law scribes can be read into what Deuteronomy has to say about prophets, the prophetic reaction is expressed in disparaging allusions in Jeremiah to "handlers of the law" and to scribes who, confident in their own wisdom as custodians of the law, falsify it with their lying pens (Jer 2:8; 8:8-9). The contrast in Jer 8:8-9 between the alleged wisdom of the law scribes and appeal to the word of YHVH, that is, to the prophetic word, points to a conflict of claims to authority in the religious sphere between prophets and Max Weber's "stratum of learned men ritually oriented to a law book" (Weber 1952: 395).

Evidence for this conflict of claims emerges more clearly when we turn to the much debated issue of Deuteronomistic editing of prophetic books. Starting out from those superscriptions to books that date the prophet's activity by reference to named kings, especially to synchronized rulers in both kingdoms (Hosea and Amos), some scholars postulate a Deuteronomistic "first edition" of the Book of the Twelve composed of (at least) Hosea, Amos, Micah, and Zephaniah (Nogalski 1993). Others have speculated that adherents of the school put together a compilation of prophetic books as a supplement to the History shortly after the fall of Jerusalem (Freedman 1963: 250-65; 1987: 29-37). This hypothesis would have the advantage of providing one explanation for the absence from the History of the canonical prophets (the so-called *Prophetenschweigen* issue), but it is not supported by evidence currently available, and there may be better explanations for the Historian's nonmention of the prophets to whom books are attributed. Most scholars would nevertheless concede that there are indications of Deuteronom(ist)ic editing in several of the prophetic books, most clearly in the prose sermons in Jeremiah.

The motivation for this editorial activity in Jeremiah appears to have been to make him over into a spokesman for the ideology of the Deuteronomistic school and a "prophet like Moses" in keeping with Deut 18:15-20. It is also possible that the editors thought of Jeremiah as the last in the prophetic succession just as Moses was the first; this hypothesis would help to explain why the final section of the History (2 Kgs 24:18–25:30) also serves to round out Jeremiah's prophetic career (Jeremiah 52). The close parallel between the call of Moses and that of Jeremiah is noted in all the commentaries, and extends to the forty years of prophetic activity assigned editorially to Jeremiah (Jer 1:2-3 corresponding to 627-587 B.C.). The prose sermons refer quite often to "his [YHVH's] servants the prophets," who throughout the history of the nation preached observance of the law and threatened disaster as the inevitable consequence of nonobservance (Jer 7:25; 25:4; 26:5; 29:19; 35:15; 44:4). The same expression (*'ăbādâv hannĕbî'îm*) appears often in the History, serving to encapsulate the school theory about the Mosaic-prophetic succession. Use of this language connotes a retrospective view of prophecy, suggesting that prophecy of this kind is essentially a past phenomenon.

The Deuteronomistic redefinition of prophecy can be traced at several other points in the Latter Prophets compilation. One of the prophets surprisingly absent from the History is Amos. The one biographical passage in the book (Amos 7:10-17), in which he predicted the violent end of Jeroboam II (either the individual or the dynasty or both), contrasts sharply with the equally brief account of the reign of this ruler in 2 Kgs 14:23-29, in which Jeroboam is the savior of his people. In this account the only prophet named is Jonah ben Amittai, who, unlike Amos, came out in support of the king's successful military campaigns. Then, out of the blue, the Historian insists that "YHVH had not spoken to the effect that he would blot out Israel's name from under the sky" (2 Kgs 14:27). The statement reads like a refutation of a prophetic pronouncement and is certainly polemical, and the only prophet around at that time who made such a prediction was Amos (Amos 8:2; 9:8a) (Crüsemann 1971: 57-63). This suggests that Amos was omitted from the History because in the judgment of the Historian he did not have the right message for that time and, in general, did not fit the profile laid down by the Deuteronomists.

The fact that Hosea also condemned the Jehu dynasty (Hos 1:4), for which the Historian shows considerable sympathy on account of its at-least-initial anti-Baalist militancy, may help to explain why he, too, is passed over in silence by the Historian (Begg 1986: 41-53). Another absentee from the History is Micah, who pronounced a categoric oracle of doom against Jerusalem: the city will be turned into a heap of ruins, a plowed field, a wooded height (Mic 3:12). But when this unfulfilled prophecy was quoted at Jeremiah's trial a century later, it was interpreted not as an oracle of doom but as a call to repentance addressed to Hezekiah (Jer 26:16-19). The trial narrative in which the elders opportunely cited this text is the sequel to Jeremiah's temple sermon (7:1–8:3), whose Deuteronomistic character is unmistakable. This, therefore, appears to be a case where an unconditional announcement of disaster is reinterpreted "deuteronomically" as conditional on repentance. We recall that repentance (*těšûbâ*, "turning") is a major concern for the postdestruction Deuteronomists.

To take one final example: it could easily escape attention that Isaiah 1–39 manifests the same contrasting prophetic profiles as we have noted in Jeremiah. The biographical or hagiographical passages in Isaiah (7:1-17; 20:1-6; 36–39) present a selection of *legenda* about a man of God and a prophet *(nābî')*[2] who performs sign-acts, intercedes, heals, works miracles, and predicts the future — in short, a kinder, gentler version of Elisha. The contrast between this profile and the Isaiah who unconditionally condemned his contemporaries and predicted disaster could hardly be more pronounced. Furthermore, these three Isaianic narratives betray as much affinity with the Deuteronomistic corpus as the prose sermons in Jeremiah. By far the longest of them, chaps. 36–39, reproduce 2 Kings 18–20 with only minor variations. The introduction to Isa 7:1-17 (7:1) is

---

2. Isaiah is called *nābî'* and *'ebed* ("servant [of YHVH]") only in the biographical sections (20:3; 37:2; 38:1; 39:3).

clearly Deuteronomistic (cf. 2 Kgs 16:5), and suggests the possibility that an author of this school has inserted this brief biographical notice about Isaiah and Ahaz into the book. The even briefer notice about Isaiah acting out the defeat and humiliation of the Egyptians by walking naked through the city (20:1-6) is linguistically as Deuteronomic as anything in the History.

It will not do to dismiss all of this as an example of "pan-Deuteronomism," a fad of the kind that seems to have a fatal attraction for biblical scholars. If it is correct to read Deuteronomy as an official, prescriptive state document, it would not be surprising if, following the fall of Jerusalem and the deportations, adherents of the school attempted to monopolize other forms of religious activity, not least prophecy. At that time, as Richard Coggins observes, "There were ideological pressures at work to impose a particular view of Israel's past, of its relation with its God, of the meaning of the various events that had befallen it, culminating in the destruction of Jerusalem and the deportation of its leading citizens" (Coggins 1999: 34).

We can summarize this stage of the argument as follows: with the publication of Deuteronomy we have a document claiming immunity from later editorial intrusion and containing a law and constitution that may not be altered. We can read Deuteronomy and the Deuteronomic corpus as a whole as the first systematic attempt to impose an orthodoxy, which involved a prescriptive reconstruction of the past in accord with the Deuteronomic ideology. A crucial feature of this reconstruction was the delineation of a normative epoch ending with the death of Moses presented as both lawgiver and prophet. This is entirely in keeping with common practice in the ancient Near East, according to which claims to authority were validated by appeal to the past, the more remote the better (Lambert 1957: 1-14; Rochberg 1984: 127-44). The project of redefining prophecy deuteronomically as "Mosaic," that is, as continuing the role and mission of Moses, was furthered by editorial incursions into several prophetic books, especially Jeremiah. I submit that we have here the essentials of canonicity, which I take to be *closure* and the neutralization by various means of claims to new revelations. With Deuteronomy we have the first decisive step toward the classic formulation in the opening pargraph of *m. 'Abot:* "Moses received Torah from Sinai and gave it to Joshua; Joshua gave it to the elders, the elders gave it to the prophets, and the prophets gave it to the men of the Great Assembly."

4

The problem is, of course, that attempts to foreclose on innovation, to impose a given understanding of the past, and to dictate morals on the basis of such an understanding are not invariably successful. So it was with Deuteronomy. In spite of its claims to finality, it came to form part of a much larger complex of law and narrative. The narrative scope of the book is limited to one day, the last day, in the life of Moses. Apart from a few ethnological musings presented en passant (Deut 2:10-12, 20-23; 3:11-14), Moses' reminiscences cover only the immediate past from Horeb to Moab, though with frequent glances back to the entry into and exit from Egypt and, beyond that, the divine promise God made to Abraham, Isaac, and Jacob (1:8; 6:10; 9:5, 27), though nothing further is said about them. At some point, Deuteronomy was incorporated into a much broader chronological framework beginning with creation and ending, in all probability, with the settlement in Canaan and the establishment of a sanctuary in Shiloh. This is the other great narrative corpus known as the Priestly source (P). The structure of this narrative suggests that the authors had in mind the Jerusalem cult in the early Persian period, either anticipated or already in place, as the focus of their concerns. We shall see that the Priestly History contains elements of religious thinking quite different from and at places incompatible with the ideology of the Deuteronomists.

Since we do not know the circumstances under which Deuteronomy was combined with the chronologically more comprehensive P narrative, we have to fall back on looking for clues in the texts themselves. The date at the beginning of Deuteronomy (1:3) — "the fortieth year, the eleventh month, the first day of the month"— corresponds to the P practice of dating from the exodus and reproduces the P chronological formulations.[3] The addition of this date inserts the entire book, including Moses' last address and the laws, elegantly and economically into the P framework, and we are told near the end that Moses died on that same day (Deut 32:48). It then became necessary to transpose the commissioning of Joshua and the death of Moses from their original position in the P narrative (Num 27:12-

3. The P formula is: year, month, day of the month; cf. Gen 7:11; 8:4-5, 13, 14, all P. Exod 40:17 and Num 10:11 vary the pattern by using ordinals instead of cardinal numbers. Exod 12:1-2 (P) marks the beginning of the epoch that dates from the exodus, and the reader is reminded of it at significant points (Exod 19:1), and as late as the construction of Solomon's temple (1 Kgs 6:1).

23) to the end of Deuteronomy (32:48-52 plus 34:1, 7-9) — passages now separated by the blessings on the tribes in chap. 33 — in order to allow Moses to promulgate the Deuteronomic law and preside over a new covenant before dying in Moab on the eve of the people's entry into Canaan. A synoptic reading of these accounts in Numbers and Deuteronomy, both of unmistakably Priestly vintage, will confirm the impression that the latter is a revised version of the former, with the addition of the actual death of Moses displaced from its original location in the wilderness narrative. That the death of Moses was originally recorded at Num 27:12-23 is apparent both from the command addressed to him to go up the mountain and die, meaning there and then and not some time in the distant future, and comparison with the accounts of the deaths of Miriam (20:1) and Aaron (20:22-29) in the same part of the narrative.

In terms of structure, the amalgamation of Deuteronomy and the Priestly history extends the narrative back to an absolute beginning in creation, but the last section of the P history, recording the settlement of the tribes and the establishment of a sanctuary in Canaan, was omitted from the Pentateuch. The result is that the Pentateuch represents, in its final shape, a compromise between different ideologies inscribed respectively in the Deuteronomistic and Priestly writings that it contains. We can now conclude our inquiry by drawing out some of the implications of this restructuring.

The first is that concluding the base narrative with the death of Moses implies that the lifetime of the lawgiver constitutes the normative epoch. Its concluding statement is significantly programmatic in this respect: "No prophet has arisen since in Israel like Moses, whom YHVH knew face to face" (Deut 34:10). The point is clear: there is a qualitative difference between the revelation vouchsafed to Moses and prophetic communications occurring after his death. Guidance for living must therefore draw on this one-time, face-to-face revelation at Sinai/Horeb rather than on the sporadic, always problematic, and often disruptive phenomenon of prophecy. This was the point of Rabbi Joshua's quoting Deut 30:12, 14: "It is not in heaven that you should say, 'Who will go up to heaven for us and get it for us that we may hear it and observe it?' . . . No, the word is very near you; it is in your mouth and in your heart, so that you can observe it."

The Pentateuch that resulted from the combination of the Deuteronomistic and Priestly compositions (D and P) was intended as God's final word, but it could not prevent other words from being spoken. In spite of the implicit warning with which the Pentateuch ends, prophetic books continued to be composed and those already in existence continued to be edited and expanded down into the Roman period, when the first commentaries, the Qumran *pěšārîm*, were written. Study of the additions to prophetic books, new prophecy generated out of old, most clearly and abundantly in evidence in Isaiah, reveals a thrust in the direction of an eschatological and eventually an apocalyptic worldview. These developments at the textual level presuppose at the level of social realities the existence of groups who drew from ancient prophecies new truths of overwhelming significance for the lives of those who belonged to them. It is this process of appropriation that constitutes the interpretative context in both the Qumran sect and the first Christian communities.

I argued some years ago that the last two paragraphs of Malachi, and therefore of the Latter Prophets, served at some point in the canonical process as the conclusion to both the Law and the (Latter) Prophets (Blenkinsopp 1977: 120-23). The first paragraph looks backward to the law of Moses and the unique revelation of Sinai/Horeb: "Bear in mind the Torah of my servant Moses, the statutes and ordinances for all Israel that I charged him with at Horeb" (4:4). The second looks forward to the end time, the final reintegration and reconciliation in Israel to be brought about by prophetic agency in the person of Elijah (4:5-6). This summary statement represents a new point of stasis beyond the coda to the Priestly-Deuteronomistic Pentateuch. In the persons of Moses and Elijah it restores the tension and the balance between tradition and innovation, institution and charisma, the claims of the past and those of the future.

Bibliography

Alexander, P. "'A Sixtieth Part of Prophecy': The Problem of Continuing Revelation in Judaism." In *Words Remembered, Texts Renewed: Essays in Honour of John F. A. Sawyer*. Ed. J. Davies et al. Sheffield: Sheffield Academic, 1995.

Alster, B. *Death in Mesopotamia*. Copenhagen: Akademisk, 1990.

Alt, A. *Essays on Old Testament History and Religion*. Trans. R. A. Wilson. Oxford: Blackwell, 1966.

Alter, R. *The Art of Biblical Narrative*. New York: Jewish Publication Society of America, 1981.

Anderson, G. "Sacrifice and Sacrificial Offerings." In *The Anchor Bible Dictionary*. Ed. David Noel Freedman. New York: Doubleday, 1992, 5:870-76.

Arend, W. *Die typischen Szenen bei Homer*. Berlin: Weidmannsche, 1933.

Audet, J.-P. "A Hebrew-Aramaic List of Books of the Old Testament in Greek Transcription." *Journal of Theological Studies* n.s. 1 (1950): 135-54.

Avigad, N. *Discovering Jerusalem*. Nashville: Thomas Nelson, 1980.

Baines, J. "Literacy: Ancient Near East." In *Anchor Bible Dictionary*. Ed. David Noel Freedman. New York: Doubleday, 1992, 4:333-37.

Bainton, R. "The Bible in the Reformation." In *The Cambridge History of the Bible*, III. Ed. S. L. Greenslade. Cambridge: Cambridge University, 1963.

Baltzer, K. *Die Biographie der Propheten*. Neukirchen-Vluyn: Neukirchener, 1975.

Barr, J. "Man and Nature: The Ecological Controversy and the Old Testament." In *Ecology and Religion in History*. Ed. D. and E. Spring. New York: Harper & Row, 1974.

———. *The Garden of Eden and the Hope of Immortality*. Minneapolis: Fortress, 1992.

———. *Biblical Faith and Natural Theology*. Oxford: Clarendon, 1993.

———. *The Concept of Biblical Theology*. Minneapolis: Fortress, 1999.

Bibliography

Barthes, R., et al. *Structural Analysis and Biblical Exegesis.* Pittsburgh: Pickwick, 1974.

Batto, B. F. "Zedeq: *Sdq*." In *Dictionary of Deities and Demons in the Bible.* Ed. K. van der Toorn et al. Leiden: Brill, 1999, 929-34.

Bauer, G. L. *The Theology of the Old Testament.* London: Charles Fox, 1838.

Bayliss, M. "The Cult of the Dead Kin in Assyria and in Babylonia." *Iraq* 35 (1973).

Begg, C. "The Non-Mention of Amos, Hosea and Micah in the Deuteronomistic History," *Biblische Notizen* 32 (1986).

Bickerman, E. *From Ezra to the Last of the Maccabees.* New York: Schocken, 1962.

Blenkinsopp, J. "The Structure of P." *Catholic Biblical Quarterly* 38 (1976).

―――. *Prophecy and Canon.* Notre Dame, Ind.: University of Notre Dame, 1977.

―――. "The Social Context of the Outsider Woman in Proverbs 1–9." *Biblica* 72 (1991).

―――. *The Pentateuch: An Introduction to the First Five Books of the Bible.* New York: Doubleday, 1992.

―――. "The Nehemiah Autobiographical Memoir." In *Language, Theology, and the Bible: Essays in Honour of James Barr.* Ed. S. E. Balentine and J. Barton. Oxford: Clarendon, 1994.

―――. "A Postexilic Lay Source in Genesis 1–11." In *Abschied vom Jahwisten.* Ed. J. C. Gertz et al. Berlin: de Gruyter, 2002, 49-62.

―――. "Saul and the Mistress of the Spirits." In *Sense and Sensitivity: Essays on Reading the Bible in Memory of Robert Carroll.* Ed. A. G. Hunter and P. R. Davies. Sheffield: Sheffield Academic, 2002, 49-62.

Bloch, R. "Écriture et tradition dans le judaïsme: Aperçus sur l'origine du midrash." *Cahiers Sioniens* 8 (1954).

Bloch-Smith, E. *Judahite Burial Practices and Beliefs about the Dead.* Sheffield: JSOT, 1992.

Blum, E. "Israël à la montagne de Dieu." In *Le Pentateuque en Question.* Ed. A. de Pury. Geneva: Labor et Fides, 1989.

Bottéro, J. *Religion in Ancient Mesopotamia.* Chicago: University of Chicago, 2001.

Bultmann, M. *A History of the Synoptic Tradition.* New York: Harper & Row, 1965.

Burkert, W. *Homo Necans: The Anthropology of Ancient Greek Sacrificial Ritual and Myth.* Berkeley, Calif.: University of California, 1983.

―――. *The Orientalizing Revolution.* Cambridge, Mass.: Harvard University, 1992.

Burstein, S. M. *The Babyloniaka of Berossus.* Malibu: Undena Press, 1978.

Carruthers, M. *The Book of Memory: A Study of Memory in Medieval Culture.* Cambridge: Cambridge University, 1990.

Caspari, W. In *Narrative and Novelle in Samuel: Studies by Hugo Gressmann and Other Scholars.* Ed. D. M. Gunn. Sheffield: Almond, 1983, 13-83, 191-94.

Childs, B. S. *Memory and Tradition in Israel.* London: SCM, 1962.

Clements, R. E. *Old Testament Theology: A Fresh Approach*. London: Marshall, Morgan & Scott, 1978.

Coggins, R. In L. S. Schearing and S. L. McKenzie. *Those Elusive Deuteronomists*. Sheffield: Sheffield Academic, 1999.

Cohen, Y. A. "Ends and Means in Political Control: State Organisation and the Punishment of Adultery, Incest, and Violation of Celibacy." *American Anthropologist* 71 (1969).

Connerton, P. *How Societies Remember*. Cambridge: Cambridge University, 1989.

Coogan, M. D. *Stories from Ancient Canaan*. Philadelphia: Westminster, 1978.

Cox, H. *The Secular City*. New York: Macmillan, 1965.

Cox, P. *Biography in Late Antiquity: A Quest for the Holy Man*. Berkeley, Calif.: University of California, 1983.

Cross, F. M. *Canaanite Myth and Hebrew Epic*. Cambridge, Mass.: Harvard University, 1973.

Crüsemann, F. "Kritik an Amos im deuteronomistischen Geschichtswerk: Erwägungen zu 2. Könige 14:27." In *Probleme biblischer Theologie: Gerhard von Rad zum 70. Geburtstag*. Ed. H. W. Wolff. Munich: Kaiser, 1971.

Culley, R. C. "Oral Tradition and Historicity." In *Studies on the Ancient Palestinian World*. Ed. J. W. Wevers and D. B. Redford. Toronto: University of Toronto, 1972.

Denzinger, H. *Enchiridion Symbolorum*. Freiburg-in-Breslau: Herder, 1955.

de Vaux, R. *Ancient Israel: Its Life and Institutions*. London: Darton, Longman & Todd, 1961.

de Vaux, R. *Studies in Old Testament Sacrifice*. Cardiff: University of Wales, 1964.

Dibelius, M. *From Tradition to Gospel*. New York: Charles Scribner's Sons, 1934.

Diez Macho, A. *Neophyti I: Genesis*. Madrid and Barcelona, 1968.

Douglas, M. *Purity and Danger*. London: Routledge, 1966.

———. *Natural Symbols: Explorations in Cosmology*. New York: Pantheon, 1970.

———. *How Institutions Think*. Syracuse, N.Y.: Syracuse University, 1986.

Dundes, A. *The Study of Folklore*. Englewood Cliffs, N.J: Prentice-Hall, 1965.

Durkheim, E. *The Elementary Forms of Religious Life*. New York: The Free Press, 1995.

Eichrodt, W. *Old Testament Theology*, I. Philadelphia: Westminster, 1961.

———. *Theology of the Old Testament*, II. Philadelphia: Westminster, 1967.

Eissfeldt, O. *The Old Testament.:An Introduction*. Oxford: Blackwell, 1965.

Fackenheim, E. L. *The Jewish Bible after the Holocaust: A Re-Reading*. Bloomington: Indiana University, 1990.

Farnell, L. R. *Greek Hero Cults and Ideas of Immortality*. Oxford: Clarendon, 1921.

Foerster, W. "Der heilige Geist im Spätjudentum." *New Testament Studies* 8 (1961/1962).

Fohrer, G. *Introduction to the Old Testament*. Nashville: Abingdon, 1968.

Bibliography

Foster, B. R. *The Epic of Gilgamesh.* New York and London: W. W. Norton, 2001.

Frankfort, H., et al. *Before Philosophy: The Intellectual Adventure of Ancient Man.* Baltimore: Penguin, 1949.

Freedman, D. N. "The Law and the Prophets," *Vetus Testamentum Supplements* 9 (1963).

————. "The Earliest Bible." In *Backgrounds to the Bible.* Ed. M. P. O'Connor and D. N. Freedman. Winona Lake, Ind.: Eisenbrauns, 1987.

Frei, H. *The Eclipse of Biblical Narrative.* New Haven, Conn.: Yale University, 1974.

Gabler, T. A., and J. G. Gabler, eds. *D. Johann Philipp Gabler's Kleinere theologische Schriften.* Ulm: Verlag der Stettinischen Buchhandlung, 1831.

George, A. *The Epic of Gilgamesh.* London: Penguin, 1999.

Gerould, G. H. *The Grateful Dead: The History of a Folk Story.* Champaign: University of Illinois, 2000.

Gibson, J. C. L. *Textbook of Syrian Semitic Inscriptions,* 1: *Hebrew and Moabite Inscriptions.* Oxford: Clarendon, 1971.

Ginzberg, L. *The Legends of the Jews,* 1. Philadelphia: Jewish Publication Society of America, 1961.

Ginsburger, M. *Pseudo-Jonathan: Thargum Jonathan ben Usiel zum Pentateuch.* Berlin, 1903.

Girard, R. *Violence and the Sacred.* Baltimore: Johns Hopkins University, 1976.

Goode, W. J. "The Theoretical Importance of Love." *American Sociological Review* 71 (1969).

Gressmann, H. "Sage und Geschichte in den Patriarchenerzählungen." *Zeitschrift für die alttestamentliche Wissenschaft* 30 (1910).

————. *Die älteste Geschichtsschreibung und Prophetie Israels: Die Schriften des Alten Testaments,* 2/1. Göttingen: Vandenhoeck & Ruprecht, 1921.

Gunkel, H. *Das Märchen im Alten Testament.* Tübingen: Mohr, 1917.

————. *Genesis.* Macon, Ga.: Mercer, 1997.

Hadas, M., and M. Smith. *Heroes and Gods: Spiritual Biographies in Antiquity.* New York: Harper & Row, 1965.

Hallo, W. W. "The Origins of the Sacrificial Cult: New Evidence from Mesopotamia and Israel." In *Ancient Israelite Religion.* Ed. P. D. Miller. Philadelphia: Fortress, 1987.

Harris, W. V. *Ancient Literacy.* Cambridge, Mass.: Harvard University, 1989.

Hecht, R. "Studies on Sacrifice, 1970-1980." *Review of Studies in Religion* 8 (1982).

Heidel, A. *The Gilgamesh Epic and Old Testament Parallels.* Chicago: University of Chicago, 1949.

Hengel, M. *Judaism and Hellenism.* Philadelphia: Fortress, 1974.

Hoffman, L. A. *Covenant of Blood: Circumcision and Gender in Rabbinic Judaism.* Chicago: University of Chicago, 1996.

Hofmann, J. C. K. *Interpreting the Bible*. Minneapolis: Augsburg, 1959 (= *Biblische Hermeneutik* [1880]).

Huehnergard, J. "Biblical Notes on Some New Akkadian Texts from Emar." *Catholic Biblical Quarterly* 47 (1985).

Huffmon, H. B. "Shalem *šlm*." In *Dictionary of Deities and Demons in the Bible*. Ed. K. van der Toorn et al. Leiden: Brill, 1997, 755-77.

Humphreys, S. *The Family, Women and Death*. London, 1983.

Idelsohn, A. Z. *Jewish Liturgy and Its Development*. New York: Schocken, 1960.

Jay, N. *Throughout Your Generations Forever: Sacrifice, Religion and Paternity*. Chicago: University of Chicago, 1991.

Jeffers, A. *Magic and Divination in Ancient Palestine and Syria*. Leiden: Brill, 1996.

Jolles, A. *Einfache Formen*. Third Edition. Tübingen: Max Niemeyer, 1965.

Kaufmann, Y. *The Religion of Israel from Its Beginnings to the Babylonian Exile*. Chicago: University of Chicago, 1960.

Kent, R. G. *Old Persian Grammar, Texts, Lexicon*. New Haven, Conn.: American Oriental Society, 1953.

Kraus, H.-J. *Geschichte der historisch-kritischen Erforschung des Alten Testaments*. Neukirchen-Vluyn: Neukirchener, 1956.

Kutsch, E. *Verheissung und Gesetz*. Berlin: de Gruyter, 1973.

Lambert, W. G. "Ancestors, Authors and Canonicity." *Journal of Cuneiform Studies* 11 (1957).

Lambert, W. G., and A. R. Millard. *ATRA-HASIS: The Babylonian Story of the Flood*. Winona Lake, Ind.: Eisenbrauns, 1999.

Le Goff, *History and Memory*. New York: Columbia University, 1992.

Lessing, G. In *Lessing's Theological Writings*. Ed. H. Chadwick. Standford, Calif.: Stanford University, 1956.

Levenson, J. "Is There a Counterpart in the Hebrew Bible to New Testament Antisemitism?" *Journal of Ecumenical Studies* 22 (1985).

Levison, J. R. "Did the Spirit Withdraw from Israel? An Evaluation of the Earliest Jewish Data," *New Testament Studies* 43 (1997).

Lewis, T. J. *Cults of the Dead in Ancient Israel and Ugarit*. Atlanta, Ga.: Scholars, 1989.

Luria, A. *The Man with a Shattered World*. Cambridge, Mass.: Harvard University, 1972.

Lust, J. "On Wizards and Prophets." *Vetus Testamentum Supplements* 26 (1974).

Martin-Achard, R. *Israël et les Nations: La Perspective Missionaire de l'Ancien Testament*. Neuchâtel: Delachaux et Niestlé, 1959.

May, H. G. "Theological Universalism in the Old Testament." *Journal of Bible and Religion* 16 (1948).

Metz, J. *Theology of the World*. New York: Herder & Herder, 1969.

Meyer, E. *Die Israeliten und ihre Nachbarstämme*. Halle: Max Niemeyer, 1906.

Bibliography

Milgrom, J. *Leviticus 1–16: A New Translation with Introduction and Commentary.* New York: Doubleday, 1991.

Misch, G. *A History of Autobiography in Antiquity.* London: Routledge & Kegan Paul, 1950.

Momigliano, A. *The Development of Greek Biography.* Cambridge, Mass.: Harvard University, 1971.

Moran, W. L. *The Amarna Letters.* Baltimore: Johns Hopkins University, 1992.

Nicholson, E. W. *Exodus and Sinai in History and Tradition.* Atlanta: John Knox, 1973.

———. *God and His People: Covenant and Theology in the Old Testament.* Oxford: Clarendon, 1986.

———. *The Pentateuch in the Twentieth Century.* Oxford: Clarendon, 1998.

Nock, A. D. *Conversion.* Oxford: Oxford University, 1933.

Nogalski, J. *Literary Precursors to the Book of the Twelve.* Berlin: de Gruyter, 1993.

Noth, M. *Exodus: A Commentary.* Philadelphia: Westminster, 1962.

———. *A History of Pentateuchal Traditions.* Englewood Cliffs, N.J: Prentice Hall, 1972.

———. *The Deuteronomistic History.* Sheffield: JSOT, 1981.

Oehler, G. F. *Theology of the Old Testament.* New York: Funk & Wagnalls, 1883.

Perlitt, L. *Bundestheologie im Alten Testament.* Neukirchen-Vluyn: Neukirchener, 1969.

Pope, M. "The Cult of the Dead at Ugarit." In *Ugarit in Retrospect.* Ed. G. D. Young. Winona Lake, Ind.: Eisenbrauns, 1981, 159-79.

Pritchard, J. B. *Ancient Near Eastern Texts Relating to the Old Testament.* Second Edition. Princeton, N.J.: Princeton University, 1955.

Propp, V. *Morphology of the Folktale.* Second Edition. Austin: University of Texas, 1968.

Robertson Smith, W. *The Religion of the Semites: The Fundamental Institutions.* New York: Schocken, 1972.

Rochberg, F. "Canonicity in Cuneiform Texts." *Journal of Cuneiform Studies* 36 (1984).

Rogerson, J. *Old Testament Criticism in the Nineteenth Century.* Philadelphia: Fortress, 1985.

Rost, L. *The Succession to the Throne of David.* Sheffield: Almond, 1982.

Rowley, H. H. *The Biblical Doctrine of Election.* London: Lutterworth, 1950a.

———. *The Growth of the Old Testament.* London: Hutchinson University Library, 1950b.

———. *The Missionary Message of the Old Testament.* London: Lutterworth, 1956.

Sandmel, S. "The Haggada within Scripture." *Journal of Biblical Literature* 80 (1961).

Schäfer, P. "Die Termini 'Heiliger Geist' und 'Geist der Prophetie' in den Targumim und das Verhältnis der Targumim zueinander." *Vetus Testamentum* 20 (1970).

───. *Die Vorstellung vom Heiligen Geist in der rabbinischen Literatur*. Munich: Kösel, 1972.

Schearing, L. S., and S. L. McKenzie, eds. *Those Elusive Deuteronomists*. Sheffield: Sheffield Academic, 1999.

Schmid, H. H. *Der sogennante Jahwist: Beobachtungen und Fragen zur Pentateuchforschung*. Zurich: Theologische, 1976.

Schmidt, B. B. *Israel's Beneficent Dead*. Tübingen: Mohr, 1994.

Scholem, G. *The Messianic Idea in Judaism and Other Essays on Jewish Spirituality*. New York: Schocken, 1971.

Scholes, R., and R. Kellogg. *The Nature of Narrative*. Oxford: Oxford University, 1966.

Schottroff, W. *"Gedenken" im Alten Orient und im Alten Testament*. Neukirchen-Vluyn: Neukirchener, 1967.

Schultz, H. *Old Testament Theology*, I. Edinburgh: T&T Clark, 1892.

Seeligman, I. L. "Voraussetzungen des Midrashexegese." *Vetus Testamentum Supplements* 1 (1953).

Sheppard, G. *Wisdom as a Hermeneutical Construct*. Berlin: de Gruyter, 1980.

Smalley, B. *The Study of the Bible in the Middle Ages*. Oxford: Blackwell, 1952.

───. In *The Cambridge History of the Bible*, III. Ed. G. W. H. Lampe. Cambridge: Cambridge University, 1963.

Smend, R. "Universalismus und Particularismus in der alttestamentliche Theologie des 19. Jahrhunderts." *Evangelische Theologie* 22 (1962).

───. *Die Mitte des Alten Testaments*. Zurich: Zollikon, 1970.

Smith, M. *Palestinian Parties and Politics That Shaped the Old Testament*. New York: Columbia University, 1971.

Speiser, E. A. *Genesis: A New Translation with Introduction and Commentary*. Garden City, N.Y.: Doubleday, 1964.

Spronk, K. *Beatific Afterlife in Ancient Israel and in the Ancient Near East*. Neukirchen-Vluyn: Neukirchener, 1986.

Steinberg, N. "The Deuteronomic Law Code and the Politics of State Centralization." In *The Bible and the Politics of Exegesis*. Ed. D. Jobling et al. Cleveland: Pilgrim, 1991.

Strenski, I. "Between Theory and Specialty: Sacrifice in the 90s." *Review of Studies in Religion* 22 (1996).

Tigay, J. H. *The Evolution of the Gilgamesh Epic*. Philadelphia: University of Pennsylvania, 1982.

───. *You Shall Have No Other Gods: Israelite Religion in the Light of Hebrew Inscriptions*. Atlanta: Scholars, 1986.

Turner, V. "Sacrifice as Quintessential Process: Prophylaxis or Abandonment?" *Harvard Theological Review* 16 (1977).

Urbach, E. E. "When Did Prophecy Cease?" *Tarbiz* 17 (1945/46) (Hebrew).

Van der Toorn, K. "The Nature of the Biblical Terafim in the Light of the Cuneiform Evidence." *Catholic Biblical Quarterly* 52 (1990).

————. *Family Religion in Babylon, Syria and Israel.* Leiden: Brill, 1996.

————, et al. *Dictionary of Deities and Demons in the Bible.* Leiden: Brill, 1999.

Van Hoonaker, A. "Divination by the *'Ob* among the Ancient Hebrews." *Expository Times* 9 (1897/98).

Van Seters, J. *Abraham in History and Tradition.* New Haven, Conn.: Yale University, 1975.

————. *In Search of History: Historiography in the Ancient World and the Origins of Biblical History.* New Haven, Conn.: Yale University, 1983.

Vansina, J. *Oral Tradition as History.* Madison: University of Wisconsin, 1985.

Vermes, G. "Hanina ben Dosa: A Controversial Galilean Saint from the First Century of the Christian Era." *Journal of Jewish Studies* 23 (1972); 29 (1973).

————. *Scripture and Tradition in Judaism: Haggadic Studies.* Second Edition. Leiden: Brill, 1973.

von Rad, G. *Old Testament Theology,* I. New York: Harper & Row, 1962.

————. *Old Testament Theology,* II. New York: Harper & Row, 1965.

————. *The Problem of the Hexateuch and Other Essays.* Edinburgh & London: Oliver & Boyd, 1966.

Vriezen, T. C. *An Outline of Old Testament Theology.* Oxford: Blackwell, 1970.

Watts, J. W., ed. *Persia and Torah: The Theory of Imperial Authorization of the Pentateuch.* Atlanta: Society of Biblical Literature, 2001.

Weber, M. *Ancient Judaism.* New York: The Free Press, 1952.

————. *Economy and Society.* Berkeley: University of California, 1978.

Weingreen, J. *From Bible to Mishna: The Continuity of Tradition.* Manchester, Eng.: Manchester University, 1976.

Weiser, A. *Introduction to the Old Testament.* London: Darton, Longman & Todd, 1961.

Wellhausen, J. *Prolegomena to the History of Israel.* New York: Meridian, 1957.

Westermann, C. *Genesis 1–11: A Commentary.* Minneapolis: Augsburg, 1984.

————. *Genesis 12–36: A Commentary.* Minneapolis: Augsburg, 1985.

White, Lynn, Jr. "The Historical Roots of Our Ecological Crisis." *Science* 155 (1967).

Whybray, R. N. *The Succession Narrative: A Study of II Sam. 9–20 and I Kings 1 and 2.* London: SCM, 1968.

Wieseltier, L. "After Memory: Reflections on the Holocaust Memorial Museum on the Mall." *The New Republic* 4.3 (1993): 4085.

Yerushalmi, Y. H. *Zakhor.* Seattle and London: University of Washington, 1982.

Young, I. M. "Israelite Literacy: Interpreting the Evidence." *Vetus Testamentum* 48 (1998).

Index of Subjects and Names

Index of Biblical Texts

220